ONE W—

Communities of Play

Communities of Play

Emergent Cultures in Multiplayer Games and Virtual Worlds

Celia Pearce and Artemesia

forewords by
Tom Boellstorff and Bonnie A. Nardi

The MIT Press Cambridge, Massachusetts London, England

For information about special quantity discounts, please email special_sales@mitpress.mit.edu

This book was set in Janson Text, Rotis Semi Sans, and Rotis Sans by Graphic Composition, Inc., Bogart, Georgia.

Printed and bound in the United States of America.

Library of Congress Cataloging-in-Publication Data

Pearce, Celia.
Communities of play : emergent cultures in multiplayer games and virtual
worlds / Celia Pearce and Artemesia.
      p. cm.
Includes bibliographical references and index.
ISBN 978-0-262-16257-9 (hardcover : alk. paper)
1. Internet games—Social aspects. 2. Fantasy games—Social aspects. 3. Role playing—
Social aspects. 4. Shared virtual environments—Social aspects. 5. Communities.
6. Community life. I. Title.
GV1469.17.S63P42 2009
794.8′1—dc22
                                                                        2008042150

10 9 8 7 6 5 4 3 2 1

This book is dedicated to my grandmother, Connie Capacchione, for a lifetime of unconditional love, support, and encouragement.

Contents

Methods of Culture

Tom Boellstorff

We live at a historical juncture in which virtual worlds and online games stand to reconfigure the very character of "culture." They will do so in a range of ways, yet with some common themes. They will do so individually and also in dialogue with each other, with other technologies ranging from web pages to cellphones, and with those broader sociopolitical changes that are too often hastily glossed as "globalization" or "neoliberalism." The stakes are high, in every sense—cultural, economic, political, and personal. Additionally, it has become blatantly clear that these stakes are pertinent worldwide, for the rich and poor, for the powerful and disempowered, and not just for elite technophiles.

Given these stakes, it is crucial that we develop the broadest possible body of scholarship exploring virtual worlds and online games from a range of methodological and theoretical perspectives. Disciplinary or topical partisanship is anathema, to be avoided at all costs: what is needed is an appreciation for the vibrant possibilities offered by a new research community seeking answers to questions that are at once novel and linked to classic dilemmas of social analysis.

It is in this context that *Communities of Play* may be fruitfully read in three different ways. First, *Communities of Play* is to my knowledge the first book-length exploration of a virtual culture formed at the interstices of multiple virtual worlds and online games. Pearce explores what she terms the "Uru Diaspora"—the movement of an online community to several different virtual worlds and games in the wake of the destruction of their own. Her work here thus usefully complements research focusing on specific virtual worlds and games, as well as work focusing on relationships between virtual worlds and the actual world.

Second, *Communities of Play* is fundamentally concerned with questions of methodology. By charting the challenges and triumphs of her research, Pearce presents to the growing body of scholarship on virtual worlds and online games a useful treatise on ethnographic practice. As an anthropologist who conducts research in the actual world (Indonesia) and a virtual world (*Second Life*), I find Pearce's ethnographic skills to be equal to any I have yet encountered: her insistence on considering method in the context of theory represents an important intervention.

Third, Pearce's experience as a game designer and her interest in the notion of emergence mean that *Communities of Play* will be valuable to those concerned with game design and virtual-world governance. Pearce shows us how in a sense all culture is emergent, since it is never intelligible solely in terms of individual actions and beliefs. She thus reaches back to classic functionalist and structuralist conceptualizations of culture in terms of an integrated whole. For instance, Ruth Benedict touched upon just this issue when noting in her classic *Patterns of Culture*, first published in 1934, that "Gunpowder is not merely the sum of sulphur and charcoal and saltpeter, and no amount of knowledge even of all three of its elements . . . will demonstrate the nature of gunpowder. . . . Cultures, likewise, are more than the sum of their traits" (p. 47). At the same time, Pearce brings in contemporary interests in reflexivity and an attention to the multiplicity of selfhood in virtual contexts quite unlike anything Benedict ever encountered. It is in this combination of an appreciation for past insights, together with an interest in forging novel tools for novel field sites, that the power of Pearce's contribution lies.

Reference
Benedict, Ruth. 1934. *Patterns of Culture*. New York: Mentor Books.

Play, Community, and History

Bonnie Nardi

The study of virtual worlds gained quick traction in academia. In a few short years, a multidisciplinary arena of scholarship emerged with participation from media studies, organization studies, education, anthropology, and computer-related fields such as human-computer interaction and computer-supported collaborative work. Celia Pearce's book is unique in this literature for situating analysis of virtual world activity in a historical frame, following the development and diaspora of an online community over several years across a series of online environments. It is remarkable that Pearce was able to attain such scope. Eighteen months of fieldwork were a part of her success, but a principled digging-into of multiple strands of virtual world history, with careful tracery of earlier games, worlds, and events that influenced her study participants, brought forth a depth and lucidness that should become a touchstone for virtual worlds scholarship.

Pearce's work is important in studying an unusual group of participants—middle-aged men and women. Typical gamers tend to be younger, and tend to be male. Pearce's research takes seriously the need to examine diverse populations; it reminds us that understanding topics such as play and play communities—Pearce's primary interests—entails developing a corpus of careful empirical work conducted in multiple contexts. Her study is so absorbing, so compelling, it issues a captivating invitation for more such work.

I am usually wary of "me-ethnography," finding it self-conscious and boring. Pearce explains how she herself emerged as a participant in the community she studied. But it's not about her, it's about the community. She uses discussions of the development of her identity as a special kind of participant not to talk about herself, but to reveal the dynamics of the community she investigated. I'm not sure most could have pulled it off. If others seek to emulate Pearce, I hope they approach the task with the humility and sense of cultural dynamics manifest in her work.

It is a pleasure to write this small bit of text, knowing that very soon you will be immersed in the abundant satisfactions of Pearce's excellent writing. Her background as a games designer is evident in the way she respectfully engages readers in clear, vivid prose structured in an original and—can we say it?—entertaining way. From its thoughtful analyses of play and community to its authoritative contextualization of games and virtual worlds, this book repays study on many levels. Enjoy!

Play, Community, and History

Acknowledgments

This endeavor would not have been possible without the support, patience, and guidance of a number of people, for whom I am eternally grateful, and whom, to varying degrees, have all had a hand in the birthing of this book.

First and foremost, I'd like to express by gratitude to the wonderful people of The Gathering of Uru (TGU) with whom my fate is inextricably linked, and who have become friends as well as collaborators. This is their amazing story and I am merely their scribe. In particular I'd like to acknowledge Raena, who not only subjected herself to numerous lengthy interviews, but also contributed to the study by doing some supplemental research and helping me navigate the group's archives; Lynn, who generously gave of her time and attention to make sure I got what I needed, including a kick in the pants from time to time; Leesa, the mayor and founder of TGU, the group's amazing leader, who welcomed me into her community; Wingman, my friend, guide, and navigator; Nature_Girl the Wise for being my go-to gal on all things *Uru*; Bette, for turning the tables on me and asking *me* the questions; Damanji, for putting up with my incessant questions; Petrova and D'evon, my guides in *Until Uru*; Tristan, who really did turn out to be a nice guy after all; Leshan, for expanding my virtual wardrobe and helping me to see my value to the community; Maesi and Shaylah, for their support and contribution to the community and to my research; and Uno, for all the virtual chocolate. (Note: all study participants are referred to by pseudonyms.)

I'd like to thank all of those who supported this work during its chrysalis period as a PhD thesis, including my advisory team, Dr. Lizbeth Goodman, Dr. Hayley Newman, and Dr. Tricia Austin, for their support, guidance, and feedback. I'd also like to thank my external advisors, who put an enormous amount of effort into this with no particular reward: first and foremost, Tom Boellstorff, who was my tour guide into the world of contemporary anthropology; Katherine Milton for her guidance in sociology and general support and friendship; T. L. Taylor for her feedback and inspiration; Neil Bennun, the proofreader and "anglocizer" of the original thesis; and Dr. Marc

Price, who asked the right questions. I'd also like to thank the SMARTlab cohort alongside whom I took this amazing journey, as well as the SMARTlab staff, including Joy Barrett, Jana Reidel, Taey Kim, Jo Gell, and Cassandra St. Louis. In addition, particular gratitude is due my extended network of UK friends who kindly housed me during my term as a PhD candidate at SMARTlab: David Furlow, Susan Benn and Gavin McFayden, Lucy Hooberman and David Triesman, and Tom Donaldson.

I'd like to thank the people I worked with on the re-launch of *Uru Live*: Blake Lewin, Laurie Baird, Cari Price, Trent Hershenson, and Eric Large (Turner/GameTap), and Rand Miller, Ryan Warzecha, Tony Fryman, Mark Dobratz, and Richard Watson (Cyan Worlds).

Special thanks are due to my colleagues at Georgia Tech, especially Janet Murray and Kenneth Knoespel, without whose sincere support and flexibility this book would never have been completed.

I also owe a great deal of gratitude to my biological and extended family. Numerous thanks are owed to Bob Rice for his emotional and technical support, his patience, and especially his continuous reminders to back up my work; my parents, Lucia Capacchione, Peter Pearce, and Susan Pearce, and my grandmother Connie Capacchione, for their encouragement and support; my sister, Aleta Francis, for her support and sense of humor; and her family, all of whom had to suffer my extended absences and lack of availability. I thank them for their patience throughout this process.

A number of friends and colleagues were instrumental in helping me think through various aspects of this research, including Mary Flanagan, my friend and college roommate; Jacki Morie, Tracy Fullerton, and Janine Fron, my partners in play in Ludica; Rob Peagler for general support and inspiration; Bernie DeKoven, my Play Guru; the Narrative Unlimited cohort; and my former colleagues at UC Irvine, especially Bonnie Nardi, Bill Tomlinson, Antoinette LaFarge, and Stuart Ross. I'd also like to thank Elizabeth Plott, Elizabeth Fricker, and Doug MacMurray, as well as Pam McCormick and Peggie Geller for their support and encouragement.

The birthing process of this book was also made possible by a small army of supporters who lent their time, efforts, and editorial talents to this endeavor: Janet Murray, Richard Kahlenberg, Clark Dodsworth, and Katherine Mancuso.

And finally, I would like to thank the wonderful people at the MIT Press who helped magically transform this book from virtual to actual: Douglas Sery, Alyssa Larose, Katie Helke, Krista Magnuson, Mel Goldsipe, and Jean Wilcox.

| I |
PLAY, COMMUNITY, AND EMERGENT CULTURES

COMMUNITIES OF PLAY AND THE GLOBAL PLAYGROUND

Communities of Play

Play communities are neither new nor unique to the Internet. They surround us in many forms, from chess and bridge clubs to sports leagues to golf buddies to summer camps; from *Dungeons & Dragons* role-playing on tabletops to outdoor historical re-enactments of renaissance faires or famous Civil War battles. As commonplace as these practices are, with the exception of sports, adult play tends to be marginalized in the U.S. and Europe. As anthropologist Richard Schechner has noted, "In the West, play is a rotten category tainted by unreality, inauthenticity, duplicity, make-believe, looseness, fooling around, and inconsequentiality" (1988).

In spite of this, anthropologists have long noted the deep connection between play and more serious traditional forms of ritual and performance, many of which involve the adoption of alternative roles or personas (van Gennep 1909, Schechner and Schuman 1976, Turner 1982). In contemporary society, this takes the form of ritually sanctioned celebrations such as Mardi Gras and Halloween (Santino 1983), which create allowances for adults to engage in fantasy role-play as part of provisional, short-term, play communities. Mardi Gras also supports a year-round culture of creativity devoted to the crafting of floats, costumes, and other ritual artifacts (Schindler 1997).

Yet in many other contexts, such ongoing play communities tend to be viewed as outside the norm. This is especially true of communities whose play cultures are deeply tied to imagination, fantasy, and the creation of a fictional identity, such as "Trekkies," who engage in role-play around the television series *Star Trek* (Jenkins 1992). Like participants in historical reenactments (Horwitz 1998, Miller 1998), live-action and tabletop role-playing games (Fine 1983), and the Burning Man festival (Gilmore and Van Proyen 2005), these play communities devote a high level of effort and creativity to their play culture, often to the bewilderment of the population at large (figure 1.1).

| Figure 1.1 |
Participants in the 2004 Burning Man festival. (Image: Jacquelyn Ford Morie)

Nonetheless, social play is a rapidly expanding category in the entertainment landscape. Cosplay, the practice of dressing up in costume, has gained widespread acceptance in Japan (Winge 2007). The Dragon*Con fan convention, which embraces a range of role-playing traditions, including cosplay and other fan practices, attracted over 30,000 participants in 2007, over twenty times the attendees of its inaugural event in 1987 (Dragon*Con 2008). The same year, over 47,000 people attended Burning Man, an annual festival/campout combining art, role-playing, and creative expression in the Nevada desert (Red Rock LLC 2007).

What do we mean when we say "play community"? As a pervasive element of diverse human cultures, anthropologists have long had a fascination with play and its social function, some devoting much of their oeuvre to the subject (Schechner and Schuman 1976, Turner 1982, Sutton-Smith 1981). Johan Huizinga, considered the father of "ludology" (a term used to describe the study of digital games), defines play as

a free activity standing quite consciously outside "ordinary" life as being "not serious," but at the same time absorbing the player intensely and utterly. It is an activity connected with no material interest, and no profit can be gained by it. It proceeds within its own proper boundaries of time and space according to fixed rules in an orderly manner. It promotes the formation of social groupings which tend to surround themselves with secrecy and to stress their difference from the common world by disguise or other means. ([1938] 1950, 13)

What type of groupings, and what do we mean by "community"? Pioneering German sociologist Ferdinand Tönnies described community (Gemeinschaft) as an association of individuals with a collective will that is enacted through individual effort. Communities take varying forms, from religious sects to neighborhoods, and are characterized by affiliations around a group identity that includes shared customs, folkways, and social mores. Typically, the will of individuals within a community is, to a certain extent, subjugated to the greater good (Tönnies [1887] 1988, 209).

I've adopted the term "communities of play" as a deliberate counterpoint to "communities of practice," a term originated in anthropology and widely adopted in Internet studies and computer-mediated communication. A community of practice is defined as a group of individuals who engage in a process of collective learning and maintain a common identity defined by a shared domain of interest or activity (Lave and Wenger 1991). The types of communities that fall under this definition tend to convene around forms of work or folk practice. Obviously, communities of practice and communities of play share much in common, and one could even argue that play is a type of practice; however, the adoption of a new term suggests that play practices warrant their own understanding of how communities form and are maintained, a subject that becomes particularly pertinent in the context of technologically mediated play.

With the emergence of digital networks, whole new varieties of adult play communities have begun to appear, enabled by desktop computers and pervasive global networks whose advanced graphical and transmission capabilities were once confined to university research labs. Some of these are extensions of nondigital forms of play, while others offer entirely new experiences and playscapes. Networks amplify the scale, progression, and geographical reach of play communities, allowing them to grow much larger much faster then their offline counterparts. These phenomena give rise to new creative playgrounds, not only within discrete networked play spaces, but also through real-world interventions, such as "alternate reality" and "big games," which take place across multiple media and in the physical world; "smart mobs," large group interactions enabled by mobile technologies; and other emerging forms of play that blur the boundaries between real and virtual, everyday life and imagination, work and play.

Marshall McLuhan coined the term "global village" to describe the shared story-telling space of television (1964). He noted that large, dispersed groups could convene over this new "electronic hearth" to engage in an intimate, simultaneous experience that was once restricted to geographic co-presence. In a similar way, networked games have created a kind of participatory "global playground" where people can now inter-act dynamically in real time and build new and increasingly complex play communities that traverse geographical and temporal boundaries.

This book is primarily concerned with the emerging genre of massively multi-player online worlds, variously known as MMOGs, MMOWs, virtual worlds, and metaverses. The most common of these new global playgrounds is the MMORPG, or massively multiplayer online role-playing game, in which players develop roles derived from fantasy literature to engage in epic fictions. Alongside this genre is the open-ended Web 2.0 "sandbox"-style environment, MMOW (massively multiplayer online world), virtual world, or metaverse, whose denizens play a part in actually shaping the world. These two genres encompass a vast landscape of networked playgrounds in which a variety of play communities and emergent social phenomena develop.

Within these pages, we will explore the ways in which play communities are formed and sustained, and the intersection between their emergent behavior and the design of the global playgrounds they inhabit. Who is attracted to different types of digital playgrounds, and therefore what initial preferences and play patterns do they bring? What is it about play environments themselves that encourages certain types of communities to form? How do their design, governance, and ongoing management affect emergent cultures of play? How do players both leverage and subvert these playgrounds to their own ends? And what happens when the powers that be decide a playground is no longer financially sustainable? What if a play community's commit-ment to each other and to its collective identity transcends the individual worlds they inhabit? What if they carry the culture of one virtual world into another?

At the heart of this book is the story of one specific play community, members of the Uru Diaspora, a group of players cast out of an online game to become refugees. It is the story of the bonds they formed in spite of—indeed *because* of—this shared trauma, and about their tenacious determination to remain together and to reclaim and reconfigure their own unique group identity and culture. It is a story about the power of play to coalesce a community beyond the boundaries of the game in which it formed, and into the real world itself.

Along the way we shall also look at some key concepts used to analyze these phenomena. In book I, we shall take a brief tour of the history of multiplayer games, starting with the first recorded examples of games played in 3500 BCE, up to the advent of the digital game. We shall briefly look at the history of online playgrounds, their context and origins in analog games, in order to frame both the core audiences and the design conventions of these games. We shall provide an overview of virtual worlds—"ecosystems of play," as I term them—and their unique properties that create a context for emergent behavior and cultures. We shall define the key concepts "emergence" and "culture" and describe criteria for their study. Book I closes with an in-depth discussion of theoretical and methodological frameworks used in the study, drawing from contemporary anthropology and sociology.

Book II chronicles the history of the Uru Diaspora and its migration to other worlds, focusing on an eighteen-month ethnography conducted during 2004 and 2005. This section is presented in the style of a traditional anthropological monograph, including a narrative of the group's history, followed by an analysis of its patterns of emergent culture. The narrative focuses on The Gathering of Uru and its journey into and around *There.com* in search of a homeland, and looks secondarily at productive play within the Uru community in *Second Life*.

Book III details the methodology used to conduct the research and also discusses the way the methodology was refined and adapted over the course of the research. This section will be of particular interest to ethnographers and game scholars who are interested in venturing into this research domain. Book IV provides a more intimate look at the day-to-day experience of playing and performing ethnography, including its stumbles and epiphanies, also of utility to ethnographers and researchers. Book V includes a coda on events that took place *after* the core study was conducted. It also provides concluding thoughts and discusses the broader implications of the study on game design and community management, as well as current trends in the global playground that will make the subject of play communities increasingly relevant in the future.

Multiplayer Games from 3500 BCE to the Twenty-First Century

While massively multiplayer online games (MMOGs) are lauded as the newest and fastest-growing genre of computer games, they could as much be viewed as a return to the natural order of things. The advent of single-player genres as the central paradigm for games is an historical aberration of digital technology (Pearce 1997, Herz 1997). Prior to the introduction of the computer as a game-playing platform, the majority of games played by hundreds of cultures for thousands of years, with few exceptions, were multiplayer. From their first evidence, such as the Egyptian Senet, the Mesopotamian Ur, and the ancient African game of mancala, to the traditional Chinese games of Go and Mah Jongg, to chess, whose multicultural odyssey spanned India and the Middle East to become a European perennial (Yalom 2004), games were predominately multiplayer.

The advent of mass production enabled new forms of single-player game, such as the puzzle, but even board games of the industrial age and playing cards, which have some single-player variants, continued primarily in this multiplayer tradition. With the rise of the middle class during the Industrial Revolution, board games became a centerpiece of the American and European parlor, joined in the mid-twentieth century by the television (Hofer 2003, Orbanes 2003).

The earliest computer games continued this multiplayer trajectory. *Tennis for Two*, a *Pong*-like demo developed in 1958 on an oscilloscope, and the 1969 classic *Spacewar!* were both multiplayer games. The first video game console, the Magnavox Odyssey, released in 1972, merged multiplayer board game conventions with the emerging medium of television to create a new form of family entertainment. Japanese console pioneer Nintendo started out as a card game company, and introduced its Famicom, later called the Nintendo Entertainment System, with a similar social orientation. Atari's 1972 arcade classic *Pong* is a highly social game, often appearing in two- or even four-player tabletop versions in pizza parlors.

The reasons a cultural practice that was definitively social for thousands of years transformed into a predominately solo activity are complex. The industrial-age arcade paradigm of player versus machine, the capability to create an automated opponent, the paradigm of personal computing, the technical constraints of platforms, and the limited availability of networks were all contributing factors. It was not until the introduction of widely available computer networks that we began to see a return to the dominant historical paradigm of the multiplayer game.

From the moment that networks began to appear in labs on college campuses, people tried to play on them. Today's massively multiplayer online games descend from the same college hacker tradition that spawned *Spacewar!*. While a complete history of MMOGs and MMOWs is beyond the scope of this book, understanding something about their origins will help to unpack fundamental questions about the complex relationship between designer and player: in what contexts are these games created, and by whom? What are their underlying values and cultures? What types of players do designers anticipate will play these games? What types do they actually attract? And what sorts of emergent behaviors are these players likely to exhibit when their play styles come into contact with the affordances of the game software?

The fantasy role-playing genre epitomized by games such as *Ultima Online, EverQuest*, and *World of Warcraft* has its roots in early text-based MUDs (multiuser dungeons or domains), which in turn derive their underlying mechanics from tabletop role-playing games such as *Dungeons & Dragons* (D&D). D&D in turn arose out of a long-standing tradition of tabletop strategy games. These can be traced even further back to eighteenth- and nineteenth-century army miniatures, revived in the twentieth century by science fiction author H. G. Wells's classic volume of war gaming rules: *Little Wars: A Game for Boys from Twelve Years of Age to One Hundred and Fifty and for That More Intelligent Sort of Girl Who Likes Boys' Games and Books* (1913). Wells's title summarizes both the ethos and intended audience of games in this tradition.

Tabletop role-playing games such as *Dungeons & Dragons*, which built their narratives around high fantasy literature, including J. R. R. Tolkien's *The Lord of the Rings* trilogy (1954, 1954, 1955), Robert E. Howard's *The Conan Chronicles* ([1932–1969] 1989), and others, were extremely popular on college campuses during the 1970s and 1980s. This was also the period and context in which computer networks were beginning to appear throughout the United States and Europe. That these two emerging trends would converge in the minds of (mostly male) computer science students seems almost inevitable, and the result was the text-based *MUD*, a networked, computationally enabled adaptation of the core mechanics of D&D-style games. More followed and soon the conventions of the genre, still confined to the ivory towers of college computer labs, became codified. These games are also tied to the development of text-based single-player adventure games that were concurrently being distributed via ARPANET, the progenitor of the modern Internet.

This lineage has deep implications for the design of contemporary MMOGs and the specific audiences they attract. Although the role-playing genre did expand this audience to a minimal extent, these games have their roots in a fantasy militaristic gameplay that, as Wells's title suggests, is almost exclusively male. The tabletop gaming tradition revolves around elaborate rules that involve dice with as many as twenty sides. In the case of role-playing games like D&D, player characters and their actions are proceduralized through a blend of statistics and die rolls that typically determine the outcome of scenarios. These can vary from combat to spell-casting to tasks such as picking a lock or obtaining information. One of the pleasures of these games is the shared imagination space generated collectively by players. Player creativity has long been a component of tabletop game culture, with players not only contributing to the

| Figure 1.2 |
Dungeons & Dragons player character fan art. (Images: The_Brave [left] and comethime [right])

storytelling process, but also creating drawings or three-dimensional figures of their characters.

The MUDs spawned by tabletop role-playing sustained a small cult following for a decade and a half, until the mid-1990s, when they were joined by a new generation of games integrating graphics with the other conventions of the genre and targeted to a mass audience. Since then, MMOGs have emerged as the fastest-growing sector of the video game industry. Each new generation of MMOG brings new refinements that include interface improvements, more sophisticated graphics, and increasingly vast worlds, yet their range remains surprisingly narrow. Games like *Meridian 59* (the first graphical game in this genre; see figure 1.3), *Ultima Online, EverQuest, Dark Ages of Camelot, Asheron's Call, Diablo* and Blizzard's second MMOG offering, *World of Warcraft* (which had 10 million subscribers as of this writing), and more recently, *The*

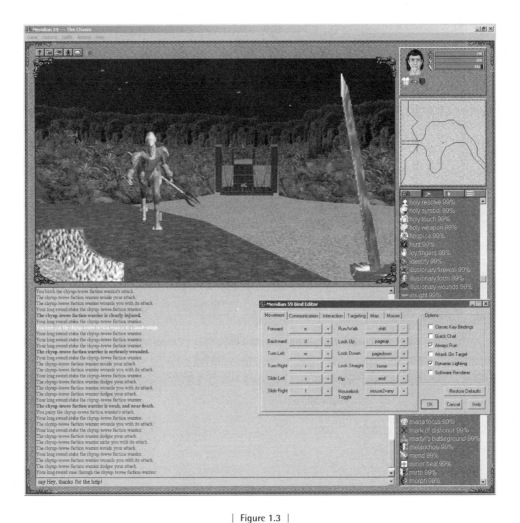

| Figure 1.3 |

The re-release version of *Meridian 59*, launched in 1996, predated *Ultima Online*, which often mistakenly is credited as the first. (Image: Brian "Psychochild" Green, Near Death Studios)

| Figure 1.4 |

Lucasfilm *Habitat*, developed for Quantum Link, a precursor to AOL, and later by Fujitsu. (Image: ©1986 LucasArts Entertainment)

Lord of the Rings Online and *Dungeons & Dragons Online*, embody this role-playing, D&D-derived, Tolkienesque fantasy genre. Variants from Korea, such as *Lineage*, *Ragnarok Online*, and *MapleStory* (the world's largest such game, with over 72 million players, and the second-best-selling content card at Target stores as of this writing) (Haro 2007), provide more accessible variants aimed at a younger audience. These are joined by science fiction-themed games such as *Star Wars: Galaxies*, *Planetside*, and *Anarchy Online*, and others with themes such as pirates, superheros, and horror, many of which build on similar conventions and focus thematically on combat and power fantasies.

Their nongame counterpart, MMOWs, have progressed, perhaps a bit more quietly, alongside MMOGs, and have arguably begun to surpass their gaming cousins in popularity among some demographics. Growing out of the budding game scene, corporate research labs, and the nascent online services industry, graphical social worlds—starting with Lucasfilm's *Habitat* in 1986—predated graphical MMOGs by almost a decade (Morabito 1986, Farmer and Morningstar 1991) (figure 1.4). Admittedly more low-tech, the earliest virtual worlds were 2-D and provided limited affordances for player creativity. *LambdaMOO*, a text-based environment created in 1991 as an experiment at Xerox PARC (the birthplace of the graphical user interface), introduced the notion of a user-created world that players could extend and expand in seemingly unlimited directions using only words on a screen (Curtis 1992). *LambdaMOO*, still in operation, is the most written-about text-based world; with journalistic, academic, and designer accounts, it has become a bellwether for studies of emergent behavior in virtual worlds (Curtis 1992; Mnookin 1996; Dibbell 1995, 1998; Schiano 1999).

As MMOGs were coming into the mainstream, virtual worlds were also experiencing a boom. Inspired by Neal Stephenson's 1992 cyberpunk classic *Snow Crash*, in the age of what Federal Bank then-chairman Alan Greenspan described as "irrational exuberance," dozens of companies were formed to either create or service the emerging virtual worlds industry. Many of these were based within a few miles of where *Second Life*'s Linden Lab stands today. *Active Worlds*, a graphical virtual world launched in 1995, was the first to follow *LambdaMOO*'s model of user-created content, and remains the longest continuously running entirely user-created virtual world. *Active Worlds* was followed by *OnLive!* in 1996, which is now available as *DigitalSpace Traveler*. Many other virtual worlds opened and closed during this period, including the 2-D chat environment *The Palace* and 3-D worlds *Cybertown* and *Blaxxun* (Damer 1997). Adobe Atmosphere, referenced later in this book, is one of the few world-building tools that survived this period, although it was eventually abandoned by Adobe in 2004.

A decade later, both MMOGs and MMOWs are experiencing another period of phenomenal growth. This has been fueled in part by significant advances in on-board graphics technologies for personal computers and the widespread adoption of broadband Internet, two prerequisites that impeded widespread adoption of early virtual worlds and MMOGs.

On the MMOG side, in addition to mainstream titles in the fantasy and sci-fi genres, smaller independent companies are also flourishing with games that could be described as category challengers. Among these are the popular casual MMOG *Puzzle Pirates*, which has added 4 million registered users since it launched in 2003, and New Medeon's *Whyville*, a science learning MMOG for tweens, which had 3.4 registered users, 60 percent of whom are female, at the time of this writing. Even *EVE Online*, a popular science fiction world with a sophisticated economy and political system, is considered highly successful and self-sustaining with as few as 250,000 active subscribers.

The MMOW space also continues to expand in a number of different directions. *Second Life* and *There.com* both opened in 2003, and while the former has taken off as, if not the most popular, at least the most publicized virtual world, the latter has managed to sustain itself through several business transitions. Newer offerings such as *Kaneva* and *Gaia Online* have expanded the range of social worlds. Simpler virtual worlds targeted to kids, which usually have free subscriptions and a virtual items-based economy, are eclipsing even the most popular of their high-end counterparts. *Habbo Hotel*, targeted to tweens, is poised to be the first virtual world to log 100 million subscriptions, albeit not all of them active. These figures, and the imminent release of Sony's *Home*, the first console-based virtual world for the Playstation 3, suggests that virtual worlds may indeed be here to stay. At this writing Google was also throwing its hat into the ring and China had just released its first MMOW, *HiPiHi*.

With all the real and imagined success of MMOGs and MMOWs, there is another more somber side to this narrative: what happens when virtual worlds fail? When new games are released, online games have been known lose audiences in a mass exodus, and the closure of MMOGs and MMOWs is a common occurrence. The very first fantasy-themed graphical MMOG, *Meridian 59*, originally published by 3DO in 1996, closed soon afterward and eventually reinvented itself as a self-sustaining indie enterprise in 2002. Another well-known closure is Microsoft's *Asheron's Call*. We know as little about why multiplayer online games fail as we do about why they succeed. The size of their publishers may be a factor but is no guarantee of success. Why did *World of Warcraft* become a smash hit, but *Star Wars: Galaxies*, built on a perennial, mainstream franchise, turn out to be a weak cult favorite at best? Should sheer quantity of players be the only metric of success? Should we count as successful the smaller, self-sustaining games, like *Meridian 59*? And why do the mid-range games and worlds, such as *Puzzle Pirates*, *Whyville*, *There.com*, and even Disney's groundbreaking but only moderately successful *Toontown*, continue to be overlooked? Even MMOGs backed by big media behemoths, such as Electronic Arts' *The Sims Online*, based on the world's most popular single-player game franchise, re-launched as *EA-Land*, and Disney's *Virtual Magic Kingdom*, were joining the death march to the MMOG graveyard at this writing, even as those same companies were in the midst of launching new products. Since corporations prefer to keep the sources of their failures under wraps, often even couching them as successes, and since there is very little follow-up research on players once they have *left* a game, it is nearly impossible to conduct postmortem analyses of why MMOGs fail.

Among the most-lamented MMOG "failures" is *Uru: Ages Beyond Myst*, the subject of this study. Based on and set in the world of the popular single-player *Myst* series, *Uru* departed from many of the traditional conventions of the fantasy-based, D&D-derived MMOGs described earlier by transporting its complex puzzles and unique style of spatial storytelling into a cooperative, multiplayer game. *Uru* had no fighting, no killing, no levels, and no point system. Players worked together to solve interconnected, brain-twisting puzzles, many of which required a familiarity with the elaborate history, cosmology, characters, story line, and even language of the *Myst* series. This included not only knowledge of the world's mythos and back story, but also facility with its arcane technologies, many of which are instrumental in the puzzle-solving mechanics.

As with the *Sims Online*, it would seem that an MMOG based on a top-selling single-player franchise should have been a sure hit. But in spite of its ardent fan base, two successive attempts at launching the game failed to draw the requisite revenue to ensure its ongoing operation. What *Uru* did succeed in doing, however, was to give rise to a small, devoted, resourceful, and tenacious play community with a distinctive play style that set them apart from players of more popular combat-based games such as *EverQuest* and *World of Warcraft*. Although the Uru community is dwarfed in scale by virtually all of the MMOGs mentioned earlier, its fanbase has exhibited endurance over the long term in the face of trials and tribulations. The phenomenon of the Uru Diaspora has outlived both commercial releases of *Uru* combined. Thus, while *Uru* was not a numerical success, I would argue that it was successful in a number of other significant aspects that will emerge as we delve into the narrative of the Uru Diaspora in more depth.

The expulsion and mass exodus of Uruvians from their "game of origin" at the precise moment when the third wave of virtual worlds was coming online created a powerful confluence of culture, technology, timing, and opportunity. Because Uru and Myst players are particularly tenacious and industrious, perhaps in part because of their decade-long encounter with the "Mensa-level" puzzles of *Myst* games (Carroll 1994), they were poised to display a unique form of emergent behavior.

As we will learn, Uru players migrated into other virtual worlds, created their own *Uru*-based cultural artifacts, and in some cases created entire facsimiles of areas in *Uru*. They created Uru mods in other game engines, including original levels for the game, and they even instigated a network of player-run *Uru* servers to allow players to run the game after its initial closure. This emergent culture, which traversed both games and virtual worlds, provides us with rich insight into the many facets of the interplay between networked play communities and the virtual worlds they inhabit.

| 2 |
VIRTUAL WORLDS, PLAY ECOSYSTEMS, AND THE LUDISPHERE

Virtual Worlds and Their Inhabitants

Virtual worlds share much in common with other media and even other game and digital play genres. But they have a number of distinctive characteristics that lend themselves to particular types of emergent behaviors. As the previous chapter highlights, there are a variety of different world types, each with its own conventions. Media conventions, such as the *D&D*-based frameworks of MUDs and fantasy role-playing games, can be particularly useful to designers, especially in a context where the underlying technologies and standards are changing at such a rapid pace. Note that even as cinema is making a dramatic transformation from film to digital projection, the core conventions of feature films provide a consistent set of guidelines that have changed little since they were initially established in the first half of the twentieth century. Meanwhile, new technologies such as sound, color, and computer special effects have kept filmmakers innovating, even within these constraints.

Similarly, virtual worlds of all genres share a set of conventions that have been proven over time to enhance player experiences and reinforce what Murray calls the "active creation of belief" (1997, 110). In the case of virtual worlds, we might further characterize this as the "collective creation of belief," since virtual worlds are, by definition, social constructions. These qualities also support the formation of what some call "virtual communities" (Rheingold 1993), but I would argue that, although the worlds may be virtual, the communities formed within them are as real as any that form in proximal space (Hyatt-Milton 2005). In this chapter, we shall investigate the core conventions that make up a virtual world and that together create a believable environment that possesses the elusive quality of "worldness."

Lisbeth Klastrup, who has written extensively on the poetics of virtual worlds, defines a virtual world as "a persistent online representation which contains the possibility of synchronous communication between users and between user and world within a framework of space designed as a navigable universe" (2003b, 27). This succinct summary provides us with a starting point from which to build. What are the defining characteristics of these worlds? What conventions do they share, regardless of whether they are MMOGs (games) or MMOWs (metaverses), and irrespective of platform, technology, resolution, or even mode of representation? Drawing from the examples given in chapter 1, as well as synthesizing the work of other authors who have tackled facets of these definitions (Damer 1997; Aarseth 2000; Klastrup 2003a, 2003b; Castronova 2005; Bartle 2003; Mulligan and Patrovsky 2003; Taylor 2006), the following list outlines the principle characteristics of virtual worlds:

- *Spatial* Virtual worlds are at their core spatial. Some would include the requirement that their spatiality must be represented graphically, but I would argue that while they are essentially spatial in nature, they do not necessarily have to be visual. Whether they are represented textually or graphically, in real time 3-D, isometric, or even 2-D graphics, is less relevant than the fact that they define a spatial construct of some kind. This inclusive definition embraces textual, graphical, and even hybrid representations of virtual space.
- *Contiguous* A virtual world is typically geographically contiguous, possessing a sense of spatial continuity or a reasonable premise for breaking that continuity. In some worlds, areas can be conceptually contiguous through a fictional construct, such as the linking books in *Myst* games, or interplanetary travel in science fiction worlds. They may also be contiguous through scale shifts, such as the tiny room a player built inside a television in *LambdaMOO*. Even in worlds such as *Second Life* or *There.com*, in which teleporting exists without a fictional construct, there is still a pervading sense of the geospatial adjacencies within the world. Put another way, most virtual worlds are mappable.
- *Explorable* The contiguous space of virtual worlds makes them inherently explorable; players may go wherever they want, although their movements may be constrained by their level or status in the world, or by available transportation modes (Klastrup 2003a, 2003b). Traversing the world can sometimes be challenging or involve complex mechanisms, and typically takes place in real time, although some foreshortening can occur, such as on a long boat ride. Transportation modes can also be used to make exploration both more challenging, more efficient, or merely more scenic. Interestingly, the vast majority of virtual worlds are built with pedestrian mobility as their baselines, augmenting this with vehicular or air travel, which in games often function as a reward for completed goals. In previous writing, I have argued that, like theme parks, virtual worlds seem to express a longing for a return

to the pedestrian community (Pearce 2007). Exploration is one of the primary pleasures of virtual worlds, as exemplified by the Explorer type in the Bartle player typology (Bartle 1996). In open-ended MMOWs or metaverses, exploration is a central activity in its own right, while in MMOGs, which have a clear goal, exploration is often a means to an end. Bartle has characterized this distinction as "Alice" (open-ended nonlinear) versus "Dorothy" (goal-oriented, result-oriented) exploration styles. (Bartle, forthcoming).

- *Persistent* Persistence is frequently cited as a defining characteristic of virtual worlds. This means that the world remains "on" at all times, and that actions taken within it are cumulative, allowing players to maintain and develop a character from one visit to the next. This contrasts with first-person shooters, in which the world is temporarily constructed for short-term, simultaneous play, but has no affordances for ongoing character development.

- *Embodied Persistent Identities* All virtual worlds include player representations, also known as avatars, another feature that distinguishes them from first-person shooters. In virtual worlds, players have bodies over which they have some creative control and that are also persistent and evolve over time through play. This is distinct from immersive virtual reality, which tends to view embodiment in terms of full sensory input with a first-person viewpoint.

- *Inhabitable* The world is inhabitable and participatory (Damer et al. 1999; Klastrup 2003a, 2003b), meaning one may enter the world and live inside it, actively contributing to its culture. Having an identity or a role is a precursor to inhabitation. Marie-Laure Ryan points out that this is the primary characteristic that differentiates virtual worlds from literature, film, and most other media (2001). In these forms, while one can be immersed in a fictional world, one cannot inhabit it as a participant in its culture.

- *Consequential Participation* The outcome of inhabitation is the consequential participation of the player in the world itself. This means is that your presence is actually a *part* of the world and of other players' experiences of it. In a novel, your absence is not detectable by the characters; in a virtual world, it is. This also distinguishes virtual worlds from traditional immersive virtual environments, which are typically geared to a single-user experience.

- *Populous* A virtual world is by definition a social world. This is what distinguishes it from single-player worlds, including "God Games" such as *Age of Empires* and *Civilization*, and explorable single-player games such as the recent sequence in the *Grand Theft Auto* series. While the population does not have to be *massive* in all virtual worlds, those with the extra *M*, such as *M*MOGs and *M*MOWs, are, by definition, populated by large numbers of people, typically in the tens to hundreds of thousands or even millions. In reality, however, these figures are deceptive: since most MMOGs (less so MMOWs) have multiple segregated servers, or "shards," they are seldom inhabitable by more than a few thousand concurrent players in a given instantiation.

· *Worldness* "Worldness" is perhaps the most elusive quality of virtual worlds. This term is used to express a sense of coherence, completeness, and consistency within the world's environment, aesthetics, and rules. To maintain a sense of worldness, a virtual world must create an aesthetic—in Klastrup's terms, a poetics (2003a)—a syntax, a vocabulary, and a framework that is extensible, sustainable, and robust. Every accessible location in the world must be accounted for in order to create the sense of contiguous, explorable space. Indeed, the very mechanisms of exploration are elements of worldness. One would not, for instance, expect to explore a Tolkien-inspired world in a futuristic spaceship any more than one would expect to see an elf in a pirate world. Worldness can, of course, be expressed in virtually any medium, and in more linear, narrative media, such as films or novels, is treated as a subset of storytelling, what J. R. R. Tolkien termed "sub-creation" (Tolkien 1983, Konzack 2006). Worldness can be gauged in terms of the "collective creation of belief," which becomes a coconspiracy between designers and players. This is a similar challenge to that faced by theme park designers. Theming, like worldness, falls apart when the world and its rationale fail to convince, or when parts of the world are in some way broken or inconsistent.

Murray has identified spatiality as one of the four expressive properties of digital media (1997, 71). In previous writings, I have argued that games are primarily a spatial medium because spatial navigation and organization has become their dominant interaction metaphor (Pearce 1997, 2002c, 2008a). Because spatiality is the unifying principle tying together these characteristic properties of virtual worlds, it becomes particularly relevant in observing patterns of emergent behavior. Players in virtual worlds are essentially playing *in* and *with* space, and, in many respects, the space is also playing *with* them. Thus, inhabiting virtual worlds requires what I term "spatial literacy" (Pearce 2008a). I define spatial literacy, like other forms of media literacy, as the ability to both "read" and "write" in the language of spatial communication and spatial narrative. Different games and virtual worlds utilize different conventions of spatial communication and meaning-making, and as we will see from the *Uru* case, it is often the situated knowledge of the language and syntax of a specific game space that gives rise to emergent behavior. In the case of Uru players, this spatial literacy guided players' understandings of the spaces and stories in *Myst* games, particularly *Uru*, and also enabled them to subsequently re-create and interpret those spaces in other game worlds (Pearce 2008a).

Playing with Identity: The Rise of the Avatar

Central to the discussion of how players inhabit virtual space is the quality of embodiment, which is accomplished through the use of an avatar. The word "avatar," originally a Sanskrit term meaning a god's embodiment on Earth, has been adopted universally in English to describe a player's representation in a virtual world, and increasingly, in online games. Originally coined by Chip Morningstar to describe player representations in the 2-D graphical online community *Habitat* (Morabito 1986, Farmer and Morningstar 1991), the term was later reintroduced independently by science fiction author Neal Stephenson in his influential cyberspace novel *Snow Crash* (1992). Initially, "avatar" was used exclusively to describe player characters in MMOWs, but it has also been adopted in MMOGs, along with "player character," "PC," or, more recently, "toon" (short for cartoon), used primarily in *World of Warcraft*. In games, nonplayer autonomous characters, also known as "bots" (for robots) or "mobs" (for mobiles), are broadly referred to as "NPCs." Some NPCs are enemies (autonomous characters that players do battle with), while others serve as helper-characters that send players on quests or serve as merchants selling gear. Although the term "avatar" (sometimes shortened to "avie" or "avi") can also be used to refer to characters in a text-based MUD or MOO (usually represented only as a text description), it is more commonly used to describe a graphical representation of the player in a two- or three-dimensional virtual world.

One of the unusual properties of avatars is that they are, as T. L. Taylor puts it, "intentional bodies," whose representation and aesthetics are defined by designers and then adopted by players. Players "wear" avatars offered to them by designers, but they sometimes do so grudgingly. In fantasy-themed MMOGs, for instance, Taylor notes "the impoverished view of online embodiment most designers seem to be operating with" (2003). Depending on character "race" (e.g., elf, orc, gnome) and "class" (mage, warlock, warrior), female armor in fantasy games typically has significantly less surface area than its male counterparts, which has prompted me to refer to it as "kombat lingerie" (Fron et al. 2007a). Embodiment can also provide clues to player motivations. In role-playing games of this sort, over half the female characters are generally believed to be operated by male players (Koster 2001; Yee 2001; Seay et al. 2004, 2001–2008). Male players frequently report playing female characters because they prefer the appearance of female avatars, especially from behind (Yee 2003). Conversely, Taylor notes that in the fantasy genre female players are often forced to bracket or ignore their discomfort with their own virtual embodiment (Taylor 2003).

Nongame MMOWs typically provide players with more options and less-hypergendered representations, but they still reveal the designers' intentions. Some older female players in *There.com* like the Disney retro aesthetic and more reasonable proportions of their *There.com* avatars, but frequently complain that they are perpetually 22 years old. *There.com*'s designers went to great lengths to make its female avatars appealing to female players, but failed to consider the possibility that older players might wish to present as such.

Uru avatar creation has affordances for wrinkles, gray hair, and even male-pattern baldness, popular features with both male and female Uru players, the majority of whom are baby boomers. *Second Life* provides a number of different adjustments for breast size and orientation, providing more options for women, but also increasing the possibility for hypergendered representations. There is a popular folk theory in *Second Life* that female avatars with oversized bosoms are likely to be inhabited by male players.

As we've seen and will explore further, in both MMOGs and MMOWs cross-gender play seldom correlates to real-world cross-dressing or transgender activity. Game designer Raph Koster plays female characters in both MMOGs and MMOWs because he prefers the quality of interaction between women. He also enjoys fashion design, which requires that he have a female avatar to test his creations (Pearce 2005). Some male players in *There.com* have female avatars primarily for the purpose of engaging in dress-up play. Conversely, I have heard *Second Life* players complain about the comparative lack of fashion options for male avatars, a problem that is more indicative of the cultural limits of emergence than of the designers' intentions. At the opposite extreme, *There.com*'s virtual fashion industry operated for its first two or three years without affordances for the creation of skirts. This precipitated among the world's predominately female fashion designers a range of emergent behaviors around faking skirt and dress-like garments, including the hoop skirt hoverpack (Fron et al. 2007a).

The relationship between players and their avatars is a complex subject that we are only beginning to understand. As suggested by its original Hindu meaning, research has repeatedly revealed that players often perceive their avatars as a medium through which one's soul, one's deep inner persona, is expressed, even though the avatar's personality may be quite distinct from that of the person controlling its agency. Again and again, both researchers and designers are finding that inhabiting an avatar can often be perceived by players as a transformational inner journey (Turkle 1984, 1995;

Heim 1993; Bartle 2003; Damer 1997; DiPaola 1997–2005, 2008; Taylor 1999, 2002a; Boellstorff 2008; Liatowitsch 2002; Turner, Mancini, and Harrison 2003; Pearce and Artemesia 2007; Bourdreau 2007).

Among participants of the study described in this book, the terms "avatar" and "player" were used somewhat interchangeably, although "avatar" was sometimes used to distinguish things happening to the virtual body of the avatar itself. It is important to note that there is always a player is in command of an avatar's agency, meaning that avatars do not make decisions on their own. (A common misconception conflates avatars and autonomous agents, or NPCs; however, avatars are always human-controlled.) However, as we shall see, the distinction between the player and his or her avatar is somewhat blurry, and players will speak about their avatars in both the first and third person, even describing their corporeal body in physical space as their "real-life avatar." As this suggests, players tended to make a distinction between the body, whether it be virtual or real, and the person or persona who was channeled through one or the other of those bodies. As Taylor has pointed out, this does not mean that an individual's persona is disembodied, but rather that it is expressed through multiple bodies (2003).

Most players in this study felt that their avatars were expressions of their "true" selves as much if not more than were their "real-life avatars." Players who had met each other in real life were able to hold multiple conceptions of each other's identities in their minds, encapsulating the personas as expressed in both the "real-life avie" as well as the avatar in virtual space. This multiplicity of identities is quite commonplace among people living online lifestyles who, in addition to perceiving their own multiple bodies/personas, learn to recognize other members of their play community as also having multiple bodies/personas. (Turkle 1995, Markham 1998, Dibbell 1998, Taylor 1999). It is sometimes difficult for those unaccustomed to virtual worlds to understand these phenomena as anything more than a form of technologically enabled (or even precipitated) multiple personality disorder. However, sociologists have long observed how people adopt or "put on" different personalities or personas in their different real-life roles: worker, parent, friend, and so on. "Performing" different personas in different contexts is a standard part of how we adapt to social situations. In fact, as Goffman has shown, the *inability* to perform appropriately in social contexts is often an indicator of psychological disorders (1963). In virtual worlds, what is viewed as appropriate behavior is often significantly different from what might be considered appropriate within real-life situations or occasions. Just as with real-world games and fantasy play, the play frame sets new constraints that enable one to take liberties with the social expectations and frameworks of ordinary life.

Taking liberties with social transactions within a play frame paves the way for communities to form emotional and social bonds unique to play. Players befriend individuals they might not otherwise have occasion to interact with. Intimacies form around shared imagination and facets of identity that are foregrounded through play. Because play is ultimately a form of expression, whether experienced in a structured game world or an open-ended metaverse, it opens up avenues for personal and social development that provide alternatives to real-life roles. In such an environment, and fueled by networks, bonds can form that are viewed by players as equally authentic, if not more so, than bonds that form in their offline, everyday lives.

Play Ecosystems

The central argument of this book is that emergent behavior in games and virtual worlds arises out of a complex interaction between players and the affordances of the play space they inhabit. This book concerns itself specifically with the genus of play space known as virtual worlds, spanning categories that include games and open-ended play environments of metaverses. The core text provides an analysis of this intersection between lived practices of play and virtual worlds through an ethnographic study of the emergent cultures of a specific play community, the Uru Diaspora. Earlier we identified networked play environments as participatory global playgrounds, in contrast with McLuhan's notion of the global village created by the electronic medium of television. We then identified the properties of virtual worlds. Now we must develop a language for talking about the relationships between these worlds and the emergent cultures they host.

Borrowing from complexity theory, which will be covered in more detail in chapter 3, we might characterize such environments as "play ecosystems." Because these software environments are designed to facilitate networked play, they have specific features and affordances that differ significantly from software we typically associate with other functions, such as work, or even social networking. Until recently, these "serious" functions of networks tended to be privileged over play, with a few exceptions (Danet 2001, Dourish 1998), perhaps because of the marginalization of play in Western culture, as noted earlier via Schechner.

Yet in spite of its marginalized status, well before the advent of digital games, play captured the attention of predigital scholars whose fields range from anthropology to behavioral psychology to philosophy, and who have examined the role of play in culture and human development. Commonly referenced in digital game studies are the canonical works of Huizinga, *Homo Ludens* (meaning "Man the Player") ([1938] 1950), and Caillois, *Man, Play and Games* (1961), but these two are by no means alone. Pioneering educator Maria Montessori ([1900] 1964) invented an entire system of "Didactic Material for Sensory Education" based on the observation that play and experimentation were integral parts of learning (Montessori [1917] 1964). Developmental psychologists Jean Piaget (1962) and Donald Winnicott (1971) both studied children's play at different ages and its impact on learning and behavioral development. Sociologists Iona and Peter Opie (1969) conducted a nationwide survey of street games in the UK. Gregory Bateson observed the astonishing ability, also noted by Piaget (1962, 110–111), of both animals and humans to distinguish between real and play fighting (1972). Anthropologist Brian Sutton-Smith's *The Ambiguity of Play*, a foundational text of digital game studies (1997), is only one of a number of books he authored on the topic (Sutton-Smith 1981, Sutton-Smith and Avedon 1971, Sutton-Smith and Pellegrini 1995). The academic journal *Play & Culture*, which he also cofounded, includes contributions from Schechner (1988), Bateson (1988), and many others. Philosopher Ludwig Wittgenstein also investigated the nature of games and their rules, especially with respect to language (1953). Bernard Suits's philosophical study of games is considered a classic in game studies (1978). Games and play have also been also an integral part of a number of social, political, and art movements, including Dada and Fluxus (Pearce 2006a), the Situationists (Plant 1992), Boal's Theater of the Oppressed (1985, 1992), and New Games (Brand 1972, Fluegelman 1976, DeKoven 1978). The New Games movement also has ties to activist and digital community practices. Cofounder Stewart Brand also founded the *Whole Earth Catalog* and, later, the WELL, one of the oldest continuously running online communities in the United States. Andrew Fluegelman is credited as the inventor of the shareware business model for software marketing.

What do we mean when we say "play" and "game"? This has been one of the principal questions explored and debated by game and play scholars. Caillois, building on Huizinga ([1938]1950), describes the essential characteristics of play as

1) free (not obligatory);
2) separate (circumscribed within the limits of time and space);
3) uncertain (outcomes are not determined in advance);
4) unproductive;
5) regulated (governed by rules); and
6) fictive, make-believe (a "second reality" or "free unreality") (1961, 43).

This definition presents us with two problematics. First is the question of circumscription. Huizinga introduced the term "magic circle" ([1938] 1950) to describe the play frame in which participants mutually agree to suspend everyday rules and social contracts and abide by a alternative set of rules or constraints. This magic circle, which resembles what Turner termed the "liminal" space of ritual (1982), can take a number of different forms: it can be an abstract construct, as adopted by children in street play; a formal ritual context, such as Halloween; an activity defined by a "boundary object" (Star and Griesemer 1989), such as a ball or a game board; a physical space, such as a sports field or arena; or a mediated environment, such as a digital game or a virtual world. There is a tendency to think of the magic circle as impermeable, but as this study shows, and as corroborated by others, while the magic circle may be sacrosanct in theory (Castronova 2004), in practice, for a variety of reasons, it is highly porous (Castronova 2005).

The second problem is the assertion, common to many definitions, that play is inherently unproductive. We have already touched on a number of contexts in which play inspires creative activities, such as *Dungeons & Dragons* figurines, costume design at fan conventions and renaissance faires, and ritual events such as Mardi Gras and Burning Man. As we shall see with the case of the Uru Diaspora, play can become an engine for a high level of creativity and innovation, which can take a variety of forms, through both leveraging and subverting software affordances (Pearce 2006b).

Taking into account the foregoing two caveats, Caillois's definition is thus serviceable, but it leaves unanswered one question of particular importance to our discussion of MMOGs and MMOWs. This is the question of distinguishing a *game* from other forms of play.

The formal characteristics of games have been a matter of particular interest to digital games scholars, and as a result, when we begin to look at formulating a clear description of "game," we find numerous variant, and sometimes conflicting, definitions. (For a comparative analysis of game definitions, see Salen and Zimmerman 2004, 71–84). While resolving this question is not the purview of this book, it warrants some attention because virtual worlds of both types are covered within this research.

Building a hybrid derived from the most widely accepted definitions, most games researchers would agree that a game is a formal system for structured play constrained by a set of rules that prescribe the means of achieving a specified goal (Suits 1967, 1978; DeKoven 1978; Pearce 1997; Salen and Zimmerman 2004; Fullerton, Swain, and Hoffman 2004; Juul 2005). Bernard Suits humorously but accurately characterizes this paradox as the deliberate contrivance of the most inefficient means of accomplishing a task (1967, 22). From here, debate takes over. Must a game's goal be definitive? Must there be a finite win/lose state that represents success or failure to accomplish the goal? Must a game's goal or even its rules be articulated at the start of play, or can they be discovered through the process of gameplay itself?

These questions become particularly contentious in the context of MMOGs, most of which do not explicitly state their goals and rules up front. Moreover, the goals of such games are typically based on the open-ended, though linear, objective of "leveling," constructed through a series of provisional micro-win/lose states associated with specified quests or tasks. Once the maximum level is reached, the gameplay actually shifts to a different mode, rather than concluding as do traditional board games or even single-player video games. In fact, losing, or even winning, is anathema to most MMOGs. Because they are subscription-based, they rely on an economic formula that precludes the closure typically associated with winning or losing in traditional games. MMOGs can also contain individual goals that differ from the main goals—player-, role- or group-specific goals, as well as missions or quests. Players can and often do augment the prescribed goals with metagoals of their own, such as becoming a successful merchant or creating an überguild. These metagoals can be categorized as forms of emergence. Other forms of emergence can occur when players do not strictly follow the teleological trajectory of the game's goals, instead "playing around," or engaging in a more exploratory, non-goal-focused way.

MMOWs add another order of complexity to the problem. While these are clearly not games, they tend to have significant elements of gameness. Most MMOWs actually contain games within them, as well as rules of various kinds, and some even contain forms of skills leveling. Players will also construct their own metagoals, such as becoming a successful fashion designer or nightclub operator. Player content-creation also introduces affordances for players to design their own games within an open-ended play space. Some environments, such as *There.com* and *The Sims Online*, provide more complex mechanisms for social networking, as well as specific point rewards for socializing, typically absent from the majority of MMOGs.

The friction between games and nongames has also been deeply embedded in discourses among game designers, reviewers, and scholars, who tend to valorize those play experiences defined as "games" over those which are characterized as open-ended play spaces or sandboxes. These arguments are deeply entrenched in power structures, market economics, and highly gendered industry rhetorics of gaming and gamers that result in entertainment software products that appeal to women often being marginalized as "not games" (Fron et al. 2007b). Even entertainment titles as popular as the best-selling franchise *The Sims*, which has sold 100 million copies worldwide, are often trivialized on this basis. Will Wright, designer of *The Sims, Sim City*, and *Spore* has described himself as "not a game maker" (Suellentrop 2007), and has characterized his titles as "possibility spaces" (Pearce 2002b).

Ludic versus Paidiaic Worlds

While the game/not game argument may seem academic in the pejorative sense, it does have some bearing on our analysis here, especially because we will be describing a case where the boundaries of each are transgressed. As Tom Boellstorff has pointed out, "crossing a boundary can strengthen the distinctiveness of the two domains it demarcates" (2008, 23). In the case of intergame or interworld immigration, it both does and doesn't, in ways we shall explore further in book II.

The game bias is deeply embedded in the discourses of technoculture and digital media, as epitomized by the very naming of the discipline "game studies," as opposed its anthropologic antecedent, "play studies." Huizinga, for instance, tended to conflate play and games and seemed to privilege more "agonistic" (or competitive) play forms that involve, in his words, "virility" ([1938] 1950, 64), "frenzied megalomania" (101), and competition for superiority. Clearly this language is highly androcentric and both Huizinga and Caillois, men of their eras, repeatedly trivialize girls' play, addressing it minimally and characterizing it as "rehearsal for motherhood" (Caillois 1961, 62). Nonetheless, Caillois begins to address our game/not game dilemma by introducing into the discourse a differentiation between games, which he characterizes as "ludus," and open-ended, creative play, which he characterizes as "paidia" (1961, 13). These two play forms exist on a spectrum and share a number of qualities in common, but also have unique properties that distinguish them from one another.

Clarifying these distinctions can help us understand both the designers' intentions and play practices within what might be characterized as ludic versus paidiaic worlds. While both styles of play occur in both types of virtual worlds, ludic game worlds and paidiaic nongame virtual worlds have distinct design goals and constraints that differentiate them in significant ways. The primary distinction is that ludic worlds present the player with a prescribed overarching goal while paidiaic worlds do not. Ludic worlds have a formal structure of objectives and a set of constraints that dictate how those objectives might be met, whereas paidiaic worlds provide players with a range of activities and options for social interaction.

Often called metaverses or social worlds, non-goal-based, paidiaic virtual worlds are characterized more as sandboxes, in which players engage in open-ended, unstructured, creative play, although they typically allow for more structured play to emerge at players' discretion. Because they generally include affordances for user-created content, such MMOW sandboxes often include more formal games within their larger open-play framework; however, because of the absence of an overarching goal, these worlds cannot be considered games in the formal sense. While the world type may guide player activity, providing a context and motivation for one type of play over another, players in either type of world frequently engage in the opposing play styles. MMOG players often engage in paidiaic play alongside, around, or in some cases, against the prescribed rules of the game; MMOW players often construct their own form of game or structured, goal-oriented play. We also see a game-within-a-game form of emergent play where players invent different games than prescribed by the software. One example of this is the Dn'i Olympics, a player-created sporting event in *Uru* that overlaid a metagame on top of, but distinct from, the existing game environment and its rules.

All virtual worlds, whether ludic or paidiaic, have rules. World rules take the form of player constraints, as well as the world's properties—its physics; its cosmology, or world view and values; its "karma system," or causal structure; its feedback systems, including rewards and penalties; its communication mechanisms and interfaces; its economic structure and transaction mechanisms; even its allowable modes of transportation. World rules constrain the ways in which players can interact with the world and each other, and the ways in which they may contribute to constructing the world, if at all.

World rules are important in our discussion of emergent behavior because they embody the affordances through which emergent behavior materializes. World rules include:

- Communication protocols—does the system allow for synchronous or asynchronous communication such as in-world email or forums? Must I be in the presence of another player or may I communicate with them in real time remotely? Can I communicate with players individually or must all communication be within a group? Do I communicate primarily with speech, text, or a combination of the two?
- Group formation protocols—how are groups formed? Can I belong to more than one group? What is the basis of group affiliation? What are the benefits or affordances of group membership? Can I send messages to my group members? Can I invite my entire group to events I plan?
- Economics—can I "own" things? Are there currencies or mechanisms for synchronous or asynchronous trading, such as an in-game auction feature? Do I have to physically go somewhere to buy/sell/trade, or may I do so remotely? Do I have to be in-world to buy things, or can I do so via a web site or other means? If I do have belongings, how are they protected?

- Land/home ownership—may I own land or a home? If so, what rights do I have there? What rights can I give others? How much control do I have over the design/décor? Can I restrict access? Can I share my home with my group or my friends?
- Avatar creation/progression—what are the constraints of avatar construction? Must I choose a race, such as an elf or orc? How much customization and control do I have over appearance, such as skin color, hair, or facial and body features, as well as attire? Is avatar clothing instrumental to gameplay or merely aesthetic? What other sorts of attributes does my character have? How might these progress over time? Can my avatar die? If so, for how long? What are the requirements for resurrection? Are there penalties involved?
- Geography/terrain/transportation—what are the features of the geography and the allowable modes of transportation? Are there mounts or vehicles? Can I fly (autonomously or via mount or vehicle)? Can I swim, or travel by boat?

While both MMOGs and MMOWs have world rules that describe the world and its properties and some constraints of player actions, MMOGs alone possess overarching goals and embedded rules that prescribe what players are to do and how they are to accomplish given goals or tasks.

It should also be noted that, in general, players in this study did not make a cultural distinction between a virtual world and a game, although they clearly understood the difference between an open-ended play environment and one with a clear goal. In practice, all of the environments explored in this study were referred to colloquially among the study participants as games, regardless of whether they met the qualifications described earlier.

Imaginations at Play: Fixed Synthetic and Co-created Worlds

Because the study of the Uru Diaspora spanned several virtual worlds of different varieties, including MMOGs and MMOWs, it became evident that, while not irrelevant, the binary distinction of game/not-game was limited in providing deeper insight into emergent behavior within online games and virtual worlds. More important than the game/not game question are the underlying architectures that support these ludic and paidiaic play forms. When we look at these architectures beyond the abstract and perhaps theological arguments about their game-like qualities, we discover much more salient and subtle properties embedded within their structures that have significant ramifications concerning emergent behavior.

Bernard DeKoven describes games as "social fictions" that exist "only as they are continuously created. They are not intended to replace reality to but suspend consequences" (1978, 1). In Monopoly, for instance, landing on the "Go To Jail" square does not result in real-life incarceration. The notion of a social fiction can be applied to both ludic and paidiaic worlds, and of particular relevance to our concerns here will be the question of whose social fiction, precisely, it is.

Game design has been described by Salen and Zimmerman as a form of "second-order design." They point out that, "As a game designer, you can never directly design play. You can only design the rules that give rise to it" (2004, 168). Thus, how do you design for meaningful play when the play itself is unpredictable, essentially out of your control? The social fiction of virtual worlds can thus be viewed as a confluence of imagination: that of the designer and that of the players. Therefore the job of the game designer is to imagine what the player might *imagine* and what he or she might *do*. In some cases, particularly in more formal games, players may also try to imagine what the designer had in mind. Each is therefore trying to create a mental model of the other's imagination. The paradox that the game designer can never entirely anticipate the player's imagination is the very essence of emergence.

As starting point, borrowing from complexity theory (which shall be explored in more depth in chapter 3), we might characterize virtual worlds as play ecosystems along a spectrum that parallels ludic/paidiaic play forms, and also helps to define the dynamics of imagination between designer and player. At one end of this spectrum is the "fixed synthetic" world, which foregrounds the designer's imagination; at the other is the "co-created world," which foregrounds the imaginations of players (figure 2.1).

This distinction is useful for two reasons. One is that the apparent ambiguity and overlap between paidiaic virtual worlds and ludic online games can create confusion and mire arguments in the question of whether something is or is not a game. Second, the relationship between MMOGs and MMOWs is in the process of shifting due in part to interworld immigration patterns that cross the game/not game threshold, such as those explored in this study. Thus placement of various worlds along this fixed synthetic/co-created worlds spectrum shifts the binary framing of the problem and allows us to understand the way underlying software architectures and designer intentions influence emergent behaviors.

Fixed synthetic worlds tend to be ludic environments more typically defined as games. These worlds, while extensible and modifiable, are defined primarily by the world's designers, who have absolute control over narratives, game mechanics, rewards and penalties, world rules, and geographical and architectural design. They tend to have strong themes and an overarching story line that comprises smaller subnarratives,

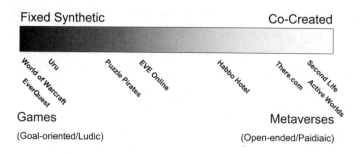

| Figure 2.1 |

Examples of different virtual worlds positioned on the spectrum of fixed synthetic vs. co-created worlds. (Image: Pearce)

as well as a metagoal comprised of smaller, relatively fixed goals. Avatar characters are usually developed instrumentally from a kit of parts defined by the designer, along a fairly prescribed trajectory of gameplay.

At the extreme, these worlds cannot be modified by players in any sanctioned way, although some do allow for limited modifications that influence the player's individual play experience, but seldom change the world as a whole. Examples of fixed synthetic worlds include such popular games as *EverQuest*, *World of Warcraft*, and, to a lesser degree, *Uru: Ages Beyond Myst*, the primary subject of this study (figure 2.2).

At the opposite end of this spectrum is the co-created world, an open-ended paidiaic environment designed for spontaneous play and creative contribution; in other words, productive play. These usually include affordances for the customization of avatars and environments, and can also contain characteristic Web 2.0 features allowing players to engage in content creation within the parameters of the world's design. At its extreme, virtually all in-world items and activities are created by players, and one could argue that all aspects of such worlds are emergent. These worlds typically do not have a set theme or story line, although they often have a unifying metaphor and/ or aesthetic direction, such as *Habbo Hotel's* use of a hotel metaphor and its bitmapped, isometric visual style, or *OnLive!'s* social metaphor of a cocktail party (DiPaola and Collins 2003).

Co-created worlds typically have affordances for creativity and allow players to build their own spaces, create their own artifacts, and vary their avatars or clothing based on aesthetic or expressive, rather than instrumental, considerations. At a more moderate level, players may be able to purchase furnishings and clothing and decorate their space or avatar. At a higher level they may be able to introduce original artifacts, alter terrain, or create animations and code. *LambdaMOO*, the text-based world

| Figure 2.2 |
World of Warcraft is a fixed synthetic world. (Image: Pearce)

created by Pavel Curtis in 1991, is the primordial co-created world and *Second Life* is perhaps its ultimate graphical instantiation to date. Other examples include Lucasfilm's *Habitat* (later Fujitsu's *WorldsAway*), *Active Worlds*, and *OnLive!*, each of which offered players varying degrees of freedom for social and creative play. Worlds and technologies that follow constructionist learning theory (Papert and Harel 1991), such as Papert's LEGO Mindstorms project (Papert 1993) or Bruckman's MOOSE Crossing (Bruckman 1997), are also examples of these types of experiences (figure 2.3).

One observation we can make is quite simply that emergence happens, regardless of where the world falls along the fixed synthetic/co-created, ludic/paidiaic spectrum. However, the types of emergence that occur are directly connected to these underlying architectures. The study also shows that emergence can and does migrate *between* both types of worlds, between other forms of mediated communication, as well as into the real world. Each of these worlds can be viewed as its own play ecosystem with its own unique characteristics. As play communities migrate between these ecosystems, traversing magic circles, they adapt to accommodate the ecosystem, and the ecosystem also adapts and mutates to accommodate them. The larger sphere of virtual worlds and supporting technologies (forums, chat, voice over IP, etc.) between which players migrate can also be viewed as a kind of metaecosystem, a web of complex relationships

| Figure 2.3 |
Virtual worlds *There.com* (left) and *Second Life* (right) are co-created worlds. (Images: Celia Pearce and Jacquelyn Ford Morie)

between these more bounded networked play spaces. I characterize this network of play ecosystems and supporting technologies as the "ludisphere."

There is often a misconception that player creativity in co-created worlds is entirely unconstrained, but the claim that a world like *Second Life* is limited only by the player's imagination is spurious. It is just as limited, if not more so, by the imaginations of its designers. While *Second Life* may place very little restriction on what players can create, the world comes heavily laden with an embedded set of libertarian, free-market, free-speech values coupled with a creation mechanism that places significant constraints on content creation. Beneath this ideological patina lies a more hegemonic governance framework in which edicts are handed down from high (Au 2008). The outcome is an implicit policy that in practice translates as: "You can do anything you want, unless we decide you can't."

Second Life's authoring environment takes place primarily in-world, thus allowing for a high level of collaboration, and also for instant gratification. Yet it falls into the classic game design ideal of being easy to learn, but challenging to master. As a result, there is a high quantity of user-created content in the world, much of which is of marginal quality; on the other hand, those who have developed mastery of *Second Life*'s cumbersome authoring system are able to create remarkably beautiful and expressive artifacts. This has resulted in the emergence of a system of economic and social status based on technical proficiency.

In a more controlled co-created world, such as *There.com*, player creation of artifacts takes place primarily out-of-world and no new player-created content can be introduced without official approval from the company's management. Thus, there is less content, but artifacts are of higher quality and more congruent with the world's overall look and feel, maintaining a more consistent aesthetic that reinforces immersion and believability. Other co-created worlds, particularly those targeted to children, such as *Habbo Hotel*, are even more constrained; thus we should not assume that players in co-created worlds have unlimited creative freedom.

Conversely, we should not regard fixed synthetic worlds as less creative or less prone to emergence than their co-created counterparts. Indeed, emergence in these worlds can be, in some respects, far more creative precisely because it is more constrained. The ways in which players appropriate and subvert the environment to their own ends can be extremely creative, and players' inventiveness in subverting game affordances can be a source of pride, respect, and social status. Part of the skill of subversion lies in a thorough understanding of the game world's deep structure—its rules and affordances, as well as its defects. Flaws in games are as much material for emergence as features, as we shall see in our case study.

Our main concern therefore will be, in what way do the design affordances of these worlds lay the groundwork for emergent behavior? The narrative of the Uru Diaspora will provide one detailed scenario of precisely these interrelationships. It will reveal the ways in which constraints and affordances, as dictated by the world's designers, serve as the raw materials for large-scale emergent behavior.

EMERGENCE IN CULTURES, GAMES, AND VIRTUAL WORLDS

Emergent Cultures

The emergent properties of real-world cultures have long been a topic of interest to historians, economists, sociologists, anthropologists, and urban planners. Urban historian Lewis Mumford described and mapped out patterns of growth in European cities, radiating from a central core, usually a cathedral (1961). Urbanist Jane Jacobs, in her famous critique of 1950s urban planning policies, spoke about the ways in which mixed-use densities in cities promote and hinder emergent behavior, both positive and negative (1961). Architect Bernard Rudofsky published an extensive study of indigenous architecture, noting the patterns created by different vernacular structures as communities expanded or migrated over time (1965). A similar study in emergent architecture is Steward Brand's *How Buildings Learn*, which analyzes the ways buildings are transformed and adapted—"modded," in gamer parlance—through use (1994).

In economic terms, Thomas Schelling described this type of emergence as "systems that lead to aggregate results that the individual neither intends nor needs to be aware of" (1971, 145). To demonstrate how such a system might work, he created a simplistic model of racial segregation using a rule-based checkerboard simulation. Individual agents of two binary types were said to be happier when neighboring agents were of their own group. Consequently, the outcome over time of a series of proximity moves would result in increased segregation, regardless of whether the agents were deliberately segregationist. He used this model to show how segregation in ghettos can self-organize in an emergent, bottom-up fashion rather than through deliberate or institutionalized exclusion.

Contemporary approaches to human cultural and historical development have taken a similar complex systems approach, and have reconfigured how we think about the notion of progress. The now-outmoded idea of cultural evolutionism, which suggests that some societies and civilizations are somehow more evolved and hence better than others, is being challenged in various ways by interpretations that frame society and history in terms of the dynamics of complex systems.

In his Pulitzer Prize-winning book, *Guns, Germs, and Steel,* Jared Diamond proposes a new reading of the historical domination of some cultures over others as an emergent process arising from the intersection of available resources and technologies, geographical conditions, and biological processes (such as disease), rather than an essentialist predisposition for superiority. Diamond illustrates the role of feedback loops, such as European exposure to and consequent immunity to disease, which served as a powerful, if inadvertent, biological weapon against the indigenous cultures of the Americas (1997).

While his approach is quite different from Diamond's, Manuel De Landa also argues for a complex systems approach to what he calls "nonlinear history" and rejects the deterministic model of cultural development (1997). Like Diamond, he critiques the notion of the dominance of Western culture as progressive, and looks instead at history as a possibility space that does not necessarily produce inevitable outcomes. He describes emergence as the "unplanned results of human agency" (17). And while some decisions made by individuals are constrained by the goals of organizations, in other cases, "what matters is not the planned results of decision making, but the unintended consequences of human decisions" (17). De Landa argues that emergent properties, which can be characterized as the whole being greater than the sum of its parts, cannot be studied using reductive methods.

These emergent (or "synergistic") properties belong to the interactions between parts, so it follows that a top-down analytical approach that begins with the whole and dissects it into its constituent parts (an ecosystem into a species, a society into institutions) is bound to miss precisely those properties. In other words, analyzing a whole into parts and then attempting to model it by adding up the components will fail to capture any property that emerged from complex interactions, since the effect of the latter may be multiplicative (e.g., mutual enhancement) and not just additive. (17–18)

Historically, emergent cultures can take hundreds or even thousands of years to develop. Yet as Diamond points out, the advent of new technology can rapidly accelerate these processes. Guns, for instance, allowed for much more rapid colonial expansion and accelerated the rate of genocide throughout the new world. Technologies of transport, as McLuhan has pointed out, accelerated the expansion of goods and people westward across the industrializing United States (1964). The Internet is just such an accelerating technology, and emergent social processes that might take years to play out in real life, such as the example of intergame immigration chronicled in this book, can happen in a matter of months, weeks, or even days. The speed of communication enabled by the Internet allows for a kind of snowball effect in terms of feedback dynamics. People tend to follow trends among their peers, not, as some might cynically suppose, because people behave like sheep, but because, as Schelling's model suggests, they wish to maintain a connection to a community. Thus, as with his segregation example, we find numerous instances of humans gathering, moving, and assembling based on a desire to join or to remain proximal to a community with which they identify.

Emergent Cultures in Games

Emergent cultures have existed in networked play spaces since their inception. Weddings in early MUDs and MOOs and MMOWs such as *Active Worlds* were commonplace. In the late 1990s the phenomenon of eBaying began to emerge, in which players of *Ultima Online* and other massively multiplayer games began to sell game accounts (in other words, their avatars), virtual objects, currency, and real estate. Supported by an extravirtual network with a highly developed feedback system, the eBay auction site, they were able to emergently spawn an entire real-world economy around the trade of virtual characters, commodities, and currency (Dibbell 2006).

This emergent phenomenon inspired economist Edward Castronova's now-famous economic analysis of *EverQuest*, in which he determined its imaginary universe, Norrath, to have the *real* world's seventy-seventh largest economy (2001). By analyzing exchange rates and trade volumes on the online black market for virtual goods and currency, he was able to calculate a gross domestic product for Norrath that placed it on an economic scale with real-world nations. Castronova's research is itself emergent, the outcome of emergent behavior on a large scale, precipitating emergent behavior on a smaller scale. His groundbreaking work has inspired a growing interest in the economies of virtual worlds. This interest has reached as far as the U.S. Federal Reserve, which is investigating both the tax and regulatory ramifications of virtual economies, as well as their utility as research contexts for the study of real world economic behavior (Campbell 2008).

While eBaying is banned by most game companies, the black market for virtual items and currency not only flourishes, but has spawned an entire global industry. In 2007, journalist Julian Dibbell, known for his early studies of the text-based world *LambdaMOO*, visited a "gold farming" factory in China. Here low-wage laborers, usually young men, live and work in barracks-style housing, spending their days playing *World of Warcraft* and gathering virtual currency, which their employers then trade on the black market for real-world profit. Dibbell noted that when these young men finish work, they go to the facility's cybercafé, where they enjoy their time off by playing *World of Warcraft*. This practice has also precipitated new emergent social behaviors within the game. Players believed to be Chinese gold farmers are shunned in a form of racism that conflates real (Chinese) and virtual (the most common characters played by gold farmers) ethnicities (Dibbell 2007).

Second Life has brilliantly leveraged these emergent economic trends as the only virtual world that sanctions the free buying and trading of its virtual currency for real money. As a result, it has attracted more publicity than its competitors as players have begun to make their real-world living through its virtual economy (Hof 2006). This policy precipitated the emergence of an in-world banking industry, and the eventual collapse of one of *Second Life*'s player-created virtual banking system. As in real-life cultures, the outcome was a run on the banks, to the tune of $750,000 in real-world financial losses (Sidel 2008). All of these examples can be viewed as emergent: they were the result of individual agency, bottom-up individual actions that aggregated into large-scale patterns of social behavior.

While some forms of emergence in games happen as a result of an aggregate of individual actions, others are more deliberate, and resemble real-world grassroots organizing. One example is a game-wide protest that was staged in *World of Warcraft* in 2005 (Taylor 2005). Warriors of all races, dissatisfied with what they felt were unfair statistics associated with their class, gathered at urban centers and even blocked a bridge to demand a change to the very software they inhabited (figure 3.1). In the process, they managed to down a server, which did not have the capacity to process such a high volume of players in a single virtual location. Game operator Blizzard, in the typically top-down approach of corporations, squelched any further uprisings by banning players found to be involved in or planning in-world protests. In other words, the company took the stance of a totalitarian regime by making civil disobedience punishable by virtual death. Because Blizzard is a company and not a nation, its players/customers/citizens had no rights whatsoever in this situation.

The totalitarian stance taken by Blizzard is common to MMOG companies. When players first initiate an account, they are required to sign an end-user licensing agreement, or EULA, that for all intents and purposes relinquishes any rights they might enjoy in the real world as a precondition of becoming a citizen of a virtual one. Most EULAs state that the company has full ownership of all intellectual property generated by players. Game companies often exercise their own intellectual property rights by prohibiting extra-virtual practices, such as some forms of fan fiction or the buying and selling of virtual game artifacts. *Second Life* is again the exception: although they

| Figure 3.1 |
Warrior protest in *World of Warcraft*. (Image: Pearce)

implemented a radical policy that allows players to retain all rights to their *intellectual* property, the company still owns the *virtual* property that represents those ideas; in other words, they may not own the ideas, but they own the bits.

As a result of some of these draconian practices, ethicists and lawyers have begun to ask, what sorts of rights, exactly, do avatars have? And how might these be reinforced? Do we need some kind of bill of avatar rights? (Reynolds 2007, Spence 2007). One thing seems to be clear: again and again, people inhabiting avatars inevitably arrive at the conclusion that they *have* rights, often based on the rights they are accustomed to enjoying in their real-world cultures. American players, for instance, expect the right to free speech as well as self-determination. These desires and expectations often come into conflict with virtual world owners, who are more preoccupied with business concerns, such as maintaining a high profit level and protecting themselves legally (Taylor 2002b). Corporations that control virtual worlds will tolerate a certain measure of emergent behavior as long as it does not threaten their bottom line. Consequently, griefing, a form of emergent gameplay in which players deliberately distrupt the gameplay of others, is generally tolerated, while mass protests and virtual currency exchange are not.

Defining Emergence

The conception of games as complex systems with emergent properties is so prevalent in the discourse of both game design and game studies that it would be impossible to cite its origins. Descriptions of emergence can be found in a diverse array of contexts, from books on popular science (Johnson 2001) to game design theory (Juul 2002, Salen and Zimmerman 2004, Sweetser 2007). So what, precisely, do we mean by "emergence?"

Emergence as a phenomenon comes out of the study of complex systems or complexity theory, another area that also serves as a fulcrum for interdisciplinary research. The Santa Fe Institute, one of the preeminent centers for the study of complex systems in the United States, encompasses fields as diverse as social science, economics, mathematics, game theory (a branch of applied mathematics and economics unrelated to game studies), ecology, evolution, the environment, organization and management, neuroscience, intelligent systems, and network infrastructures (Santa Fe Institute 2008). The Human Complex Systems group at the University of California, Los Angeles embraces every permutation of its theme, from economics to urban planning and computer-generated synthetic cultures, to multiplayer online games (UCLA 2008; Sanders and McCabe 2003, 6, 44). The term "emergence" describes how complex, often decentralized systems self-organize in ways that cannot be predicted by their underlying structures or rule sets, nor by the individual behavior of agents within the system (Bar-Yam 1997). Anthills, freeways, neural networks, stock markets, terrorist cells, cities, the Internet, and computer games are examples used to describe emergence (Johnson 2001). These disparate systems have in common a display of collective behaviors and even collective intelligences that arise out of, and yet transcend the actions of, the individual parts or elements.

According to Steven Johnson, author of *Emergence: The Connected Lives of Ants, Brains, Cities, and Software*, complex systems exhibit emergence because they

. . . solve problems by drawing on masses of relatively (simple) elements, rather than a single, intelligent "executive branch." They are bottom-up systems, not top-down. They get their smarts from below. In more technical language, they are complex adaptive systems that display emergent behavior. In these systems, agents residing on one scale start producing behavior that lies one scale above them: ants create colonies; urbanities create neighborhoods; simple pattern-recognition software learns how to recommend new books. The movement from low-level rules to higher-level sophistication is what we call emergence. (2001, 18)

It is significant that one of the key characters Johnson features in his discussion of emergence in all its permutations is Will Wright, designer of the games *SimCity*, *The Sims*, and *The Sims Online*, and games make repeated appearances throughout the book. The notion of emergence as a property of games is pervasive. Media scholar Janet Murray has described one of the properties of computational media as being "procedural," or rule-based (1997). Rule-based systems have a greater tendency toward emergence because they have a larger possibility space with affordances for more varied outcomes. Even simple rules systems can produce complex, emergent outcomes.

Using examples of board games, sports, most action games, and all strategy games, ludologist Jesper Juul argues that emergence is "the primordial game structure, where a game is specified as a small number of rules that yield large numbers of game variations, that the players must design strategies for dealing with." "Progression" he describes as "the historically newer structure" in which we find "cinematic storytelling ambitions" in this otherwise indigenously procedural and hence emergent medium (2002). In *Rules of Play*, Salen and Zimmerman look in depth at notions of games as complex systems and emergence as an outcome of the interaction of rules (2004). In my 2002 paper on emergent authorship, I described a new model for storytelling in which players themselves contribute to narratives in games such as *The Sims*, *Ultima Online*, and *EverQuest* through emergent processes (Pearce 2002a). Cindy Poremba's master's thesis provided a further analysis of the player as co-creator within the context of these emergent story systems (2003). These ideas parallel Henry Jenkins's notion of "textual poaching," in which fan cultures, such as Star Trek fans, aka "Trekkies," develop their own emergent narratives from the kit of parts provided by the television series (1992).

So what, precisely, is emergence, and how might it be studied? In his essay for the book *Virtual Worlds: Synthetic Universes, Digital Life, and Complexity*, Yaneer Bar-Yam, president of the New England Complex Systems Institute, defines emergence as a set of "collective behaviors" in which all the parts are "interdependent," arguing that the more distinct and specialized the individual interdependent behaviors, the more complex the collective behavior likely to arise (1999). Bar-Yam describes emergence as

1. what parts of a system do together that they would not do by themselves; collective behavior.
2. what a system does by virtue of its relationship to its environment that it would not do by itself.
3. the act or process of becoming an emergent system. (2003)

Further:

According to (1) emergence refers to understanding how collective properties arise from the properties of the parts. More generally, it refers to how behavior at a larger scale of the system arises from the detailed structure, behavior, and relationships at a finer scale. In the extreme, it is about how macroscopic behavior arises from microscopic behavior. (Bar-Yam 2003)

In discussing methodology, Bar-Yam suggests a holistic approach to observing the relationship between the parts and the system as a whole:

. . . emergent properties cannot be studied by physically taking a system apart and looking at the parts (reductionism). They can, however, be studied by looking at each of the parts in the context of the system as a whole. This is the nature of emergence and an indication of how it can be studied and understood. (1997, 11)

To describe this process, Bar-Yam invokes the metaphor of "[seeing] the forest and the trees at the same time . . . We see the ways the trees and the forest are related to each other" (2000). Sociologist C. Wright Mills has drawn upon the same metaphor to describe the essential character of what he calls "the sociological imagination" (1959).

The forest/tree metaphor illustrates the key challenge of studying emergence in large-scale social systems. This type of research necessitates a methodology that enables one to observe and analyze phenomena at different scales simultaneously. In other words, it must enable us to look at the behavior of individual units in a complex system, their relationship to each other, and the overarching patterns of the system as whole, all at the same time. We cannot, as De Landa has pointed out, calculate the patterns within a complex system by the reductionist method of studying the properties of its parts. It is also crucial to be able to observe the system's dynamics, as well as their outcomes, in progress. Capturing their evidence exclusively after the fact, either through surveys or forensic evidence, such as artifacts, will not allow a complete understanding of patterns of emergence. In addition, we are faced with the problem of observing the relationship between the play community and the play ecosystem, which can only really be understood as a lived practice.

As Bar-Yam points out, "One of the problems in thinking about the concepts of complex systems is that we often assign properties to a system that are actually properties of a relationship between the system and its environment." This is particularly significant to the research described here, where relationships between players, as well as the players' relationship to the environment of the virtual world, are central: "When parts of a system are related to each other, we talk about them as a network, when a system is related to parts of a larger system, we talk about its ecosystem" (2000).

Returning to our earlier discussion placing MMOWs along a spectrum of fixed synthetic versus co-created worlds, we can begin to look at these environments as play ecosystems in which networks of players engage in various emergent behaviors. This is where the distinctions between different types of worlds become important: each ecosystem provides particular designed characteristics and affordances that affect the emergent behavior of networks within it. As we shall see, a play community can exhibit patterns of emergence that transcend any particular virtual world, but these are made explicit through interactions unique to the affordances of each play ecosystem.

One of the critical properties of complex systems is feedback. In cybernetics, feedback is defined as a phenomenon in which some portion of the output of a system is passed through the input. This can be used to describe machines that use feedback systems, the classic example being a thermostat on a heater (Wiener 1948, 96). The thermostat continually reads the temperature and makes adjustments accordingly.

Within networked social systems, feedback can be a powerful engine for large-scale social emergence, and the accelerated forms of emergence seen in these systems are a direct result of the designed affordances of the software. Examples of this on the Internet include iTunes, MySpace, and YouTube, each of which has grown exponentially since its inception through feedback. This process, epitomized by YouTube, can be described thus: the more people who watch, the more people who upload videos; the more people who upload videos, the more people who watch. Networks are particularly good at processing feedback since many units of input can move quickly through the system and be distributed to a large number of outputs. This research concerns the ways in which both the social context of play and the design of the game software itself facilitate this feedback process.

The qualities of properties of play are critical. Play can be viewed as a particular type of engine for emergence by virtue of its feedback dynamics. Play is inherently spontaneous and experimental, and therefore players will find themselves responding

| Figure 3.2 |
A wedding in *Active Worlds* c. 1996. (Image: Bruce Damer)

to social feedback in a very different way than they might in other contexts. The common types of emergence seen within virtual multiplayer games and virtual worlds illustrate this point. As we've seen, they include online weddings (figure 3.2), game-wide protests, social organizations such as guilds or social groups, various types of social and fashion trends, and extravirtual phenomena such as fan sites and the selling of virtual characters, items, or currency.

The play frame sets the stage for many of these phenomena, but the virtual environments themselves also have particular properties that lend themselves to emergence:

- *Discrete* Virtual worlds are (mostly) closed systems, discrete synthetic environments that possess and maintain a consistent set of internal rules. Within that closed system, we can observe classic properties of emergence, such as feedback, and multigenerational patterns. In addition, they also have a variety of transactions with worlds outside themselves, which can both influence in-world emergence and produce extravirtual forms of emergence.
- *Open-ended* Both social virtual worlds and game worlds are open-ended; they do not have a finite win state or conclusion.
- *Persistent* Persistence allows for cumulative action, without which emergence would not be able to play itself out over time.
- *Synchronous and asynchronous* The property of allowing for both synchronous and asynchronous inhabitation also provides another feedback mechanism to support the propagation of emergent behaviors.
- *Long-Term* Engagement in multiplayer games and virtual worlds is long-term. Persistence also allows for one player's behavior to build on another's, so even with the effect of "churn" (players leaving a game) we can still see extended emergent behaviors over time. Churn can also produce emergent behavior, as we've discussed, such as a mass exodus to a new world.
- *Accelerated* Social phenomena in MMOGs tend to happen at an accelerated rate. In spite of the fact that tasks often take significantly longer to perform than in the physical world, players often report losing track of time and of having the sense that "time flies." Simultaneously, there appears to be a phenomenon of time compression in which social processes that would ordinarily take much longer are perceived and observed to occur at a highly accelerated rate. Friendships and romantic relationships appear to develop more quickly, and the growth and decline of communities seems to progress much faster than would be the case in real-world settlements, although no systematic comparison has been done as part of this or other research that I am aware of.
- *Networked* As mentioned earlier, MMOGs and MMOWs are by definition populated. The more people, the larger the possibility space for emergence.
- *Diverse* As Bar-Yam points out, the more specialized and diverse the units in a complex system, the more complex the system, and the more opportunities for emergent behaviors. In more homogenous systems, behavior is relatively uniform, so emergence is less likely to occur, as behaviors are less likely to diverge from their initial purpose and more likely to arrive at equilibrium rather than exhibiting change over time (2003). James Surowiecki, author of *The Wisdom of Crowds*,

points out that collective intelligence emerges at a much higher level in groups that are diverse than in groups whose individuals have uniform skills and abilities (2004).

One of the challenges of studying emergent behavior is that we sometimes only know it by its forensic evidence. We know, for instance, that thousands of players abandoned *The Sims Online*, but we do not have any way to understand what happened after the fact. In addition, emergence often happens at such a large scale that it is very difficult to observe in any meaningful way, other than in terms of demographics or quantitative data.

In order to explore the main research focus of emergent behavior in virtual worlds, the challenge was to identify a subject that met all the criteria for emergence, but was imminently studyable. The Uru group fit these criteria for the following reasons:

- *Emergent behavior* The Uru group exhibited emergent patterns of behavior that fell outside of the formal structure of the game as intended by its designers, and which exhibited the bottom-up process described earlier.
- *Events over time* The eighteen-month time frame was identified as a period commensurate with traditional anthropological field studies, and also aligned with the churn rate that many developers have identified as typical of MMOGs (Appelcline 2004). This was an ample duration to gather sufficient data, especially given the phenomenon of social acceleration mentioned earlier. It should also be noted that emergent processes don't necessarily end when the research stops, and as we'll see, the emergent cultures of this group have continued far behind the formal part of the study.
- *Scale* The study of emergent behavior requires a sufficient group size to obtain significant results. It would not have been feasible for a single ethnographer to study the entire Uru Diaspora, who numbered 10,000 at the game's initial closure. A smaller subset was thus chosen, The Gathering of Uru, which comprised between 160 and 450 players during the course of the study, a manageable number for a qualitative study. This figure is also considered statistically significant for quantitative research.
- *Components versus system* By definition, emergent phenomena transcend the life cycle of any one of the elements within the complex system. Therefore, the emergent phenomena studied had to demonstrate recognizable patterns across a diverse sampling of individual participants.

- *System versus environment*   Emergent phenomena happen when a system comes into contact with a specific environment or ecosystem. In the case of the Uru Diaspora, the network actually traversed several different virtual worlds, giving us a glimpse at how its emergent behavior adapted to each ecosystem.
- *Method*   The study had to use a multiscaled method that would allow observation of the forest and the trees at the same time: in other words, it had to be possible to observe the three components—system, parts and ecosystem—concurrently.

A methodological conundrum confronts us at this point. What tools and methods should we use to observe the emergent phenomena we have defined here? There are a number of different established methods in game studies. Quantitative methods, such as surveys, and in-game data mining can provide us with very useful information; they are excellent at understanding the scope of individuals' attitudes about their gameplay experience. They are also effective at getting at the larger patterns of behavior and attitudes displayed by individuals. Quantitative methods are, however, less effective at getting at larger patterns of interaction *between* individuals. Large-scale surveys help us understand that people are spending an average of twenty hours a week in online games, but not specifically what they are doing, who they are spending time with, and how they interact in social contexts within the ecosystem. Data mining, such as capturing chat logs in a fixed location, is an excellent method for discourse analysis in specific contexts, although it does not give us the attitudinal data of surveys, nor measure larger cultural patterns across multiple locations. Social network theory, used extensively in Internet studies and computer-mediated communications, branches of sociology, and organizational theory, provides excellent methods for understanding the movement of information and the overall structures of social networks. Yet it lacks the tools we need to study the intersubjective social transactions of meaning-making from which cultures are constructed. Thus we need to identify a method that is particularly strong at analyzing and interpreting the dynamics and formation of culture.

READING, WRITING, AND PLAYING CULTURES

Situating Culture

What do we mean by "culture?" Some, especially lawmakers and mass media, would assert that "game culture" is an oxymoron. Indeed, games are viewed as so low a form of culture, at least in the United States, that some judges have ruled that they do not warrant the same speech protection rights as other media because they do not qualify as a form of expression (Au 2002). Most media scholars would disagree.

Video games have been called the medium of the twenty-first century. The fact that video games are part of the mass media landscape can no longer be sufficiently argued against in light of the data. According to several reports, the number of digital game players in the United States has been steadily growing, reaching about two-thirds of Americans by 2007, roughly a quarter of whom are over 50 (a bit higher than the percentage of baby boomers as in the overall population) (NDP Group 2007, Entertainment Software Association 2008). In 2007, Nielsen media research reported that nearly half of American households had a game console by the fourth quarter of 2006 (Nielsen 2007). And judging by the fact that there are now sufficient peer-review-quality academic papers to justify the publication of a journal titled *Games and Culture*, it is safe to say we have arrived at a point where the previous debates about whether these two terms can coexist in the same phrase can be put to rest.

In the context of media, culture is usually thought of in terms of cultural production, such as arts, entertainment, and literature. But to anthropologists and sociologists, "culture" has the much broader connotation of the entire repertoire of collective symbols and forms of meaning-making, including language, arts, ritual and mythology, and everyday practices that are shared by a given group or society. Such practices are said to be "intersubjective," meaning that they are constructed through interactions between people, rather than by the strict agency of individuals. Anthropologist Clifford Geertz describes culture as "webs of significance [man] himself has spun," the analysis of which is "not an experimental science in search of law but an interpretative one in search of meaning" (1973, 5). Geertz sees these webs of significance as public systems of meaning that are necessarily the collective property of a group. Culture is both constructed and learned, is iterative, and is constantly in flux. Most importantly, culture is shared.

The concept of intersubjectivity provides a useful framework to think about the ways culture is constructed, learned, and propagated. The culture of a networked game can be viewed as a social construction of shared meanings between designers and players. These shared meanings are constructed with what Thomas Luckmann called the individual's "life-world" through everyday social or cultural practices (1983). Sociologist Herbert Blumer, building on Herbert Mead's previous work, coined the term "symbolic interactionism" to describe this shared meaning-making (1969). In essence, individuals interpret objects through a lens of meaning that arises out of a process of social interaction and has the capacity to change over time.

Intersubjectivity is what Seale defines as "the common-sense, shared meanings constructed by people in their interactions with each other and used as an everyday resource to interpret the meaning of elements of social and cultural life" (2004). Intersubjectivity is used largely as a means to look at the world through the lens of social transactions, rather than individual psychology and motivation (Blumer 1969). Many aspects of culture, such as language and ritual, are considered intersubjective because they both arise from and become materials for social transactions.

Michael Jackson argues for intersubjectivity as a useful lens through which to observe the construction of culture (1998). He notes Joas's notion of the "intersubjective turn" (1993) in which "subjectivity has not so much been dissolved as relocated" (Jackson 1998, 6). To Jackson, intersubjectivity helps us better understand how different cultures construct different conceptions of the relationship between "the one and the many." It "resonates with the manner in which many non-Western peoples tend to emphasize identity as 'mutually arising'—as relational and variable—rather than assign ontological primacy to the individual persons or objects that are implicit in any intersubjective nexus;" it also "helps us unpack the relationship between two different but vitally connected senses of the word subject—the first referring to the empirical person, endowed with consciousness and will, the second, to abstract generalities such as society, class, gender, nation, structure, history, culture, and tradition that are subjects of our thinking but not themselves possessed of life" (Jackson 1998, 7).

The advent of digital social networks brings new resonance to this intersubjective turn, materializing the abstract notion of the "noosphere" (Teilhard de Chardin 1961), a kind of shared knowledge space that Marshall McLuhan observed as being realized through electric media (1964). The results of this study suggest that such networks are connecting modern culture to traditional, non-Western forms and reconfiguring our sense of the relationship between the one and the many.

At its core, this research explores everyday practices of popular "fan" culture. As such it may be seen to overlap to some degree with the concerns of ethnographers such as Paul Willis, who builds on De Certeau's theory of "the practice of every day life," suggesting that "consumption" in industrial societies is an act of production, perhaps even an art form (De Certeau 1984). Willis applies this notion in describing the cultural practices of British "bike boys," motorcycle gangs who modify and customize their motorbikes as a form of personal and creative expression (1978). Willis argues for an approach to ethnography that frames the process of meaning-making in everyday life as an art practice. Similarly, this study explores the relationship between play and creativity, and celebrates the artistic instinct that underlies all play practice. Because the ethnographer must also engage in the creative act of consumption—in other words, playing the game—she is also intimately implicated in these cultural practices.

Willis also points out the strong connection between subjective and intersubjective processes, the social construction not only of meaning, but also of identity: "Cultural practices of meaning-making are intrinsically self-motivated as aspects of identity-making and self-construction: in making our cultural worlds we make ourselves" (1978, 100).

In other words, according to Willis, individual identity and the construction of culture are in constant discourse, and each feeds the other. Far from the Cartesian model of "I think therefore I am," Willis suggests that individual identity cannot be so neatly separated from culture. "Of the relationship between social constructs and individual behavior, Willis asks, "Do we speak language, or does it speak us?" (2000, 15). We could easily reframe the question: "Do we play games, or do they play us?"

Interestingly, Jackson also touches on issues directly relevant to play culture when he speaks of "playing with reality":

If life is conceived as a game, then it slips and slides between slavish adherence to the rules and a desire to play fast and loose with them. Play enables us to renegotiate the given, experiment with alternatives, imagine how things might be otherwise, and so resolve obliquely and artificially that which cannot be resolved in the "real" world. (1998, 28)

Drawing from Willis and Jackson, life might be construed as both a game and an art practice comprising both the exploration of and the bending of rules. Wills envisions ethnography as a puzzle to be solved, a position that this project explicitly embraces as integral to its methodology (2000). Thus ethnography itself also becomes both a game and an art practice.

Just as players themselves are in a sense creating through consuming, the ethnographic process here is ultimately also framed as an art practice, one which is reflexive, and which tries to unravel some of the classic dichotomies of both ethnography and games: what is real, and what is virtual, what is fiction and what is fact; how the subjectivity of the ethnographer affects the study subjects, and even more interestingly, how the study subjects affect the ethnographer. Just as the magic circle is porous, this reflexive, performative approach also reveals the porousness of the research process itself: in human matters, boundaries are never as clear as we idealize them to be.

One place that this boundary has been idealized is in attempts to enforce the magic circle and maintain a strong boundary between virtual worlds and the real world. Edward Castronova has approached some of the inherent tensions with this concept, initially making a case for maintaining the integrity of virtual worlds as "a world apart" from real world laws, customs, and culture (Castronova 2004); he later conceded that such a utopian goal is impractical and ultimately unenforceable, and has characterized "The Almost-Magic Circle" as more of a "membrane" (2004, 147) than an impermeable boundary in the strict sense (Castronova 2005). In practice, because most massively multiplayer games and virtual worlds are played on computers (as opposed to game consoles), they vie for attention with other PC functions such as e-mail, forums, instant messaging and voice-over-IP, and productivity and creativity software, as well as other games. And because many virtual worlds are open, allowing creative input from players, as offensive as this cultural "miscegenation" may be to some MMOG purists, it is an inevitable outcome of emergent behavior.

This point, along with the findings of this research, brings us to one of the main challenges we face in the study of both emergence and play: both are, by their very nature, unpredictable. When you introduce the variable of intergame immigration, with players dispersed not only geographically but also virtually, within multiple play ecosystems, you are faced with a methodological conundrum. Addressing this challenge is part of an ongoing effort by myself and others to develop methods by which to study and interpret the emergent and labile cultures of play.

Methodology: Multi-sited Cyberethnography

What research strategy could possibly collect information on unpredictable outcomes? Social anthropology has one trick up its sleeve: the deliberate attempt to generate more data than the investigator is aware of at the time of collection. Anthropologists deploy open-ended, non-linear methods of data collection which they call ethnography; I refer particularly to the nature of ethnography entailed in anthropology's version of fieldwork. Rather than devising research protocols that will purify the data in advance of analysis, the anthropologist embarks on a participatory exercise which yields materials for which analytical protocols are often devised after the fact. In the field the ethnographer may work by indirection, creating tangents from which the principal subject can be observed (through "the wider social context"). But what is tangential at one stage may become central at the next. (Strathern 2004, 5–6)

Marilyn Strathern's description of the anthropological method, quoted by anthropologist Tom Boellstorff in the inaugural issue of *Games & Culture* (2006), resonates on a variety of levels with the larger project of the study of game cultures. In particular, her description suggests that ethnography itself is an emergent process, and thus is uniquely suited for studying cultures of emergence in online games and virtual worlds, and potentially elsewhere. The ludic environments of online games are characteristically open-ended, nonlinear and participatory, unpredictable and labile, and thus require an agile and responsive approach to research. They are also characterized by lived experience, which is one of the central concerns of ethnography. Contemporary, postcolonial, post-structuralist cultural anthropology avoids arriving at cultural contexts with hypotheses or preconceived scenarios about what might occur and what it might mean. This is a particularly useful approach in the social studies of games because of their inherent unpredictability and emergent qualities.

Ethnography has been widely adopted among researchers from computer-mediated communication, computer-supported collaborative work, game studies, and a range of other disciplines related to networked communication. Variants of this method have been used to study diverse aspects of network culture, including the World Wide Web, IRC/chat, MUDs and MOOs, forums, and blogs (Turkle 1995, Hine 1998, Mnookin 1996, Paccagnella 1997, Markham 1998, Bell and Kennedy 2000, Nocera 2002, Kendall 2002, Reed 2005). Ethnography is also used in computer-supported collaborative work (Nardi and O'Day 1999; Nardi, Whittaker, and Bradner 2000; Nardi 2005), as well as Garfinkel's related "ethnomethodology" (1967), the study of shared (folk) methods (Dourish 2001). Ethnography can also be used as part of a participatory design process (Salvador and Mateas 1997; Salvador, Bell, and Anderson 1999; Barab et al. 2004).

"Virtual ethnography" (Mason 1996) has come into popular use in Internet studies, although I prefer the term "cyberethnography" because of the baggage that "virtual" inevitably carries with it. Christine Hine has described virtual ethnography as:

particularly provocative in exploring the ways in which the designers of technologies understand their users and the ways in which users creatively appropriate and interpret the technologies which are made available to them. Among the questions preoccupying workers in this field has been the extent to which values, assumptions and even technological characteristics built into the technologies by designers have influence on the users of technologies. A view of technology emerges which sees it as embedded within the social relations which make it meaningful. (1998)

It is unfortunate that the design of these environments, let alone their underlying values, is so often overlooked. Many of the articles featured in the *Journal of Computer-Mediated Communication,* for instance, have little reference to the software or interfaces within which the social interaction being described takes place. Social network analysis, similarly, often lacks the sense of context that is vital to understanding games from a cultural perspective. Scholars of human interface design, in particular those who study networked collaborative workspace, devote far greater attention to software design (Salvador, Bell, and Anderson 1999; Dourish 2001; Nardi and O'Day 1999). Approaches drawn from this discipline, such as Nardi's studies of social interaction and collaboration in *World of Warcraft,* can help us better understand the specificities of how software serves as not only a context but as a medium for social interaction (Nardi and Harris 2006). While there is a significant body of writing about the underlying values of software (Friedman and Nissenbaum 1996), as well as the cultures of the environments in which software is produced (Born 1995), it has not been until fairly recently that either the values or cultures of virtual world creation have been a subject of study (Losh 2006, 2009 [forthcoming]; Malaby, forthcoming), although we do have some precedents from practitioners (Curtis 1992, Damer 1997, Kim 1997, Horn 1998, Bartle 2003, Mulligan and Patrovsky 2003, DiPaola 2008, DiPaola and Collins 2002, 2003). There is a great deal of room for further exploration of the game design process, both in terms of methods used and the socioeconomic and cultural contexts in which game design takes place.

Borrowing from Marcus's concept of "multi-sited ethnography," which addresses the problem of anthropology in a global system (1995), the method used here blends techniques from anthropology, sociology, and "virtual ethnography," which I characterize as multi-sited cyberethnography. Although not originally developed as a method for studying networked cultures, Marcus anticipated the applicability of multi-sited ethnography to media studies, which he describes as "among a number of interdisciplinary (in fact, ideologically antidisciplinary) arenas" that might find utility in such a concept (97). Because of the nature of this study, which concerns the migration of game communities between virtual worlds, Marcus's multi-sited ethnography provides a means to, in his words, "examine the circulation of cultural meanings, objects and identities in diffuse space-time" and it "investigates and ethnographically constructs the lifeworlds of various situated subjects " as well as "aspects of the system itself through the associations and connections it suggests among sites" (96).

This last point is key because Marcus sees multi-sited ethnography as a means of understanding a "world system," or in this case a "virtual world system," encompassing the totality of networked games and virtual worlds on the Internet—what I am calling the ludisphere. Marcus's framework for understanding the complexity of anthropology within the world system, and especially the transmigration of peoples, cultures, and artifacts across borders, is highly applicable to the project at hand in which players are migrating across the borders of magic circles in virtual worlds. It also allows for the multiscaled approach of studying both the individual players and the system as a whole, our repeating theme of looking at the forest and the trees concurrently.

Thus, in a multi-sited ethnography, comparison emerges from putting questions to an emergent object of study whose contours, sites, and relationships are not known beforehand, but are themselves a contribution of making an account that has different, complexly connected, real-world sites of investigation. (Marcus 1995, 102)

In describing this method, Marcus outlines a number of approaches, each of which entails following some aspect of culture across borders. The three being applied here are "Follow the People" (1995, 106), specifically, the migrations of players between different game worlds after the closure of the original *Uru* game; "Follow the Thing" (106–107), in this case intellectual property of the *Uru* game and its emergent fan cultures; and "Follow the Story" (109), the narrative of the refugee status of the Uru Diaspora. I would also add to this the methods of "following up" and "following leads," which often entail taking on the very tangents to which Strathern alludes earlier, and are particularly relevant in a play space where much of the activity is unstructured and unscheduled. Not only do "Cultures . . . not hold still for their portraits" (Clifford and Marcus 1986, 10), they constantly change their orientation to their portraitists. This is particularly true in ethnographies of play, where the strategy of following requires a highly improvisational approach, and one which I would characterize as opportunistic: being in the right place at the right time and going with the flow of whatever is happening in the moment. Play is by nature spontaneous and unpredictable, requiring what Janesick describes as a choreographic approach (2000) that is flexible, responsive, and playful.

Playing and Performing Ethnography

All the world is not, of course, a stage, but the crucial ways in which it isn't are not easy to specify.

—Erving Goffman, *The Presentation of Self in Everyday Life*, 1959

Live in your world. Play in ours.

—Sony Computer Entertainment, Marketing Campaign Slogan, 2003

At a historical moment when the roles of audience and performer increasingly conflate, Erving Goffman's "dramaturgical" approach to sociology (1959) is experiencing a renaissance. In his manifesto *Performance Ethnography*, Norman Denzin invokes Goffman when he points out that "We inhabit a performance-based, dramaturgical culture. The dividing line between performer and audience blurs, and culture itself becomes a dramatic performance" (2003, 81). To illustrate, Denzin draws our attention to the "nearly invisible boundaries that separate everyday theatrical performances from formal theater, dance, music, MTV, video and film" (81). Yet Denzin somehow neglects to include in his analysis the medium that has, more than any other, brought the conflation of performer, audience, and stage to its fullest realization.

With its proliferation of personal web sites, blogs, photo sites, forums, and Web 2.0 applications such as YouTube and MySpace, as well as online games and virtual worlds, the Internet is perhaps the largest stage in human history. A number of digital media scholars have made this correlation (Laurel 1991, Murray 1997), and networks have only enhanced the performative nature of computing. The Internet has transformed computers from singular participatory theaters to complex and populous discursive performative spaces where every participant is both performer and audience. Online games and virtual worlds, with their fantasy narratives and role-playing structures, are arguably the most dramatic instantiation of the digital stage. While all the *real* world may not be a stage, it can be argued that all virtual worlds most definitely are.

Performance ethnography has been defined in two ways. The first, epitomized by the work of Turner and Schechner, as well as van Gennep, entails the study and analysis of the role of performance and ritual in cultures (Schechner and Schuman 1976, Turner 1982, van Gennep 1909). This form of anthropology has typically embraced play and games as a subset of ritual and performance, although generally not as its focal point. In this regard, Victor Turner's notions of the "liminal" and "liminoid" space are particularly apt. Both concepts, like Huizinga's magic circle, define a space outside of the everyday. For Turner, the liminal space of ritual serves as a kind of transitional gateway from one dimension or stage of life to another (such as between seasons or phases of life, or between the world of the living and the dead), while liminoid space serves as a respite between daily activities of production, characterized by leisure practices in industrialized, Western cultures (1982). Ritual events such as weddings in virtual worlds suggest a blending of the liminal and the liminoid. They redefine virtual worlds as a "space between," as well as a site of transformation (as mentioned earlier and corroborated by other research; see Turkle 1995, Dibbell 1998, Taylor 1999, Bartle 2003).

Turner and Schechner also collaborated to pioneer the second type of performance ethnography described by Denzin, the theatrical performance of ethnographic texts and narratives, often with audience participation (Manning 1988). Yet Denzin's assertion that "performance approaches to knowing insist on immediacy and involvement" (2003, 8) suggests a third type of performance ethnography, one in which the ethnographic method of participant observation is itself framed as a performance. The study of game culture demands such an approach because its object, play, can only be adequately understood through immediate and direct engagement.

Virtual worlds present us with a unique context for ethnographic research because they are inherently performative spaces. Unlike traditional ethnography, one cannot enter into an online game or virtual world without joining in the performance. There is no defined distinction between performer and audience; they are one and the same. Goffman's concept of the performance of everyday life (1959), especially in the context of public space (1963), provides us with a starting point for understanding networked play space as a kind of everyday co-performance. Thus when we talk about the phenomenon of "seeing and being seen," we are also implicating the importance of both *having* and *being* an audience. As has already been discussed, this co-performative framework can be seen in myriad forms of participatory culture, from fan conventions (Jenkins 1992) to renaissance faires and costume play (Miller 1998) to the annual Burning Man festival (Gilmore and Van Proyen 2005), all of which blur the boundaries between Turner's liminal and liminoid spaces.

Play contexts where behavior that might not ordinarily be sanctioned is not only allowed, but also lauded, recall Goffman's concept of "occasioned" behavior (1963). Here, and in his essay on frame theory, Goffman points out that our roles are constantly shifting depending on the context (1974). Similarly, when people enter into a play frame, they are literally and figuratively playing by a different set of social rules that allow them to take liberties with their roles and identities that they might not take in ordinary life.

The entrée into this co-performative space is the creation of the avatar, a pseudo-fictional character, an alter ego. The first step of a player entering a virtual world is to invent a character name. This becomes the signifier of her situated identity going forward: the marker of reputation, the vehicle of her agency, and the representation of her cumulative actions. This character and even its appearance may change and be transformed over time, but the name remains the same. The player also crafts her initial visual representation in the world, given a kit of parts provided by the designers. This creative act, much like choosing a costume for a masquerade ball, is the first performative gesture, the scaffolding on which her future identity will be built. From this point forward, players both play and play *with* their emergent identities through an intersubjective process.

Far from being singly a creation of the individual, the avatar is a mechanism for social agency, and the player's identity-creation will emerge in a particular social context through a set of interactions with a particular group of people. Avatars do not exist in isolation, and through this intersubjective co-performative framework players may discover sides of themselves that may not have avenues of expression in the other aspects of their lives, even sides of themselves of which they may not previously have been aware. At times, these forms of expression can be subversive, in both negative and positive ways. Part of what this study reveals is the relationship between the emergence of individual and group identity through the performance and practice of play.

For in practicing the ethnography of play, we are playing ourselves. The ethnography is a mystery to be unraveled, and the identity we form in this context is at once a scientific discipline and an art practice. When he coined the term in 1984, science fiction author William Gibson characterized "cyberspace" as a "consensual hallucination." When we enter an online game or virtual world, we enter a space of the imagination, and as researchers, we take on the task of studying consensual hallucinations populated by real people, all of whom share in this performative and productive act. The ethnographer is no exception, and very quickly will find that she is drawn into the play space. Yet she also stands outside the magic circle to some extent. As an observer, she must play the game, but at the same time, she plays a metagame, the game of ethnography itself. And like her subjects, she never knows where this identity will take her. In spite of her objective stance, she is not immune to the very emergent processes she seeks to understand.

Feminist Ethnography

Feminist anthropology has a useful set of frameworks to bring to the study of game cultures. Early anthropologists concerned themselves almost exclusively with male aspects of culture, in a way not dissimilar from the extreme yet unstated male bias that pervades both the game industry and, as a consequence, contemporary game studies. Game scholars, as some have already done, might take a lead from feminist ethnographers such as Margaret Mead and Zora Neale Hurston, who tried to amend this bias by including or even highlighting female subjects. In *Fictions of Feminist Ethnography*, Kamala Visweswaran points out the ways in which female anthropologists draw an entirely different reading from a culture by gaining access to women's cultural practices and perspectives, harvesting different insights than their male counterparts (1994).

The work of anthropologists such as Mead (1949), Hurston (1935), Shostak (1981), Powdermaker (1966), Smith Bowen (1964), Behar (1993), and others gives us insight into female attitudes, practices, and rituals to which male ethnographers would not have been privy. At the same time, women ethnographers, viewed as outsiders by the cultures they study, can also gain access to aspects of male culture that females native to that culture cannot. Men may also find the female ethnographer less threatening, and thus reveal different information than they would to her male counterpart. Thus, women ethnographers may have an entirely different angle of access to the culture overall as a result of their renegotiated gender status.

In addition to shifting the gender focus, feminist ethnography has long challenged boundaries between subjectivity and objectivity, individual and society, researcher and subject, fact and fiction, self and other, and art and science, and is frequently dismissed as "subjective" and hence "unscientific" (Visweswaran 1994). But as Ruth Behar argues, taking the role of the "vulnerable observer" and accepting emotional engagement as a legitimate part of the ethnographic process may ultimately lead to a deeper truth (1996).

Feminist ethnography also challenges structures of power and authority and casts subjects in the roles of collaborators, or even as the drivers of the research. Ruth Behar was chosen by her research subject because Esperanza wanted the anthropologist to tell her story (1993). In the aptly titled *Stranger and Friend*, Hortense Powdermaker describes being drawn into the preparations for a dance ritual by her Lesu subjects, who eventually invited her to participate in the ritual itself (1966, 111–112). Feminist ethnographers Eleanore Smith Bowen (nom de plume Laura Bohannan, 1964) and Zora Neale Hurston (1937) blurred the boundary between fact and fiction. Hurston's work is often categorized as autoethnography, a common methodological approach among MMOG researchers, particularly women, who frequently select their own play communities as a subject of study. "In Hurston's ethnography," states Visweswaran, "community is seen not merely as an object to be externally described, but as a realm intimately inhabited" (33). Likewise, the play community may be best studied when "intimately inhabited," as communities can be seen with greater depth when viewed from their interiors. As this study shows, such intimate inhabitation may be the inevitable outcome of participant observation within play cultures.

Also integral to practices of feminist ethnography is our position toward the authoritative voice of the subject. Not unlike Hurston's folklore, this research serves as an oral history, a kind of folklore, with the subjects' voices front and center.

Even if the particular subjective position of the female ethnographer were not privileged in this study, it might still be categorized as a feminist ethnography strictly on the basis of demographics alone. The group of Uru refugees this study concerns represents a disproportionately high percentage of women, exactly 50 percent, relative to other MMOG studies, even those conducted by women. This figure parallels the larger Uru demographics overall, suggesting that *Uru* also stands out as a game with a distinct appeal to nontraditional MMOG audiences, including not only women, but also older players.

In addition to its subject matter, this study is philosophically aligned with the concerns of feminist ethnography and expands them into the realm of digital cultures. As such, this research takes a particular stance toward observing and interpreting cultures, and draws on feminist ethnography to address the challenge of exploring and transgressing borders between fiction and reality.

Reading and Writing Cultures: Ethnography of Fictional Worlds

If we agree that one of the traditional ways to think about fiction is that it builds a believable world, but one that the reader rejects as factual, then we can easily say of ethnography that it, too, sets out to build a believable world but one that the reader will accept as factual. Yet even this distinction breaks down if we consider that ethnography, like fiction, constructs existing or possible worlds, all the while retaining the idea of an alternative "made" world.

—Kamala Visweswaran (1994, 1)

This study is not a fiction. Rather, it sets out to create a nonfictional account of a fictional world, and explores the emergent culture of a "fictive ethnicity," an identity adopted around an imaginary homeland (Pearce 2008c). Proponents of Baudrillard's theory of simulacra (1994; Schechner and Schuman 1976) might find such a notion alarming. In his disdain for the synthetic, Baudrillard failed to recognize the immediacy and *reality* of imagination, and the human need for alternative modes of being, a fact that is well documented by Victor Turner (1982) and others (van Gennep 1909, Schechner and Schuman 1976).

Although denizens of fictional worlds, the Uru Diaspora shares discursive qualities of real-world diasporas, which, according to James Clifford, represent "experiences of displacement, of constructing homes away from home" (1983, 302) and relating to such notions as "border, creolization, transculturation, hybridity" (303). In conceiving a contemporary definition of diaspora, Clifford cites Rouse, who describes a diaspora as a single community that maintains "transnational migrant circuits" through "the continuous circulation of people, money, goods and information" (1991, 162). However, as Safran (1991) and Anderson (1991) both point out, some real-world diasporas may ultimately be just as mythological as the fictive identity of the Uru Diaspora, whose communal identity is of choice, rather than geopolitics or genetics. This fictive identity presents us with a unique conflation of global corporate culture and fan-based media subversion. While on the one hand, the Uru identity is built upon an artifact of corporate media, namely the *Uru* game, on the other, it provides its denizens with the freedom to build and extend their own vision and values around a fictional identity that provides an augmentation to, rather than an escape from, their various real-life roles. Furthermore, Uruvians frequently make a point of highlighting their nonviolent ludic values, as juxtaposed against those of most other MMOGs and their players.

While this notion of a fictive ethnicity may seem like a conundrum, anthropology is a discipline that has long blurred the boundary between science and art; anthropologists have written along a spectrum from the more formal style of the ethnographic monograph to anthropologically informed works that are baldly framed as fiction. The question of whether anthropological texts can or should be viewed as literature has vexed anthropologists going back to ethnography pioneer Bronislaw Malinowski, who wondered whether or not ethnographic writings should adopt a literary style (1967). At its heart, this struggle is about the role of narrative: should anthropologists be storytellers, or merely interpret data? To what extent is an anthropologist a folklorist, and to what extent a scientist? Margaret Mead's research on female adolescence in Samoa was famously critiqued as fiction (Freeman 1983), an assertion that is itself likely to have been fiction (Patience and Smith 1986). Thus anthropological perspectives, even at their origins, provide a theoretical context for reflexively exploring the contested territory between real and fictional cultures, and the role of the ethnographer in their construction.

In large part because of its historical relationship with colonialism, contemporary anthropology also provides us with a means to reflect on and interrogate the relationship between the researcher and her subjects, both in the field, and in matters of representation. As Clifford and Marcus point out:

Since Malinowski's time, the "method" of participant observation has enacted a delicate balance of subjectivity and objectivity. The ethnographer's personal experiences, especially those of participation and empathy, are recognized as central to the research process, but they are firmly restrained by the impersonal standards of observation and "objective" distance. In classical ethnographies the voice of the author was always manifest, but the conventions of textual presentation and reading forbade too close a connection between authorial style and the reality presented. (1986, 13)

They add that "States of serious confusion, violent feelings or acts, censorship, important failures, changes of course, and excessive pleasures are excluded from the published account" (13). Ironically, these types of events are often the most important and can also have significant implications for the research. Ethnography is a messy business, and while the common practice is to present a cleaned-up version of events, there can also be value in exposing the ethnographer's process of what Edward Shils calls "learning as he stumbles" (1957).

I grappled with this extensively, and finally decided to address these issues in book IV, which attempts to address some of these stumbles while avoiding "interrupting the flow of the main ethnographic narrative" (Behar 1996) or allowing my own narrative to eclipse that of my subjects (Wolcott 1990). In fact, some of the more challenging moments of rupture also yielded significant epiphanies, precipitated a stronger relationship with the subjects, and ultimately caused me to modify my research methods. Therefore, although these narratives may be perceived as personal, they were germane to the research and thus warrant inclusion in the account of the results. Far from being trivial, they illuminate facets that a traditional "objective" account cannot reveal. If this is a polyphonic text, then in a sense, Book IV is devoted to my inner voice, reflecting on the process. This includes both a detailed account of the methods, tools, and techniques that were used to conduct the research, as well as the emergent quality of the ethnographic process.

In the same way that it is important to remember that the design of online games and virtual worlds is a social construction, it is equally important to remember that any ethnography of their cultures is also socially constructed. However, the assumption that the ethnographer, as "authority," may have a larger role in constructing the cultures she studies than the other way around is not only naïve but arrogant in the extreme. Clifford and Marcus have pointed out that "Hermeneutic philosophy in its varying styles . . . reminds us that the simplest cultural accounts are intentional creations, that interpreters constantly construct themselves through the others they study" (1986, 10). Thus the researcher must take a reflective stance toward her relationship to her subjects, and acknowledge the ways in which each constructs the other. "It has become clear that every version of an 'other,' wherever found, is also a construction of a 'self' . . ." (23). Furthermore, they add that culture is ". . . contested, temporal, and emergent. Representation and explanation—both by insiders and outsiders—is implicated in this emergence" (19). Thus the representation itself also becomes part of the cultural process. This is particularly the case in network play culture, where cultures are constantly shifting in a highly compressed frame of both time and space.

This privileging of authority, which is often coupled with an anxiety about the biases the researcher brings to the table, overlooks the possibility that the subjects have an active role to play not only in constructing their own accounts of their culture, but in constructing in the ethnographer herself. Time and time again, especially in the feminist ethnographies described earlier, we see that the researcher is as much constructed by the subjects as the other way around. Far from being passive objects of study, a mutual construction may take place that transforms the researcher as much if not more than it does the subject. As with anything else, the construction of ethnographic texts and their authors (and in this I include the subjects) is an intersubjective enterprise.

While book II, the heart of this story, both structurally and conceptually, is the story of the Uru Diaspora and specifically The Gathering of Uru, there is also a metanarrative of the relationship between researcher and subjects, which is explored in book V. As with Behar's study of Esperanza and Smith Bowen's experience of losing herself to a dance ritual that her subjects drew her into (1964), the narrative of this study is as much about the social construction of the ethnographer as the other way around, perhaps more so. While I acknowledge that my engagement with the group had an impact on the subjects, it is clear to me that their impact on me was far greater than mine on them. In the final analysis, they crafted me as a researcher as well as the research itself, to as much if not a greater extent than I have crafted, constructed, and written my interpretation of their culture.

| **II** |
THE *URU* DIASPORA

AN IMAGINARY HOMELAND

A Polyphonic Cultural History

What follows are the findings of an eighteen-month ethnographic study of The Gathering of Uru, a "neighborhood" of the online game *Uru*, and the group's immigration into *There.com* and other virtual worlds that took place from March 2004 to September 2005. It also draws some comparisons between immigration by other *Uru* groups into multiplayer virtual worlds, most notably *Second Life*, and explores the role of the player-run *Until Uru* servers in community cohesion.

The study can be characterized as a design research approach to applied ethnography, employing a method for sociological/anthropological research that serves to inform game design. Building on my background as a game designer, my primary focus was to study the ways in which the design of games and online virtual worlds influences or constrains the emergent social behavior that takes place within them. I was also interested in the broader question of how play communities are formed and sustained, and how they change and evolve across virtual play spaces.

The spirit of this project was one of collaboration. From the start, members of The Gathering of Uru (TGU) embraced me as part of their community, and were highly supportive of this research. As the semiofficial ethnographer/folklorist of the TGU group, I spent many hours talking, visiting, and playing with many of them, both individually and in groups in different contexts, and I studied and documented their activities and creative output in detail. Some members of TGU actively participated in the research by gathering data, editing interviews, and providing pointers to key threads on the forums, for which I am extremely grateful. They helped shape the development of the methodology in a very active and productive way. The findings were then posted on a "participant blog," an online web site that group members were invited to annotate.

It should be noted that the *Uru* story does not end with this eighteen-month ethnography, and the coda at the beginning of book V describes events that took place subsequently and the author's ongoing role within the Uru community.

A Note on Anonymity

Anonymity is a complex issue in Internet research. Virtually all the subjects in this study were amenable to the use of their real avatar names. This became a particular challenge with regard to issues of authorship. I was also aware that while participants might not have a concern about their privacy in-world (what happens if your avatar becomes famous?), there may have been some unanticipated consequences from using actual avatar monikers. I thus adopted the standard ethical practice of maintaining study subjects' and informants' anonymity through the use of pseudonyms for individuals, groups, and locations that are described throughout this account.

History and Context: *Myst, Uru*, and *Beyond*

Laying the Groundwork: Myst Players Come Together

Uru: Ages Beyond Myst was a massively multiplayer online game based on the Myst game series by Cyan Worlds (Ashe 2003). *Myst*, first published for the Macintosh in 1993, was ranked the top PC game of all time for eight years in a row until it was surpassed by *The Sims* in 2001. *Myst* was heralded as the first CD-ROM game to garner a significant audience of adult women. One of the first computer games to be considered a work of art, *Myst* was often referenced as an indication that computer games had "come of age" (Carroll 1994, Tiscali 2003). Some early computer business analysts posited that the bundling of *Myst* with PCs sold in the mid-1990s was instrumental in establishing a market for PCs in the home.

Myst was described in the online game magazine *Game Revolution*:

There are only a few truly monumental moments in video game history, a small number of games that have fundamentally changed the cultural landscape. However, it is clearly the case that *Myst* was one of those games, and its heyday was one of those moments. When *Myst* became the best-selling PC game of all time (a title it held for eight years), video games were no longer just for kids. Gaming had suddenly risen to a new level, a respectable and artistic level, and it was no longer possible to simply dismiss it as childish entertainment.

In the original *Myst*, players slowly wandered around beautiful, fantastical environments composed of pre-rendered, two-dimensional stills. To progress, you had to solve mind-bending puzzles designed to challenge Mensa veterans in an effort to slowly unravel

| Figure 5.1 |
Myst's compelling environments and complex puzzles made it the top-selling PC game for eight years running.
(Image: Pearce)

the story of two deranged brothers, Sirrus and Achenar, and the strange book-worlds their father created, which eventually became their prisons. (Ferris 2004)

Key to *Myst*'s unprecedented success was its groundbreaking use of high-quality graphics and audio production, and its story line (see figure 5.1). Many computer games up until this point had devoted the PC's limited processing power to pixilated animation, poorly compressed video, and the classic electronic, low-resolution audio associated with early arcade games. The conventional wisdom was that action was essential, and high-quality visuals and audio were of secondary concern. *Myst* inverted this equation and sacrificed speed and action for the highest possible visual and audio quality. With a very small team and a garage band ethos, the Miller brothers' technique involved using 3-D software tools to create vividly rendered still images of a complex imaginary world. Technically, the game was deceptively simple—it was merely a branching matrix of still images, augmented by a moody, ambient musical score. The interface was elegant and minimal. Players navigated the eerily abandoned game world in a first-person perspective. There were no controls on the screen. Instead, as you dragged your cursor around, it would change shape to indicate that a choice was available; most of these choices were directional, but could also involve opening drawers or books to obtain clues and information. There were very few occasions when one saw any characters in the game, and these generally appeared in the form of rough video clips seen in the pages of books. Simple puzzles integrated into the world caused unusual large-scale transformations of the environment. The images were so breathtaking, so elaborately thought-out and intricately rendered, that players almost relished in the slow pace of the gameplay. Like other popular imaginary worlds, *Myst* had an entire culture, history, and language, symbols and technologies, and a sustainable mythology that spawned a perennially popular multigame franchise.

Understanding Uru Players

The decade-long history of *Myst* fandom is key to understanding the *Uru* phenomenon in general and the TGU community in particular. In-game interviews and surveys of the online forums revealed the following:

- Most TGU members had been *Myst* fans prior to joining *Uru*, many since the game's inception.
- Because of the diverse and perennial appeal of the *Myst* franchise, TGU members range in age from mid-teens to mid-seventies, with the majority in their forties and fifties. This remains a surprisingly diverse figure relative to other MMOGs, and represents an unusually wide age range.
- The gender mix, which is consistent with the *Myst* demographic overall, is exactly equal, a statistical anomaly where PC games, and especially MMOGs, are concerned.
- Many players did not like or play any other games; most had never played an online game prior to playing *Uru*.
- Players' longtime immersion in the *Myst* world made them both facile at its unique style of puzzle-solving and experts in the game's narrative, history, and culture.
- Players had been inhabiting the *Myst* world for a decade by themselves, although a handful communicated through a rich fan culture infrastructure; *Uru* was the first opportunity they had to actually *play* with other *Myst* aficionados within this well-loved world.
- Because the game is intellectual in nature, players tended to value intelligence and problem-solving; most players expressed an aversion to games with killing and violence.

These qualities are important because they serve to reinforce an observation that was echoed in player interviews. At the core of a play community's character is the sort of people the game attracts. This blend of people with these characteristics was drawn to this particular game for a particular reason. They arrived on the scene with a certain set of values and a predisposition toward certain emergent social behaviors. They brought with them a long-term devotion to and deep knowledge of a classic game, combined with an aversion to many of the play mechanics that are presumed to be fun in the contemporary commercial game landscape. These are all prerequisites to understanding the ways in which The Gathering of Uru formed and developed over time.

It would appear that, to a certain extent, the game's own values and ideologies predispose it to attract a certain type of player, even before the game is actually played. Once those players come together, their community forms and develops around these shared values, which also intersect with the values embedded in the game itself. In many game communities, players may not even be aware of the values and ideologies that attract them to a game in the first place, let alone the ways in which they influence play and social interaction. This remarkably self-reflective group, however, was well aware that part of their uniqueness originated from their connection with the *Myst* series, its narratives, play patterns, individual and group identities, and values.

Comments

"At the core of a play community's character is the sort of people the game attracts."
Does this observation illuminate the root of Uru's failure? Has the gamer world changed? Much has been written about first person shooter and "EverQuest" type games and certainly they are very popular, particularly with the most recent generation (or two) of gamers. Is World of Warcraft the "Myst" of the current gamer generation?
This raises a question in my mind. What sorts of people are attracted to the Uru game? Is the Uru community you have studied an anachronism?
Posted by: Raena | February 05, 2006 at 05:04 PM

Myst Uru: Story, World, Game

The narrative and rules of the *Myst* world are rich and complex. They have evolved and expanded for over a decade, while remaining internally consistent. The original *Myst* designers, minister's sons Rand and Robyn Miller, embedded implicit Christian spiritual themes in the game and its narrative, although this was executed in a subtle way that has often escaped the awareness of even long-term players. This may be comparable to the way Christian themes appear allegorically in the fiction of C. S.

Lewis (Caughey 2005). The game was intended for a secular audience and, although the designers spoke openly in interviews of its Christian subtext, there were no direct references to Christianity, nor was there any evidence that the game had an evangelical agenda.

The overarching mythology of the *Myst* series revolves around the epic tale of the D'ni people, a human-like race who had the power to call into being entire worlds (game levels), called Ages, through writing. Special "linking books" serve as transport mechanisms between these Ages, prompting some game scholars to interpret this as a metaphor for computer programming. The basic premise of world creation through writing serves as a mechanism for extensibility, allowing for the easy addition of new Ages. The proliferation of books is key to the *Myst* mythology, and books are a recurring motif shared in different instantiations of *Myst/Uru* culture across all the virtual worlds it occupies. The notion of who can and should create Ages became a topic of deep philosophical debate among Uru players as they began to move into other worlds and create their own instantiations of Uru culture. In spite of the popularity of and scholarly interest in *Myst*, I found no other scholars writing about *Uru* itself. In fact, most game scholars I spoke with were not even aware of the game's existence.

The Uru Experience

The first thing players were asked to do when launching the game was to design their avatar. Avatar features were limited and aesthetic rather than skills- or statistics-based. The avatar choices offered were male or female human, with a limited choice of hairstyles and outfits and an unlimited color palette, as well as the ability to make the avatar look older, add wrinkles and graying hair, or even present male-pattern baldness.

With their immersive first-person perspectives, all the prior *Myst* games placed the player in the game narrative with an ambiguous identity, sometimes referred to as "the Stranger." Messages throughout the game were left for Catherine, wife of Atrus and mother of their two sons, who were the focus of the game. Giving the player a unique, customizable identity was a first for the *Myst* franchise.

Once they entered the *Uru* world, players found themselves called to a mysterious cleft in the middle of an unnamed desert, presumed to be in New Mexico. Descending into this underground cave, they eventually discovered the ruins of an abandoned city. Dispersed throughout the city were numerous clues, as well as linking books to various Ages, each one of which had a *Myst*-style puzzle integrated into its environs. Along the way, players also had to discover "journey cloths," left behind by Yeesha (the main character in the story, and daughter to Atrus and Catherine). At the core of *Uru*'s narrative was the controversial restoration of the lost world of the D'ni people,

| Figure 5.2 |
Avatar exploring the *Myst Uru* world. (Image: Pearce)

a culture one player described in an interview as created by "taking a tribe of New Mexico Indians and adding water."

This player went on to point out the resemblance between the artwork and iconography in the *Myst* games *Riven*, *Uru*, and *Myst Exile* to caves built by Native Americans in New Mexico, where the Miller brothers once lived (Carroll 1994). According to players, the D'ni culture bears many resemblances to these Native cultures, down to the architecture built into rockwork, although some also hypothesize that it is the mysterious Bahro "beast people" who most closely resemble these cultures. Unlike the settlements of New Mexico's indigenous people, in D'ni Ae'gura, as in most *Myst* worlds, water was plentiful.

In D'ni Ae'gura, players took on the roles of explorers to solve various puzzles integral to both the environment of each Age and to the story line, as shown in figure 5.2. Solving each puzzle resulted in the resumption of some feature or service of the world, the activation of a technology or mechanism, and/or the opening of access to new zones. Most of these puzzles were spatial in nature, including made-up numbers and languages and requiring a level of spatial literacy and cryptography. Puzzles were embedded seamlessly into the environments and their solutions often transformed the space itself. Turning on a power supply with the correct combination of moves, for instance, would activate a rotating room or a lift system that would allow access to another part of the Age. Closing the correct combination of steam vents would allow the player to ride a puff of steam over a rock formation into a secret area containing additional clues and more journey cloths. Indeed, the narrative was so deeply embedded in the space that the two were indistinguishable from one another. In order to solve both the game and the narrative, players had to become expert at reading the space. As with all *Myst* games there were no explicit instructions given as to the game mechanics or rules.

Uru was unusual in that it could be played as a single-player game (known as *Uru Prime*) or a multiplayer game. Players who were so inclined could request an invitation to the multiplayer server-based version, initially known in beta testing as *Uru Prologue*. They would then be put on a waiting list until the next round of invitations was issued. At one point, a "clerical error" resulted in invitations being issued to all players on the waiting list, resulting in what amounted to an accidental public beta test of the game. New *Prologue* players were randomly assigned a neighborhood, or "hood." These "newbies" began in one of the generic D'ni Restoration Council (DRC) hoods, but they later had the option of joining a player-created hood or starting one of their own. Though there was no direct competition in the game, there were factions, and trouble was fomented by Cyan through the use of paid actors. Cyan's attempt to perpetuate drama in the game met with mixed responses from players. Some enjoyed the artificial drama and conflict, while others found it intrusive and divisive.

There are six key geographical components to *Uru*, which will become relevant, particularly in the discussion of player-created artifacts.

The Desert and the Cleft

When players entered the game, they found themselves facing a volcano-like hill surrounded by a barbed wire fence. Exploring this area, they would discover a number of clues, including the first few in a series of journey cloths left by Yeesha, which was one of the primary game mechanics. Completing each Age required finding seven of these journey cloths. At the foot of the hill was a camper and a mysterious gentleman who identified himself as Zandi, and who informed the player that "she" has "left a message for you" in the Cleft. Once you had scoured the area for journey cloths, including exploring remnants of earlier *Myst* games, such as a toppled water tower and the skeleton of a mysterious creature, you would make your way down into the Cleft. The Cleft was the entryway to the Cavern, as the underground city was called.

Descending a ladder, players would find themselves in a cave with chambers carved into the rock and a pool of water at the bottom. While not a tutorial in the strict sense, the Desert and the Cleft introduced the game basics: jump and climb, collect journey cloths, solve puzzles, decode things, and learn how to operate machines. Once the puzzles were completed and the mechanism running properly, Yeesha would appear as a 3-D hologram, giving players a cryptic explanation of what they were to do in the game. En route to the City, you would pass into a tunnel where you were presented with a linking book that served as a teleport to your main home in the game: your Relto.

The Relto

Uru employed an unusual combination of private and public spaces. The most private of these was the Relto, the individual player's home base, a small adobe cottage on an island in the clouds, as seen in figure 5.3. As a player progressed in the game, her Relto would change, based on Ages visited and Relto pages gathered in the different Ages. New features were added with each new Age solved, including weather, landscaping (waterfalls, volcanos, rocks, trees, flowers), birds and butterflies, and linking books to allow access to the parts of the world the player had thus far discovered. Linking books were stored in a small built-in bookcase inside the Relto hut, or within special columns in front of the building. Players traveled from Age to Age via these books. Linking books could only be obtained by finding them in-world or by accessing them through the Nexus. They therefore functioned as a reward for exploration and would accumulate in the bookshelves and columns in the Relto as the player progressed through the game.

The Nexus

The Nexus was a small chamber that contained a mechanized library of linking books. Players could access the Nexus via linking books in the City or from their Reltos, allowing access to the Neighborhoods and their Ages, as well as other players' Ages when invited.

The Neighborhood

In *Uru Prologue*, there were many identical instantiations (shards) of the hood, each of which was home to a particular group, also called a hood (figure 5.4). The hood contained a number of features, the most notable of which was a central fountain. There was also an archaic device called an Imager, on which players could post text

| Figure 5.3 |

The Relto is the player's home base in *Uru*, and where they store their library of personal Linking Books. (Image: Pearce)

or images within the hood. There was also an auditorium with a lectern and a library with linking books to the Nexus and other Ages and areas in the game. The hood was also the site of the Egg Room, a mysterious chamber that housed a floating, ornately decorated egg, the meaning of which remained an enigma. Players could visit other hoods besides their own via the Nexus, but each had a single Neighborhood book in her Relto in order to access the hood to which she belonged.

The City (D'ni Ae'gura)

D'ni Ae'gura was a shared space, the large ancient city apparently abandoned by its creators, uninhabited and in various states of disrepair, and now occupied only by explorers (other players) and the D'ni Restoration Council (figure 5.5.) The City contained an inoperative ferry terminal, a large library (where new linking books would periodically appear), Nexus books, and linking books in various places. Large chunks

| Figure 5.4 |
The "hood" was both the group and its gathering place in *Uru*. (Text blurred to protect subject anonymity.) (Image: Pearce)

of walls were missing, and the streets were adorned with barriers and orange traffic cones placed there by the DRC. Players could explore the city, search the rubble and debris to the extent they were allowed, and attempt to gain access to locked or seemingly inaccessible areas. Central to the city was a large tree, known as Terokh Jeruth, the Great Tree of Possibility. One of the Cyan-created mythical controversies revolved around whether or not the city should be restored. As with all *Myst* games, things were seldom as they appeared, and there was always a dark side to every *Myst* story.

The Bahro Caves

The act of collecting all of the journey cloths left behind by Yeesha provided access to hidden caves formerly inhabited by the Bahro "beast people," referred to by Yeesha as "The Least." The D'ni's relationship to the Bahro, who appear to have been enslaved and even tortured, suggests a darker side to the D'ni culture. The Bahro Caves, secret

| **Figure 5.5** |
The abandoned city of D'ni Ae'gura. (Image: Pearce)

| Figure 5.6 |
Eder Kemo, the Garden Age. (Image: Pearce)

rooms in the city, and glyphs throughout the Ages hinted that these beings, which may or may not have been "human," were marginalized and persecuted by the D'ni, a potential deterrent to wishing to restore the D'ni culture.

Ages

Once each linking book was discovered, each player would have access to her own unique instantiation of each of the Ages. Ages typically included fantastical features, both natural and man-made, a large part of the series' appeal. Examples of these features are shown in figures 5.6 and 5.7. Some were termed "Machine Ages," and involved the deciphering of elaborate and sometimes arcane devices and equipment often embedded in massive structures with large moving parts. Solving Age puzzles involved manipulating contraptions, deciphering words or numbers in the D'ni language or Bahro petraglyphs, matching patterns, starting up machinery, opening portals,

| Figure 5.7 |

A typical *Uru* Age contains mysterious puzzles and machines. (Image: Pearce)

and the like. In *Uru*, the Ages were persistent and would remember their state so that players could work on Ages with repeated visits. Players could also invite other people into their own Ages, accessible via the Nexus, allowing for group puzzle-solving and exploring. Some Age puzzles were nearly impossible to solve by oneself, thus encouraging social interaction and cooperation. Players also used Ages for formal and informal social gatherings, and to play other sorts of made-up games.

Each player also carried two personal devices on her avatar: a Relto book, a small linking notebook enabling players to transport themselves back to their Reltos, and a Ki, a small PDA-like device that facilitated remote communication and the location of other players, as well as the ability to capture and store in-game screenshots, which could be sent to other players' Kis or posted on hood Imagers.

IDENTITY AS PLACE

The Gathering of Uru: Birth of a Hood

The Gathering of Uru was one of the larger and more influential hoods within the Uru community. It was formed unofficially prior to the so-called public release of the game during the beta-test period, but officially began accepting members on November 17, 2003. In an in-game interview in *There.com*, Leesa, the founder and mayor of TGU, described its creation as follows:

I was a beta tester for *Uru* and created The Gathering neighborhood but to start with it was private and I was the only member. I had never been in a multiplayer game or chatted on the net—was quite a loner. Then as part of the beta I had to make my hood public and see how it worked with visitors and other members so that also meant I was going to have to speak with people . . . which terrified me. One night I was walking by a new beta tester and he asked if I would help him. I couldn't be rude so I started my first chat. He became my first member. Got a few more members. To my surprise people started asking to join. They would ask me what I wanted the hood to be and I guess they liked my answer. Then so many started joining I realized I would have to become organized and set some ground rules. And it grew from that.

In the first hood there were 138. Then a second shard was opened and I started another TG on it. It grew to 157. Then a third shard opened for the last few weeks of *Uru Prologue* and I got 49 members. When we came here [There.com] I said I'd start TG up again but other Uru and Myst people wanted to join so I renamed it here to The Gathering of Uru.

. . . I was very flattered because people were coming in the last night of *Uru Prologue* and asking to join before they pulled the plug.

Once the plug was pulled, they were, in Leesa's words, "bound and determined to stay together in any way we could." They were prepared to apply a great amount of time, effort, creativity, and resourcefulness to this end.

The Rise and Fall of *Uru*: Becoming Refugees

Uru went on sale to the public in November 2003, after having been out in a private beta since January of that year. Although the game itself was officially released, the online version was never actually launched in commercial form. Instead, Cyan and Ubisoft launched a semi-public beta. Like Leesa, a number of the members of The Gathering were part of the original private beta test and thus were already established in the *Uru* community prior to the public beta opening. Many of these beta testers (including Leesa) were also part of the League of Welcomers, a hood devoted to helping new players.

As mentioned earlier, *Uru* had a somewhat unconventional structure: it could be played as a single-player game, *Uru Prime*, or players could apply to be in the multiplayer beta version, known as *Uru Prologue*. Once they had submitted their applications, they were put on a waiting list until the next slot opened up. This was a way to "gate" the world and control throughput, possibly to avoid potential server problems. Players who were not yet enrolled in *Uru Prologue* could learn about the game through the *Uru* forums. One player told me she was afraid to play the online version because she had read on the forums that there were actors playing game characters whose job it was to foment conflict and pit players against each other in different factions.

Players were apparently admitted to *Uru Prologue* in batches of about 500 people at a time. However, in the last two months of the game's life, two mass invitations were issued, allowing the majority of eligible players into the game. The first of two "clerical errors" by Cyan, often couched in historical terms, occurred in late December or early January, inadvertently generating invitations to all eligible players. Accounts of what caused this error remain vague and unclear, but the game was again closed to new players and the queue resumed until the end of January when, again, the entire list of qualified players received invitations. Many Uru refugees now believe that the second so-called error was deliberate—for *Uru Prologue* was to close down only a few weeks later, and the full-blown commercial release, *Uru Live*, was never to be. Events occurred very quickly from this point forward. Many key members of The Gathering hood were not admitted into *Uru Prologue* until this second mass invite. They therefore only played the online game for about two weeks before the servers were shut down. Other players arrived on the heels of the announcement, posted by Cyan on November 4, of the game's imminent closure.

As is the case with almost all online games, the actual facts behind the closure have never been completely revealed by either developer Cyan or publisher Ubisoft. Differing accounts can be found on forums and blogs on the Internet, but according to Ubisoft's *Uru* community manager, a total of 40,000 people ended up receiving invitations to *Uru Prologue*, of which only 10,000 actually signed up. Ubisoft was both surprised and disappointed by what they perceived as low turnout, although it should be noted that at this point, there were no subscription fees charged to players. A much more challenging problem stemmed from the instability of the client-server architecture, also related to the gated entry. Because of the way the client (player's software) processed incoming data from the server, the more players who were logged on, the more unstable the client would become; this caused both excessive lag and frequent client crashes. As mentioned before, Leesa actually had to have three shards to accommodate the 350-plus members of her hood, but even groups as small as 30 concurrent players could cause lag and crashes. So in fact, had the game been as popular as Cyan and Ubisoft had hoped, it still might not have survived because of challenges with the client/server architecture. The instability of this architecture became much more apparent to players later when they began to use the server software on their own player-run *Until Uru* servers.

When weighed against this evidence, Ubisoft's claim that the game's closure was due to insufficient players does not ring true with many members of the Uru Diaspora. Rather than admit that the game's failure was the result of poor marketing (a common complaint of players, reinforced by the fact that the game is virtually unknown in game research circles) or a faulty technology, it was much more convenient for Ubisoft and Cyan to blame the "market" for its demise.

Comments

Well I have really enjoyed reading this and can see how much work and thought has been given. When I first heard of this, I was a bit skeptical (as you know), but having read this and thoroughly enjoyed it. It's been a pleasure.

As the author has taken a long look/time to be part of our TGU community, by joining us "in-Game," she has produced a wonderful piece of writing, and after many interviews with various members, I think she has done a brill job. [sic]

Thank you for doing this, its great to be seen as a community, and to be expressed in this way. Good luck with the project and it's been good to get to know you as well.

Posted by: Tristan | April 03, 2006 at 04:17 AM

I find it interesting that the creators of MMOs, whose survival depends upon the communities which arise from them, have so little understanding of those communities and make little effort to learn. When things go wrong they blame finances, low membership, software, hardware, etc. but never look to their own ignorance of the community as a major cause.

Posted by: Leesa | April 10, 2006 at 01:23 PM

Virtual World/Real Grief

The *Uru Prologue* server shutdown is the key historical event for the Uru Diaspora. In my interviews with Uru refugees across several MMOWs it was referred to variously as "Black Monday" and "Black Tuesday," and I was told that it took place on February 9 or February 10. I later learned that in fact both dates were correct. The server closed at 9:00 PM Pacific Standard Time on February 9 and concurrently for players in Eastern and European time zones (midnight and 5:00 AM, respectively, on February 10). (Because so many MMOW/G servers are based in California, Pacific Standard Time has become the GMT of cyberspace.)

This crucial date is extensively documented in a number of locations, and has become a kind of "national" holiday for members of the Uru Diaspora throughout the ludisphere. In anticipation of the imminent server closure, The Gathering's deputy mayor Lynn and hood member Henry set up Koalanet, a forum enabling hood members to stay in communication with each other after their world was destroyed. The forum included a mechanism for asynchronous discussion via topical threads, as well as a live text chat environment. Koalanet quickly became the community hub, as well as a conduit for intense expressions of grieving both before and after *Uru*'s closure. The forum also became essential as a transitional space, in the planning and ongoing maintenance of the TGU community, and ultimately enabled the group to support its intergame diasporic community. (It should also be added that this archive proved a valuable research tool; as all participants were asked to register and enter details such as their membership date, birthday, and gender, demographic data was culled primarily from this source.)

Players were made aware by Cyan and Ubisoft of the imminent server shutdown about five days prior to the event, although staff and community managers were aware of it earlier (a source of great anguish to *Uru* staff). The announcement was made jointly by Cyan and Ubisoft via a personal letter from developer Rand Miller that *Uru Live* was not to be and *Prologue* would be shut down. In the weeks following the news, over 2,000 players petitioned, offering to pay subscription fees for an entire year in advance, in order to keep the game running.

The last day of *Uru*, many players assembled in-world, gathering in hoods, or visiting each other's Ages. (figure 6.1) Owing to varied time zones, not all players were able to be online at the strike of midnight PST, the scheduled shutdown time. A core group of TGU members gathered in the garden of Lynn's Eder Kemo Age, talked, told each other stories, and played hide-and-seek. As the time approached, they moved into a circular configuration close enough so that their avatars would appear to be holding hands. Several players recall the clocks in their "rl" (real-life)

| Figure 6.1 |

Players embrace in a group "ki hug" during the final hours of *Uru Prologue.* (Image: Raena)

homes striking midnight, the screen freezing, and a system alert message appearing on the screen: "There is something wrong with your Internet connection," followed by a dialogue box saying "OK." As one player recalled: "I couldn't bring myself to press that OK button because for me it was NOT OK." (figure 6.2)

In the minutes and hours immediately following the shutdown, a number of TGU members regrouped in the chat area of the Koalanet forum. This was not prearranged, but occurred spontaneously. Players experienced what they characterized as a "shock and catharsis" and many described symptoms of posttraumatic stress. This collective trauma, and the ability to share its aftermath together via their own self-created chat and forum, was absolutely critical in cementing the bond that carried the group forward to its eventual immigration and ongoing survival. At this point the players had been made refugees, and the impact of this shared trauma on long-term community building cannot be understated. It is difficult to determine what would have happened to the group had the game stayed open indefinitely, but many continue to cite this shared trauma as a factor in their deep emotional connection to one another. In fact, all former Uru players, even those previously unknown to each other, seem to share this common bond when meeting in other virtual worlds. Added to this were

| Figure 6.2 |

The last thing *Uru* players saw was a screen indicating an Internet error. (Image: Raena)

additional personal revelations, such as the fact that some of the members were disabled, which seemed, on an individual level, to literally add insult to injury. In some sense, the turning point for players was when they realized that it was, as many put it, all about the people, not about the game. Koalanet quickly became a daily shared ritual, a place where players could check in with each other, as well as express their feelings about their collective experience.

The examples below of writings created by TGU members in the days immediately following the close of *Uru Prologue* are an indication of player's reactions to what for many turned out to be a harrowing experience.

To all who are grieving our loss.
February 12, 2004, 01:52:48 am
The tears the tears why can't I stop the tears
It was only supposed to be a game, no violence, no fears
A neighborhood? A community?
It was just a game to me
but the more that I played the more I could see
this was becoming so much more for me
I have a family, I have friends,
my busy schedule it never ends
Out to a meeting, out to lunch,
Can't wait to get home to spend time with this bunch
Then as I played day after day
my opinion, it began to sway
This is no longer a game to me
These people are part of my family
—Aria of Katran

I walk in Uru
A Poem by ScarletMoon
Yesterday I walked in Uru
A gathering as it were
A meeting of friends
In ages unknown
Today I walked in Uru
Soaking up tears of those I know
Their eyes a color of red

Crying till we go
Tomorrow I walk in Uru
The time I know not when
Yet I know my friends will wait
For the gathering to begin again
Posted on: February 20, 2004, 10:40:16

When darkness falls. . . . . .
Open spaces, fallen graces, bring eyes that look anew,
Heart felt moments in dim lit places, remind me of Uru
Ancients' relics, tumbled and derelict on mountains in dark hue,
solemn traces of forgotten races, remind me of Uru.
Friendly chatter, a distant clatter of machines that we pursue
a book of pages, to the ages, reminds me of Uru.
A final bow, to what is now, in a garden of eternal dew,
one more rainstorm, one more feeling, reminds me of Uru.
—Tristan

Yearning for the Homeland

My Homeland Uru
From my beautiful homeland
From my beloved homeland
I hear the Bahro cry
and Kadish's wife sing her song of despair

And a refrain is sung by a sister who lives far from her homeland
And the memories make her cry
The song that she sings springs from her pain and her own tears
And we can hear her cry

Your homeland strikes your soul when you are gone
Your homeland sighs when you are not there
The memories live and flow through my blood
I carry her inside me, yes its true

The refrains continue, as does the melancholy
And the song that keeps repeating,

Flows in my blood, ever stronger
On its way to my heart

I sing of my homeland, beautiful and loved
I suffer the pain that is in her soul
Although I am far away, I can feel her
And one day I'll return

I know it
–Raena

This poem, posted by TGU member Raena on May 13, 2004, about three months after the server shutdown, expresses this sense of losing one's homeland, a sentiment that many TGUers shared. To an unknowing reader, it would be hard to recognize that its writer was talking about a fictional place. In reality of course, she knows it is a virtual world, but her deep attachment to *Uru* as "homeland," and the implied ethnic identity that goes with that, is clearly expressed in this text.

In discussing the Uru group at large and the TGU group in particular, I adopted the terms "refugee" and "diaspora." The former term I adopted directly from the Uru community, who regularly referred to themselves as refugees. Diaspora is my own term for the dispersion of Uru players that now inhabit other games and virtual worlds. *The American Heritage Dictionary* defines a diaspora as "A dispersion of a people from their original homeland" (2000). As mentioned before, a diaspora is characterized by "experiences of displacement, of constructing homes away from home . . ." (Clifford 1994). Refugees are persons who have left their homeland because of persecution. It may be more proper to call the Uru Diaspora exiles, but the term "exile" implies individual rather than group expulsion. (Ironically, one of the games in the series is entitled *Myst Exile*). "Refugees" also implies a wandering from place to place, which was precisely what occurred. In addition to TGU, there are a number of other communities of the Uru Diaspora in a number of MMOW/Gs; the Welcomers' League (of which Leesa is also a member), for instance, has had, at various points, chapters within *There.com, Star Wars: Galaxies*, and *The Matrix Online*, extending its original mission to welcome and help Uru newbies to other games. Especially in the beginning, as TGU members and other Uru players searched for a new homeland, there persisted a hope that they might someday return to *Uru*.

Immigration: The Quest for a New Home

With Koalanet as their main convening site, the TGU group began to gather, either using the online chat or contributing to the asynchronous discussion forum. Koalanet provided a communication hub for the group, but it was clear that they missed sharing the avatar experience within the *Uru* milieu. Certainly they could talk to each other, but they needed to *play* together and "see" each other. It was also clear in talking to players that *Uru*'s spatial environment was part of what they missed; they often spoke in interviews of the game's visual beauty. Even before the server shutdown, they began to investigate alternatives. Most players did not perceive this as having happened in an organized fashion; rather, different players began to take it upon themselves to explore options and share their findings with the group.

Two branches of research emerged. One was geared toward recreating *Uru* using virtual world authoring tools. Players investigated a range of options, including sophisticated game development packages such as Virtools and online 3-D technologies such as VRML. They also looked at virtual environments that had affordances for player-made content, among them *Active Worlds*, a ten-year-old player-built virtual world. The second branch was more interested in a ready-to-play solution that did not require any technical skills and to which the group could immigrate as soon as possible in order to maintain some momentum. A debate surfaced at this time and one of the outcomes was that different activities could go on concurrently.

As an interim solution, two members, Basil and D'evon (who later served as TGU's shard administrator for *Until Uru*), created a text-based MUD of the hood. It provided a context for chatting and employed skillful writing and humor, but many players had difficulty navigating the interface. Players seemed to long for the visual experience of the *Uru* world, for their own and each other's avatars.

Meanwhile, the ready-to-play camp was considering a number of potential candidates for migration. Self-appointed scouts began to investigate other possible virtual venues. *Ryzom* and *EverQuest* were two games under early consideration, but most players found them too violent and competitive for their liking. The two primary candidates that came to the forefront were *Second Life* and *There.com*, both online virtual worlds that were less games and more virtual recreation zones; each of these worlds also had mechanisms for players to create their own virtual artifacts and environments. Another group of about 200 Uru players had settled in *Second Life*. Of these, a small subset, varying in size from six to nine players, began to construct D'ni Island, the heart of which was a facsimile of areas of the *Uru* game, taking advantage of *Second Life*'s flexible in-game modeling and scripting capability. A resourceful and dedicated group, they managed to re-create several key areas of *Uru*, complete with scripted linking books that, if clicked on, would take players to another zone within their *Uru*-themed area in *Second Life*. They also created a Nexus with links to a series of Reltos

| Figure 6.3 |
TGU scouts posted screenshots of their adventures in *There.com*. (Image: Raena)

and private group member homes. This group was a secondary part of the study, and more will be said about them in the section on artifact creation. In the summer of 2005, another group consisting of former Myst and Uru players built an entirely new *Myst*-style game in *Second Life*.

Uru's community managers, concerned for the well-being of their players, tried to support the newly formed diaspora in whatever way they could. When they became aware that Uru players sought to migrate into other virtual worlds, they alerted a number of operators, including *There.com* and *Second Life*, in hopes of securing them a new home. This top-down approach did not result in any formal relocation program, but did serve to alert community managers to the incoming refugees.

The way in which the search for a new home took place also seems to have the classic hallmarks of emergence. Rather than a centralized, top-down effort, players dispersed and explored different worlds, bringing back travelogues. Self-appointed scouts Katsushiro, Felion, Raena, and a few others reported back with screenshots of activities from *There.com* (figure 6.3), while Ezra brought back a report on *Second Life*. Erik, whose primary interest was in making a new hood from scratch, continued to report on the various tools he was investigating that might be suitable for this task.

This discussion of where to migrate to was one of the few instances in the Koalanet forum where there were obvious disagreements among TGU members. Players had strong feelings, pro and con, as to the various options presented—although all agreed that any substitute for *Uru* would pale by comparison. This debate, primarily comparing *Second Life* and *There.com*, revolved around two areas of world design: avatar expressiveness and navigation. Because the avatar served as the representation of player identity in-world, players had very strong feelings about its expressive features in each of the worlds being considered. (More details on avatar expressiveness will be covered in chapter 7.) The other issue of paramount concern was navigation. As explorers, players felt that ease of navigation was critical, and *Second Life* was deemed weak in this regard. In addition to more refined navigation, *There.com* also offered a method of loading graphics to the client that allowed for more scenic vistas, whereas *Second Life*'s loading schema did not load objects in the distance, thus making scenic vistas impossible.

Although these differences of opinion appeared to present a major rift, the group finally arrived at a compromise. This key moment in their development could easily have torn the group apart, but it seems that TGU's main priority was to stay together, and they were willing to find a way to overcome their differences in order to assure their long-term sustainability.

Ezra, who Leesa later appointed deputy mayor of TGU in *Second Life*, brought this to light in a March 5, 2004 post on the Koalanet forum:

I was thinking about this more last night and realized the reason I was feeling upset was because my worst fear when the cancellation [...] was first announced was that the Uru community would fracture and fall apart. I had met so many wonderful people in Uru and didn't want to lose that connection. Thinking of TGU fracturing into different sites/chat rooms/games/etc. that I couldn't/wouldn't participate in was very distressing.
But then I had a thought! Why can't we "fracture" into different places? What's wrong with that? If various groups of people hang out in various places online, it will be no different than real life. We should have a Meeting Place presence everywhere—in any area people want to hang out. Heck, if some TGU folk want to hang out in EverQuest or The Sims Online, more power to them!

The very process of this debate made it clear to TGU members that the Koalanet forum itself had become their primary communication hub, a home base that transcended whatever virtual world they ultimately chose to inhabit. This was articulated a few hours after Ezra's post by TGU founder Leesa, who demonstrated her role as "thought leader" by explicitly giving members permission to settle wherever they wished:

First, there is no competition between "There" and "Second Life" or any other place. We go where we want. And like Petrova said, we had three shards in Uru. I had to spend time on all three, obviously, but most people seemed to settle into one shard they liked the best.

Secondly, this forum and chat are our home not "There" or "Second Life" or anywhere else. Those places are for us to interact and play. So no matter where you are: There, Second Life, Ryzom, somewhere else or nowhere else, you are a TGUer and this forum is where you come home to (and when Erik is done we'll probably all stop going to those other places anyway).

The outcome of this dispute was that ultimately *There.com* was to become the main settlement for a majority of TGU members, although there was no official decree to that effect. Rather it was a spontaneous chain of events coaxed along by a few members. Raena, concerned that if they didn't find a new home quickly the group would fall apart, acted as an informal ambassador and made contact with her appointed *There .com* mentor, Alice, telling her their plight. She also managed to convince Lynn and Leesa to try it. Even though no formal dictate was given, once the two group leaders decided they would settle in *There.com*, it was only a matter of a few weeks before the bulk of remaining TGUers followed suit. Alice, an established Thereian, offered the refugees some space near her community, Emerald City, as a settlement.

A small number of original TGUers chose not to make *There.com* their home. Some visited occasionally; others did not go at all. Concurrently, TGU continued to maintain a small contingent in *Second Life*. Ezra, who was one of the strongest *Second Life* proponents, eventually retired as deputy mayor (primarily because of real-life priorities); Katsushiro, one of the original *There.com* scouts, eventually moved to *Second Life* but visited *There.com* on occasion. A few players, who will be discussed later, took central roles in creating and/or maintaining other TGU zones.

Initially The Gathering of Uru, one of about a half a dozen Uru refugee clubs in *There.com*, had about 300 members. Most of these were members of the original TGU group in *Uru*. During the first six months, the group actually grew; new members formerly of *Uru* but not from TGU joined, as well as Thereians who hung around the TGU group and enjoyed their culture. At the midway point of this study, The Gathering of Uru in *There.com* had around 450 members. At the end of the eighteen-month study, this number had waned to about 160, although most of the key members of the community remained active.

For a small and growing virtual society like *There.com*, the sudden onslaught of a large group of players en masse placed a significant burden on the system. Once again, the clients and servers were overworked. The TGU community that had settled near Alice's Emerald City grew to about sixty people in a matter of four weeks, creating huge problems with lag and "blockheads" (avatars reducing to low-polygon representations). There were also festering resentments among the "indigenous" Thereians and Emerald City residents, a number of whom moved out. TGU then moved to an adjacent lot to create more space between the two communities. Emerald City then moved, in part to get away from the server congestion caused by the growing immigrant group; however, TGU followed as a gesture of support for Alice, allowing still more space between the settlements to mitigate the lag. Nonetheless, the TGU group continued to grow steadily, and eventually was forced to move away from Emerald City entirely. In each case, the move was brought on either by a battle for processing resources, or "griefing" (harassment) from other players.

The primary form of griefing entailed players running over avatars with dune buggies. While the avatar suffers no long-term damage, the impact is very disruptive to whatever the avatar might be doing at the time. Another form of griefing was what one TGUer described as "sign wars." Because players in *There.com* could not "own" land per se, settlement was done more or less on a squatting basis. Thus any unclaimed land near or around the physical structures placed by the group was up for grabs. Whenever the TGUers would create a new settlement, they would plant a sign identifying it as their area. Griefers would then place another sign in front of theirs, such as a billboard advertising cybersex.

A significant faction of existing Thereians was suspicious and fearful of this sudden inrush of "outsiders." Many were afraid that, by sheer numbers, the Uruvians would take over *There.com* entirely, turning it into *Uru*. Some *There.com* denizens thought the "Uru people" a bit odd. They were clearly a very close-knit group, and often greeted each other in a foreign language with words like "Shorah!" (D'ni for "peace"). They were intelligent, resourceful, and, some felt, potentially dangerous. Some Thereians even took up the matter with *There.com* management, complaining about the refugees. As a result, TGUers became very protective of one another, and the persecution from Thereians only served to further strengthen their bond.

There.com management had the opposite response to the new arrivals: they were conciliatory and accommodating. After all, the Uru immigrants represented an instant market. There, Inc. (the world's owner at the time) was more than happy to nurture this growing population and the subscription fees it brought. In the long run,

| Figure 6.4 |
Uruvian immigrants romping in the Moroccan fountain in the first TGU Center in *There.com*. (Image: Raena)

Uruvians would go on to spend quite a bit of money in *There.com*, paying many additional fees related to keeping up PortaZones (temporary arrangements of structures and objects), and buying and selling numerous items in auction (for which players are charged a transaction fee). Because they were older and more committed than the average online game player, they were willing and able to spend money. The combination of their economic sway, their maturity, and their experience of suffering at the hands of an MMOG company contributed to their forthright and demanding manner with *There.com* management. The perception, not entirely unfounded, that the Uru people had undue influence with the powers that be only served to exacerbate the tensions between the new immigrants and native Thereians.

Between February and April 2004, TGU moved no less than five times to avoid harassment before settling in its sixth and finale locale. Finally, *There.com* management was able to secure an available island for the group, although some Thereians believed

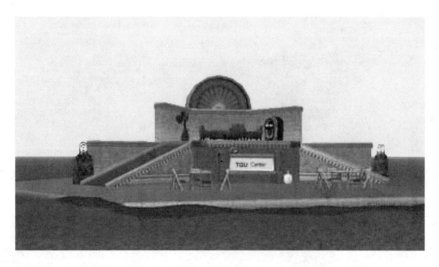

| Figure 6.5 |
The second instantiation of the Center on Yeesha Island. (Image: Pearce)

its occupant had been pushed out to accommodate the immigrants. This became their permanent settlement in *There.com*.

The TGU Community Center, a PortaZone (PAZ) that followed the group around from place to place, was originally created by Ember using a Moroccan kit available from *There.com* (figure 6.4). Although there were other kits that were stylistically better suited to *Uru*, the Moroccan was selected for the simple reason that it had a fountain. With each move, the Community Center PAZ had been carried along with the group and repositioned at each new location. This structure became the focal point of the new island, initially called Leesa Island, and later changed to Yeesha Island, shown in figure 6.5. Eventually, the Community Center was rebuilt using *Uru*-style architectural components designed by Damanji, who emerged as one of TGU's leading artisans. The centerpiece of the Community Center was a replica of the *Uru* hood fountain (made by another player), shown in figure 6.6.

Throughout the period that TGU was in a state of flux in *There.com*, and even after settlement on the island, many group members had a sense that this was a temporary arrangement until they could build their own self-contained virtual homeland, Erik's special and still-ongoing project. In early interviews, TGU members frequently commented that once Erik was done, they wouldn't need *There* anymore.

Implied in this was a deep desire for self-determination. Having already been "wronged" by the operator of a virtual world, TGU consistently harbored a sense that

| Figure 6.6 |
The final iteration of the TGU Center in *There.com* complete with *Uru* hood fountain and *Uru*-style architectural components.
(Image: Pearce)

the best solution would be one not controlled by a corporation. This desire became particularly acute during brief periods when there was some possibility that *There.com* would be closing. The uncertainty of the status of their world was, understandably, unsettling to the displaced Uruvians. Perhaps fuelled in part by this anxiety, two key group members, D'evon and Erik, never visited *There.com* for the duration of this study, although Erik eventually did set up his first *There.com* account after meeting other TGUers in real life.

A Home of Their Own

Throughout TGU's trials in *There.com*, Erik continued his effort to create a new version of *Uru* with the Atmosphere 3-D world-authoring environment, a technology he had never before used. Erik described his motivation as follows:

this may sound a little silly, but it was because of a promise I made to leesa on black tuesday . . . she was utterly devastated . . . she didn't make it to the hood where the rest of us were and just sent messages to us. and i was pretty upset over uru closing as well.

anyway, i promised leesa that i would rebuild the hood—for her, for me, and for the rest of us. got a bit carried away here, i think it is safe to say. especially since i didn't know anything about 3-D environments . . . or 3-D at all really.

Erik was so motivated that he was willing to learn an entirely new set of skills in order to create something that would serve as a home for his community. His goal was to create a self-contained re-creation of the hood, rather than attempt to create something in another 3-D world. "To me, *Uru* wasn't only about the people—it was the people AND the place . . . the mood, atmosphere, ambience."

Erik did not like the atmosphere or ambience presented by the alternatives. He felt *There.com* was too cartoonish and he did not care for the aesthetics of *Second Life*; nor did he care for the cultures of either world. Working entirely on his own, he taught himself to create 3D models using Caligari TrueSpace, an easy-to-use, less-expensive alternative to more high-end programs such as 3-D Studio Max, and used Adobe Photoshop, with which he was already familiar, to create textures. Erik also created replicas of his friends' avatars for use in this new hood. He created the textures by hand, rather than appropriating them from the *Uru* game software, because he did not want to infringe on any of Cyan or Ubisoft's copyrights. For the same reason, he also alerted Cyan and a representative of the company came and viewed the Atmosphere hood, but did not contact him further. Erik took this as an indication that it was safe to proceed.

In an interview, Erik cited his favorite aspect of *Uru*: "the water . . . that was the genius of the hood—as well as other places (in *Uru*). Placing a fountain in the hood meant that people would gather there . . . because people are drawn to water—esp running water." Architects and urban planners are aware that water, whether as a natural feature or a man-made element, is a major attractor in public space. As Erik put it, "look at any piazza in any italian city. or the water cooler at the office for that matter. water is life, therefore people seek water." Erik began his re-creation of the hood with the fountain, "the centerpiece of anything Uru." Indeed the importance of the fountain can clearly be seen, as it is a recurring artifact that appears in many different player-created instantiations of *Uru* (figure 6.7).

Initially, Erik released the fountain courtyard and other areas of the hood (figure 6.8), and then later added some other rooms of his own invention (figure 6.9). Using

| Figure 6.7 |

Erik's custom-made avatars hanging out at a re-creation of the *Uru* fountain in his Atmosphere Hood. (Image: Pearce)

their custom-made avatars, players began to meet in the "Atmos Hood," as players came to call it, typically ten to twelve players concurrently, at a fixed weekly time. A previously established regular meeting time for the MUD—Saturday noon (to accommodate European players)—was supplanted by Lynn to encourage people to gather in Erik's Atmosphere Hood on a regular basis. This scheduling activity on Lynn's part exemplifies the ways in which TGU members worked to support each other's efforts to keep the community together. It is also interesting to note that while Erik was considered a very active member of the community, the only instantiation of Uru immigrant culture in which he actively participated was the Atmosphere Hood.

Assimilation/Transculturation

In the context of immigration, the term "assimilation" generally implies an immigrant group adapting to its new locale. In the case of TGU, it is clear that, over time, a process of mutual assimilation occurred between TGUers and Thereians. This

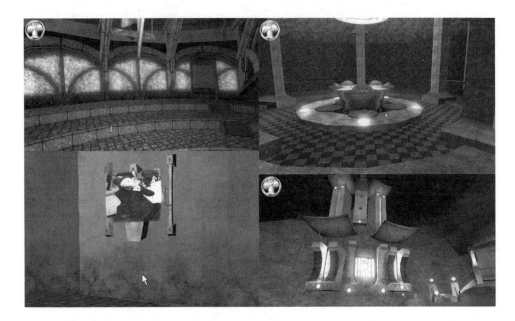

| Figure 6.8 |
Details of Erik's Atmosphere Hood. (Image: Pearce)

might equate to what Fernando Ortiz called "transculturation" (1947), in which a cultural context adapts to new arrivals as much as the immigrant group adapts to its new milieu. Over time, TGU players made major contributions to the *There.com* community, and eventually became fully integrated, while still maintaining their group identity. The University of There, for instance, founded by TGU member Wingman, was composed primarily of Damanji's *Uru*-inspired "Cone Houses." Damanji became not only TGU's lead artisan, but also one of the top developers in *There.com*. Other TGU members took leadership roles in fashion design, art creation and curating, sporting events, event hosting, performance, and building, as well as on *There.com*'s Member Advisory Board. Through the social mediation of the world, Uru immigrants have become Uruvian-Thereians, in the same way that Italian immigrants to the United States became Italian-Americans. As a result, Uruvians have become an integral part of *There.com*'s culture, economy, and political structure.

TGU member Cola, in an essay titled "A Thereian Makes Peace with the Urufugee Within," makes several word plays based on *Myst* content (including the last line, which is quoted from *Uru*) and voices the merging of the two cultures this way:

| Figure 6.9 |
Erik's attempt at creating a new *Uru* Age in Atmosphere. (Image: Pearce)

The merging of the soul of the Urufugee into the citizen of There is happening. It wasn't without its tantrums of not wanting to merge, not wanting to believe Uru was gone and the guilty feelings of actually enjoying something other than Uru. But time does tell and there will always be the memories of D'ni and having been together there. Perhaps we could have a dual citizenship; Uruvian and Thereian. I have **Myst** being in D'ni, my soul, heart and being were **Riven** from D'ni, I am an **Exile** from the place where I want to be yet **Uru** has been put to bed. But perhaps the ending has not yet been written.

It is hard to say what percentage of the *There.com* population is comprised of Uruvian immigrants, as *There.com* management will not release subscriber numbers. However, of the estimated 10,000 players who played *Uru Prologue*, TGU appears to be the largest single group of Uru refugees, and is considered by many in the Uru community at large to be the strongest in terms of group cohesion.

The trajectory of the TGU experience in *There.com* demonstrates the power of play communities to remain together even in the face of adversity. The profound and

| Figure 6.10 |
Visitors to Yeesha Island in *There.com* are greeted by the player-designed banners of The Gathering of Uru (left) and the League of Free Welcomers (right). (Image: Pearce)

deep connection formed by partners in play suggests that play activity has unique social qualities relevant in forming sustainable long-term affiliations. With the help of online communications tools, these can be sustained well beyond the term of the original play context in which they were formed. The unique style and personality of the group can also be transplanted into another play context or ecosystem, where it will adapt to new conditions while maintaining its essential attributes and group cohesion (figure 6.10).

Uru Reclaimed

Concurrently with Erik's Atmos Hood and the TGU migration into *There.com* and other virtual worlds, and the *Second Life* re-creation of *Uru*, a group of Uru fans/hackers who were actively working on restoring the original game succeeded in reverse-engineering the server software. Because of their loyalty toward Cyan, however, they approached the developer with a proposal: grant special permission to players to run Cyan's *Uru* server software on their own servers. This arrangement came to fruition in summer 2004 under the auspices of *Until Uru*, and the TGU shard became active in August 2004. The *Until Uru* game was, as one player put it, "exactly as we left it"; in other words, there were no new Ages or new gameplay. The hacker group also continued to conduct experiments with their reverse-engineered server infrastructure, including attempting to create new Ages.

The origins of the creation of *Until Uru* seem deeply embedded in the gameplay. As Xploros, *Uru*'s community manager, who held that title until the summer of 2005, described it:

There had always been a segment of the community that "hacked" and reverse engineered the *Uru* software. ... The Myst world is very dedicated to puzzle solving, and self-reliance, and that the experience of the participant could be immersive in many ways. And when Uru was hacked, it was found that there was additional material that made it clear that some expectation of such hacking was built into the game ... which had no internal game function, but were enjoyed immensely by those who discovered this hidden material.

After that, and especially after the closure of *Uru*, the community (congregating mostly on one of the fan sites ...) began reverse engineering the *Uru* servers, and quickly gaining enough success to be able to predict a public run server to be released at some point. At this time they began talking to Cyan so as to secure permission for this effort.

Based on prior posts and conversations, one would have assumed that players would return to *Until Uru* and abandon their settlements in other virtual worlds. However, this was not the case. Uru refugees had already, to a certain extent, assimilated to their new environs. Rather than the anticipated return to their homeland, *Until Uru* was lauded as something special. TGU members began meeting there regularly at noon on Sundays, a date and time that allowed for all of the international members to participate. Players also conducted special events in the *Until Uru* shards, such as a St. Patrick's Day parade and the D'ni Olympics, originally founded by TGU member Maesi. A number of TGU members remained disinclined to visit *Until Uru*; they saw it as a symbol of the past, and preferred, in their words, to move forward.

The introduction of *Until Uru* also provided the opportunity for newer members of TGU who had never played *Uru* before (including the author of this study) to experience the game firsthand. My own experience of *Until Uru* came in the fall of 2004, shortly after the TGU shard was opened. Having heard about and seen *Uru* through the eyes of players, via their homages and simulations, for about six months, entering the world about which I knew so much but had never before visited brought another dimension of insight to the research.

I was already familiar with the places and artifacts of *Uru* through both player-created instantiations and descriptions of them. TGU members were very excited to take me through the different Ages of *Uru*, help me with the puzzles, and show me the different areas of their beloved home world. They knew the nooks, crannies, and nuances of the game in detail, and one of their greatest pleasures continued to be showing the original *Uru* game to the uninitiated. Furthermore, almost everything in *Uru* has special meaning, which players relished sharing. For those new to *Uru* who knew TGU members in other games, venturing into *Until Uru* explained a great deal about the group and its unique characteristics. Visiting *Uru* exposed one to the source of key symbols, images, and artifacts that were referred to repeatedly by Uru groups in other virtual worlds. Understanding the importance of those artifacts to Uruvians was key to understanding the group and its particular personality, which will be described in more detail in the chapters on communities of play and TGU play styles.

Although *Until Uru* did not include any new Ages, Cyan did release extension packs for the game after the server closure, and the hacker group behind *Until Uru* also created some new add-on packs. Players invented, both by using these new capabilities and by exploiting design features or bugs, a plethora of new gameplay activities within the *Uru* world.

Comments

"Based on prior posts and conversations, one would have assumed that players would return to Until Uru and abandon their settlements in other virtual worlds. However, this was not the case. Uru refugees had already, to a certain extent, assimilated to their new environs . . ."

Perhaps this group would have returned in a more substantial way to Until Uru if there was the promise of more content. The community has now settled in a variety of worlds which are being maintained and are moving forward with new content and new members. I believe there would be greater numbers returning to the cavern if there was the ability for members to create new content as they have become accustomed to in THERE, Second Life and other places.
Posted by: Raena | February 05, 2006 at 05:13 PM

Self-Determination

Because of the trauma they had been dealt at the hands of Cyan and Ubisoft, *Uru* players felt particularly sensitive about their relationships with the corporations that governed them. This trauma reared its ugly head once again on "Black Friday," May

21, 2004, when only a few months after TGU's arrival, *There.com* threatened to close. Players petitioned and the company agreed not to close the game if current players could find a way to increase subscriptions. In very short order, subscription rates were brought up and *There.com* was saved. It is likely that this experience of feeling as though they were at the wrath of corporations is also what fueled TGU's ongoing involvement in *There.com*'s Member Advisory Board. They did not want a repeat of the *Uru* eviction.

Technical savvy is one means of empowerment against the tyranny of corporate governance. Erik was motivated to learn two entirely new software packages in order to assure total control of his instantiation of *Uru*. And the *Until Uru* hacker group used their ability to hack the server as leverage in negotiations with the game's developers. They astutely understood that the demonstration of power was better than its use. Cyan, well aware that *Uru* players were part of the core fan base for all their games, supported the hacker group's efforts. Conversely, although Ubisoft and Cyan were aware of the various *Uru*-derived projects taking place throughout the ludisphere, they never attempted to intervene or interfere with any *Uru* player initiatives.

For TGU members, Koalanet became their safe haven of self-determination. It was the clearinghouse for all things TGU, and spanned all of the TGU settlements across multiple MMOWs. Through it, TGUers could safely traverse the ludisphere and still maintain control over their collective identity and destiny.

Over time, *Uru* players, both TGUers and others, have slowly taken over ownership of the *Myst* brand. While many players began by simulating artifacts from the original *Uru* games, eventually they began to create their own *Uru*-esque objects. *Uru* fans like collie, who, at a recent Mysterium fan convention presented her *Uru*-themed quilts, are even taking the *Uru* culture out into the real world. Players who may ultimately know more than developers about the worlds they create feel both inspired and empowered to add their own creative contributions to the "database" of the game's narrative and culture. This type of emergent fan culture can clearly be seen in cases such as *Star Trek*'s Trekkie phenomenon (Jenkins 1992); thus we find player creations such as the "D'ni Pocket Dictionary" among the new extravirtual artifacts that players have created. In the summer of 2005, *Myst* and *Uru* fans in *Second Life* even created *Inara*, a completely new game designed in the *Myst/Uru* tradition.

A year and a half after *Uru Prologue* was put to bed, players still entertained hopes that the game would some day reopen, with all the planned Ages added. These hopes were put to rest when Cyan announced in September 2005 that they were retiring the *Myst* legacy. While this news saddened fans, they themselves were already taking the initiative to transition the *Myst* world into a fan-owned and operated phenomenon.

Uruvian-Thereians had successfully deployed their "emergent Age" strategy, *Second Life* players had already created an entirely original Age, and the hacker group that had instigated *Until Uru*, which had been in negotiation with Cyan to release their Age-building tools, released a beta of the first player-made *Uru* Age in November 2005.

These trends in productive play suggest that *Uru* and *Myst* players have already taken on the task of keeping *Uru* and *Myst* alive by preserving the game's culture in other virtual worlds, and by expanding and extending the *Myst/Uru* world through the creative application of their own skills and imaginations.

But as players were fond of saying, the ending had not yet been written. *Uru* was to reopen . . . and then reclose . . . only a few short years later.

THE INNER LIVES OF AVATARS

Avatar Representation

The avatar is the essential unit within the network of the play community, and is the means whereby the individual player interacts with both other players and the ecosystem of the play environment.

While the avatar is the primary form of expression provided to players in an MMOW, it is as much if not more the expression of the world's designers as it is that of the players. Designers determine what modes of representation, and thus what forms of expression, are available to players. "In doing so," points out media artist and theorist Allucquére Rosanne Stone, "they are articulating their own assumptions about bodies and sociality and projecting them onto the codes that define cyberspace systems" (1991). T. L. Taylor calls these "intentional bodies," because they reflect the intentions (or lack thereof) of game designers when they articulate the qualities that player characters in games are to have (2003). These sometimes unconscious assumptions and intentions permeate every aspect of every virtual world, from the design of individual avatars, to the world's narrative and values, to its "karma systems" of cause and effect. Player rewards naturally influence behavior, and as discussed earlier, players with certain sets of values tend to gravitate toward certain types of games and virtual worlds whose values they share.

If the avatar is framed as a form of personal expression, as performance medium, it is not hard to see the ways in which the components of the avatar kit dictate the forms of expression that occur. In most MMOGs, avatar creation involves an elaborate system of races, classes, and skills statistics that are deeply tied to game mechanics; body types tend to be hypersexualized, and wardrobe options are tied to the statistical value of the gear in combat (as shown in figure 7.1). In *Uru* and the other virtual worlds described here, avatar creation is primarily aesthetic, the choices limited but straightforward (figure 7.2). Since *Uru* has no points, avatar design is not tied in any

| Figure 7.1 |
A *World of Warcraft* avatar, showing armor stats. (Image: Pearce)

way to point values or game mechanics. Avatars are clearly human, with reasonably natural proportions, and for each gender players can pick from a menu of hairstyles, facial features, unusually modest clothing items (for an MMOG), and color palettes for skin, hair, and clothing, including the ability to show thinning or graying hair. This was an astute design choice, possibly made in anticipation of the game's demographics, and building off the *Myst* games' known fanbase. It is interesting that the designers chose not to follow the conventions of a traditional role-playing game, which would have put players in the roles of D'ni or Bahro. Rather, they invited players to become explorers in the *Myst* world, giving them the implied option to do so as themselves.

Uru players' interworld migration presented the need to compare aspects of avatar expressiveness in different virtual worlds. When TGUers began to look at alternatives to *Uru*, they had already formed strong attachments to their *Uru* avatars; therefore, one goal was to replicate their *Uru* avies within the constraints of the new game's avatar creation system. For some, the cartoony avatars of *There.com* looked too much like Mattel's Barbie and Ken dolls of the 1960s, and forced players to present as twenty-

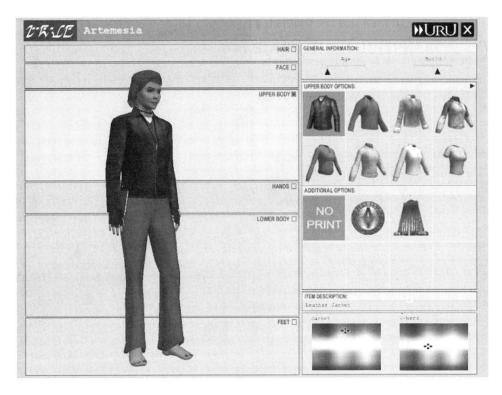

| Figure 7.2 |
Avatar creation in *Uru* is primarily aesthetic. (Image: Pearce)

two-year-olds. Avatars tended to be shapely, although there was some leeway to create more plump physiques. Some players actually liked the Disneyesque aesthetic, and one player posited the theory that this style might also have resonated culturally with the generation represented by many members of the group, the majority of whom who were in their forties and fifties. They also argued that *There.com* avatars were more expressive in terms of animation and gesture. "Here," TGU mayor Leesa pointed out with reference to *There.com*, "our avatars breathe."

Those in favor of *Second Life* argued that the avatars were more realistic and allowed for more customization, making it easier to re-create their *Uru* avatars; however, some found *Second Life*'s avatar animations to be stiff and unnatural.

All of these nuanced arguments evince the importance of players' feelings about their avatars in both their sense of identity and their comfort within the virtual world. These arguments also highlight the fact that the avatar, at least in the case of these

| Figure 7.3 |

Avatar modification at one of *There.com*'s spas. (Image: Pearce)

players, was viewed more as a form of expression than a symbol or measure of skills and status. Because these were persistent identities, for most players, the appearance and expressive qualities (such as animation) of avatars were a key factor in their migration preferences.

Becoming and Losing an Avatar

As mentioned earlier, the introduction of the avatar into the *Myst* world was a new feature to the *Uru* game, the importance of which cannot be overemphasized. All of the *Myst* games that preceded *Uru* put the player in the first-person perspective with an ambiguous identity. These games were effective at simulating immersion, the panacea to virtual reality at that time (Rheingold 1993).

As enjoyable as they were, however, *Myst* and its derivatives were very lonely games in which most of the world appeared abandoned. Few characters appeared during gameplay, and the player was not embodied in any way. From a game studies

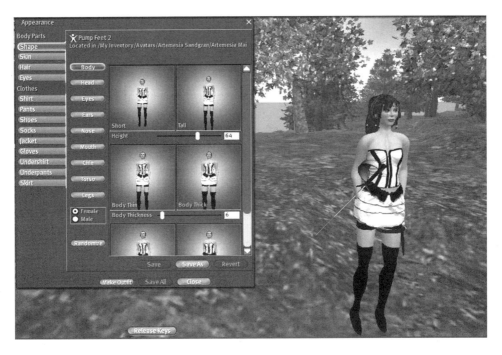

| Figure 7.4 |
Avatar modification in *Second Life*. (Image: Pearce)

perspective, I am not aware of any other game franchise that provides the opportunity to compare a first-person versus an avatar-based experience, but it is clear that even before entering the multiplayer world, this new feature produced a paradigm shift in the effect of the player experience.

Having an avatar—that is, a representation of yourself—is a prerequisite to being in a multiplayer world. However, even before players encountered other avatars in the multiplayer *Uru Prologue*, they had already had the experience of avatar embodiment through *Uru Prime*. Because *Uru*'s avatar creation left open the option to play themselves in game (as opposed to a fantasy role) many players created modified versions of themselves to inhabit the game. Compared to other games, there were remarkably few instances of cross-gender avatar creation. In the case of TGU, of 450 people at its maximum group size, only 3 known cases of cross-gendered play occurred, whereas in typical MMOGs as many as half the female avatars in-world may actually be played by male players. As Wingman put it: "I suggest their avatars resemble the way they want to think of themselves."

All of the TGU players interviewed also described feeling that their avatars were the same person across all the virtual worlds they inhabited. One recurring theme among the TGU players I spoke to was that the avatar was a window into the soul through which you could see the real person. This seemed to be the case regardless of whether avatar representation was fixed (as in *Uru*), somewhat flexible (as in *There .com*), or entirely malleable (as in *Second Life*). Thus persistent identity seemed more relevant than consistent representation, although the visual recognition of the identity is clearly also a factor, especially in the development of long-term relationships.

Raena, a long-standing TGU member and the group's cartographer, described it this way: "Uru was the first game I ever played where I was an actual avatar . . . I discovered after spending all those hours . . . I kind of felt that I was living vicariously through the avie who was exploring the game . . . it was nice to see yourself, or think of yourself as a person within the game." She equated it with the real-life phenomenon of proprioception, that is, the perception of where our bodies are in space, and this added another dimension to the game. Part of what Raena enjoyed were the ways in which embodiment afforded new forms of play within the world she knew and loved so well. She cites jumping as one of the fun things she could do with her new avatar. A sense of embodiment gave new and perhaps more resonant meaning to the virtual space she was inhabiting. She also found that over time she identified more and more with her avie and also with those of other people. "I found in Uru," she says, "I was kind of 'feeling' the avie."

Lynn, the deputy mayor of both the TGU group en masse and its settlement within *There.com*, enjoyed the avatar instantiation for other reasons. Because of a spinal condition, the once-active Lynn was confined to a wheelchair. The avie had two significances for her:

I . . . didn't even know what an avatar was until Uru. And all of a sudden I would be able to run and jump and walk and not have to worry about a damn (wheel) chair . . . or if a curb got in the way . . . it was to me a total sense of freedom to be the type of person that I was before. I was a very active person. And when I lost that I had no idea this opportunity existed . . . It just gave me such a great feeling. And I think that's why I asked when (Uru) closed if we could come to a place that would also have avatars . . . because we have a chat program on Koalanet that would hold up to 600 (people). In avie you get to still play and run.

Thus for Lynn, the avatar became a kind of social augmentation. The level playing field enabled by the avatar liberated her from her bodily constraints. It also availed her

| Figure 7.5 |
TGU deputy mayor Lynn exploring *Until Uru.* (Image: Pearce)

community of her energetic play style and considerable leadership skills. Lynn's case contrasts sharply with arguments that online life is disembodied. On the contrary, in Lynn's case the avatar experience has been a case of reembodiment. Being able to help people brought her out of a deep depression she suffered as a result of her physical condition. "I volunteered all of my adult life. This situation that we're in with avatars allows me to continue to feel like I'm a productive citizen, a helpful person, where I can still be useful."

Seeing oneself inside the *Myst* world had a profound effect not only on Lynn but also on all the TGU members. Indeed, part of the anguish of the initial loss of the *Uru* server stemmed from this deep connection that players had formed with their avatars. Once again, Raena gives expression to this experience:

February 13, 2004, 02:31:48 pm
Inspired by Scarlet and Aria I have written a few awkward words about our avatars and our relationship with them. For through our avatars in D'ni we made relationships with each other.

Avi in D'ni

by Raena of Katran

It began as a request: "Create Player"

and you were led to the wardrobe to make choices.

To pick hair, color and clothes.

To be old or be young, or maybe rotund,

you could even change the length of your nose.

Those choices you made created an avatar that day,

your new life as Avi in D'ni.

Remember when you first felt scared,

of thunder or strange looking creature?

Did your heart skip a beat when you fell off a cliff?

Did you feel better when you wound up in Relto?

That moment was when you and Avi became one,

your true innerself.

Your soul free from the physical world

to be the person inside.

So precious!

In Uru your Avi found a level playing field.

Free from cultural pressures and bias.

Free to express emotion, say how you feel.

You could walk, run and dance,

see and be seen,

love and be loved.

We were family as Avi in D'ni.

Now our avatars are gone,

our souls are stripped bare.

We cry tears for our loved and lost Avi.

And here we will stay, as we wait for the day,

when we're once again Avi in D'ni.

—Raena

The way Raena's poem builds on others that preceded it highlights the role of social feedback, helping to generate a discourse by building on a shared experience. The ability to safely express feelings that might otherwise be frowned upon is a significant characteristic of this group. Safety begets safety, and as each player came forth with his or her deepest feelings, others followed in kind with their own expressions.

This poem also gives us additional insight into what the loss of the server meant; one lost one's friends and one's virtual self. As Raena explained, it was a kind of death. This is quite distinct from the kind of death avatars in games like *EverQuest* experience—these are frequent and temporary deaths, similar to restarting a level in a game. You are revived, respawned, perhaps penalized by a loss of gear or experience points, but your avatar identity lives on. This was a permanent death, not of the people, but of their avatar personae in the virtual world.

What this suggests is that the avatar is neither entirely "me," nor entirely "not me," but a *version* of me that only exists in a particular mediated context. When that context, and with it the avatar, ceases to be, that part of the self dies as well. That part of the self, expressed and projected through the avatar in a shared virtual world, is as much a creation of the group as the group is a creation of the individuals within it. This echoes Winnicott's "me/not me" paradox, as described by Schechner and alluded to earlier (Schechner 1988, Winnicott 1971).

Comments

Looking back I find my fondest memories of this time frame are the poems we read and the poems we wrote. Safety among friends? Perhaps. For me at least it felt like we all were of one mind, writing with one hand and one heart.

Posted by: Raena | April 07, 2006 at 01:58 PM

The Social Construction of Identity

Rather than being a matter of individual agency, these findings suggest that avatar identity evolves through a process of interaction with others. Thus, the avatar identity is what sociologists would call an "intersubjective accomplishment," the product of an ongoing and dynamic set of social transactions and feedback—in other words, emergence (Pearce and Artemesia 2007).

The oft-forgotten node in these transactions is the game designer. The game itself, the play ecosystem, is the medium through which these transactions occur, and the mediation is of their making. Thus the intersubjective achievement is really a three-way collaboration between the individual player, the community, and the designers of the world, who present not as avatars but as the game and its ecosystem.

Perhaps the best illustration of the process of emergent identity formation is the way in which Leesa became the reluctant leader of a group of over 450 people. Ordinarily, one might think of leadership as anathema to emergence, which is by definition a bottom-up process. However, Leesa did not really set out with the objective of being a leader. Rather, she grew into the role through a process of social feedback—as more and more players joined the group, she developed a sense of leadership and responsibility toward them, as indicated by her making a point of spending equal time in each of the three TGU shards in the original *Uru*. Even the fact that she did not post her rules until *after* the group had begun to grow supports this bottom-up theory of leadership.

Later, when she moved into *There.com*, most TGU members followed her, although she made it a point to avoid making any official decree on the subject. In fact, shortly after the migration, Leesa made an attempt to abandon the group entirely, because of stress and real-life health problems. But TGUers begged her back and she returned to the fray. One tactic she used to mitigate the pressure that came with leadership was to create the TGU Council; this created a way to distribute both responsibility and power. Throughout this process, Leesa had a growing awareness of her importance to the group, and this awareness of who her avatar was becoming also had an impact on the person *behind* the avatar.

This pattern of social identity construction appears again in the case of artisans. The more positive feedback they received, whether social or economic, the more motivated they were to create. Damanji, who made architectural elements, vehicles, and clothing; Maesi, who made clothing; and Shaylah and Raena, who created virtual paintings and later artifacts, are just a few examples within the *Uru* group. Within *There.com*, player designers become minor celebrities, known for their aesthetic style and productivity. Furthermore, the more positive feedback players get, the more they tend to experiment. Thus even personal, individual style appears to evolve through a process of social feedback.

One of the most interesting cases of the social construction of identity arises around gender. As mentioned earlier, cross-gender play is a common practice in online games, although in general, it does not seem to equate with real-life transgender behavior. Designers of *Ultima Online*, for instance, were surprised to discover that while 50 percent of the avatar characters in-game were female, only 20 percent of the actual players were, suggesting that a little less than half the female avatars were being played by men (Koster 2001). A small amount of gender switching did occur within the TGU group. In each case, the player eventually revealed his true gender (all three cases were of men playing women), and in each case, the outcome of how this should be dealt with was largely decided by the group.

One TGUer played a female consistently and effectively, even with the introduction of voice, for eighteen months before revealing the gender of her real-life avie. When the decision as to whether or not to continue playing the female avatar was vetted with the group, it became clear that, although they supported the player's personal choice, the majority of TGUers had become attached to the female character.

After a brief period of adjustment, including attempts by the player to use a male avatar, eventually, by something of an unspoken consensus, he returned to the female avatar as his primary in-game character. He continued to use the female voice in-world, even though other players were now aware he was male.

In some respects, it is difficult to tell where group identity ends and individual identity begins. While Western culture tends to reify individual identity and agency, this apparent ambiguity between group and individual identity may be more reflective of non-Western cultures, which view the individual on more of a continuum with the group as a whole (Jackson 1998). In the case of TGU, self-identifying as *Uru* refugees meant that the individual avatar identity was inextricably tied to the group identity. This collective identity both compelled and enabled the migration of individual identity to other virtual worlds.

In interviews, players would often speak in the collective we, identifying qualities and values of the group. The majority of these group indicators were couched in terms of play styles; for example, "We are explorers; we are puzzle solvers; we do not like violence," suggesting that a large factor in group identity had to do with their signature play style and values. Other qualities were tied to social interaction styles. "We are tolerant and respectful of others; we do not join factions; we avoid drama."

Many of the play styles cited are directly tied to the play patterns of *Uru*, but the group style of TGU is distinctive, even within the *Uru* community, for its particular social values, epitomized by "Leesa's Rules." On the other hand, most TGU players asserted that those social values also arise out of the type of person that is attracted to a game like *Uru*. In interviews with key TGU leaders, all agreed that most in the group would never have gravitated toward a first-person shooter or medieval role-playing game. Thus, even social values are intermingled with the game insomuch as they may be an attractor for certain player types.

An interesting linguistic idiosyncrasy highlights the relationship between the individual and the social. The word "Uru" has a double meaning in the D'ni language. Colloquially (according to both players and designers) Uru means "you are you," a fitting name for a game involving avatars. However, both the official game web site and fan-created D'ni dictionaries give the meaning of Uru as "a community or large gathering." This seeming contradiction provides a clue to the core quality of both TGU and Uru at large: that the individual and group identities are integrally related to one another.

One of the most surprising outcomes of the study was the extent to which my own role as ethnographer became socially constructed through interaction with the group. I was conscious of the fact that my presence was going to have some kind of impact on the group, but even from the beginning was surprised by how this played out. When I first began interviewing TGU members, it was clear that my presence in their midst was having a therapeutic effect. Clearly they needed to talk about their experiences, and they appreciated having a willing ear. Far from meeting resistance, players were more than happy to talk to me, often for hours, about what they had been through. I was amazed at how forthcoming they were, and over time I began to develop an integral role in the group.

This role, however, developed and transformed. In the fall of 2004, a crisis precipitated by a magazine interview, and described briefly in chapter 13, caused me to rethink some of my methodological assumptions, but also shifted the dynamics of my relationships with the participants. It was at this point that I began to develop personal friendships with individual TGU members. Two members, Bette and Wingman, conspired to turn the tables on me by requesting an interview for the University of There newsletter. This created a further shift in the dynamics with the group. By the time I attended the There Real Life Gathering, I had become a fully matriculated member of TGU, and it became clear that the group had had much more impact on me than I had on the group.

Avatar Presence and Intersubjectivity

Based on interviews with TGU members, it appears that over the long term, players form strong emotional bonds with their avatars, as do members of their social circle. This may explain why losing the avatar can be so traumatic, and switching to a different avatar identity can often be a difficult transition, not only for the player but also for other members of the play community. Players also reported missing their own avatars, as well as the avatars of players who had switched characters, even if the players themselves were still present in the game using a different avatar.

Avatar experiences described by players contrast sharply with earlier theories about presence handed down to us from the high-end virtual reality research of the 1990s. This branch of research focused on the notion of first-person immersion as the best means to create a sense of presence—in other words, the quality of "being there" —within a virtual world. Enhancing and perfecting sensory inputs and so-called embodied interaction were seen as the primary means of increasing this quality of presence. However, this and other avatar research suggests a different conclusion: that having a representation of the self visible inside the world may actually enhance the sense of presence, as well as the sense of embodiment.

Based on the outcomes of this research, this seems to stem from four contributing factors, each of which has to do with intersubjectivity. First, seeing a representation of oneself projected into the virtual world appears to enhance one's ability to emotionally project into the world, whether it be single- or multiplayer. Second, the sense of proprioception (the awareness of where our bodies are in space) produced by the avatar may create a more direct embodied relationship with the 3-D world, particularly through play—running, jumping, and the like. Third, the emotional attachment to the player's character seems to create a deep connection both to other avatars and to the virtual world they share. Finally, it may be that one of the key aspects of experiencing presence in an online virtual world is the quality of being perceived within a play context, or, as MacKinnon put it, in cyberspace "I am perceived, therefore I am" (1995). I would take this one step further and argue that the ability to be perceived through one's play identity creates a unique mode of being perceived that may not be shared in other modes of computer-mediated communication. I term this "seeing and being seen" (Pearce 2006c).

Thus it may be that a sense of social presence within the play space is more emotionally compelling to some players than a sense of physical presence. Part of the reason for this may be the relationship between social presence and flow, which will be covered in more depth in the subsequent section.

Comments

Perhaps "immersion" technology is not sufficient to allow one to look down and see one's avatar hands and feet, or look into a mirror, or gain an adequate feel for one's presence spatially. THERE offers a first person mode, which is rarely used. Uru has a first person mode as well but was only useful to get a close up look at some clue or other object intrinsic to gameplay. As in THERE, first person in Uru is rarely used for person-to-person interaction.

The ability to see your avatar on the screen defines where you are in-world in relation to the others. Called "third person mode" my mind quickly adapted to this and as they say in sports "be the ball." In "third person" mode you "be the avi". I have observed people in the Uru group excusing themselves when violating each other's space. A good example is in Uru where it is possible to pass through each other when moving. It is common to hear someone say "sorry," or "I felt that."
Posted by: Raena | February 05, 2006 at 05:20 PM

It is interesting the number of people who dream about their online worlds on a regular basis and who are their avie in the dreams, not their "real life" self.
Posted by: Leesa | April 10, 2006 at 01:28 PM

COMMUNITIES AND CULTURES OF PLAY

The Power of Play

As discussed earlier, even game studies shares the implicit assumption in Western culture that play is a waste of time. Early game scholars whose work has become canon in the field, while stressing the cultural importance of play, also assert that "unproductive" was one of play's defining characteristics (Caillois 1961, Huizinga [1938] 1950). Contemporary writers in video game studies have carried on this tradition (Salen and Zimmerman 2004, Juul 2002), although some are beginning to question this core assumption. This study shows that, to the contrary, the time spent on play is not only not wasted but can also be highly productive, both in terms of creative enterprise, and of effort placed on community building. It can also be argued that play is, in fact, an act of cultural production, as players engage in the dynamic creation of entertainment experiences, in addition to the contribution of artifacts to the play environment.

Conversely, anthropologists such as Richard Schechner and Victor Turner have argued that play is crucial to human culture and development and manifests in more "serious" forms such as ritual, which both anthropologists feel has play at its core (Schechner 1988, Schechner and Schuman 1976, Turner 1982). Play theorist Brian Sutton-Smith has also suggested that play should be viewed as important in its own right, and not simply as a mechanism for accomplishing more "serious" ends like education (1997). In terms of society at large, particularly in the United States (although this is less the case in other countries, such as Japan), adult play is considered somehow trivial and in some cases even immoral. While video games have been the subject of intense scrutiny in recent years, games in general are part of a larger tradition of the suppression of entertainment throughout history, ranging from theater in Shakespeare's day to film during the McCarthy era. Even a game as seemingly innocuous as chess was repeatedly banned throughout history because it was presumed to promote decadence, gambling, violence, and immoral sexual behavior (Yalom 2004).

Even among TGUers, the common remark that "it's not just a game" reveals the depth of this cultural bias that somehow a game is an inferior form of human social experience. Although one could argue that *There.com* is more of a metaverse than a game, players also made the same comment of *Uru*. In both cases, players saw that these play spaces had profound implications in their lives. The TGU experience suggests a repositioning of adult play space from its presently marginalized status to acknowledging its central role in developing unique and enduring friendships. The TGU data presents a compelling argument that games can be not only a context for personal transformation, but also a catalyst for strong and powerful social bonds. For many TGU players, playing within the social context of their group is a sublime and even a spiritual experience, a revelation that surprised most members. As suggested earlier, at least a part of this spiritual aspect of game-playing is derived from the content of the *Myst* series itself, but this was amplified and in some ways transformed by the additional social dimension of play in *Uru*.

The power of this social dimension was perhaps the biggest surprise for players. Very few TGU players entered *Uru* with the intent of forming social bonds. Most informants were somewhat dismayed at their intense emotional reaction to the closure of the game, as well as their ongoing commitment to the group. Furthermore, many were surprised by the transformative power that play had had on them as individuals. All agreed that their experience with *Uru* and TGU had changed them in one way or another.

Comments

As a Biological Anthropologist/Primatologist, I am not surprised at the power of play. It is an extremely important learning and socializing tool in the animal kingdom. Animals kept from play (usually because of human interference in the name of science and research) almost always demonstrate some degree of developmental, psychological and/or social problems.
Posted by: Leesa | April 10, 2006 at 01:35 PM

A Community of Loners

As discussed earlier, *Uru* marked the transition of the *Myst* world from a solitary experience to a context for social interaction. Like Leesa, TGU's founder, the vast majority of players interviewed for this study self-identified as "loners" or "shy." Some suffer from fairly extreme cases of shyness, such as a variation of agoraphobia, some are hindered in social and public activities by physical disabilities, and some live in remote regions.

For many players, the experience of *Myst* had meant a decade of solitary exploring and puzzle-solving. Given this, it is not surprising that only a quarter of eligible players ever actually signed up for *Uru Prologue*. Some who eventually did join *Uru Prologue* reported being hesitant. Once inside the multiplayer world, many engaged with other players with trepidation.

One experience conveyed by some players was the joy in discovering comrades in this formerly lonely world they knew and loved. With *Uru Prologue*, it was as if a portal opened up in which people who had been playing alone in the same beloved imaginary world for many years could share this experience with others.

This transition from lone player to community player is expressed in this poem by Teddy, written a few days after the server closure:

(I was working in my garden yesterday when this came to me. . . .)

An Avatar's Lament

I am but a figment, the imagination of my creator.
I was created for one purpose: to explore.
I was sent on a journey, to learn things my creator already knew.

I discovered great monuments and beautiful gardens and a cavern beyond belief.
A world was created for me and it was my duty to learn its ways.

One day, I met others like me. Explorers, figments, dreams.
Though we didn't share creators, we shared a common goal.
With them, I changed. I was no longer just an explorer. I was more.
I was now a friend, confidant, buddy and playmate.

I grew beyond my purpose, I became more real.
And with my friends, we began to touch our creators, and they grew, too.
Our play was their play.
We became.

That day came that our world was shattered.
Our Lives were coming to an end.
A new twist to my being, I had emotions and I didn't want to lose my friends.
But we consoled each other, we played as much as we could.
We climbed the walls, and hid and danced,
And together, we passed beyond.

I am but a shade now, roaming a shadow realm.
A place where once was life, is quiet as a tomb.
D'ni sleeps and a cherub guards its gates.
Our creators dream.

We were not made in our creators' likenesses,
but in some way, there is more of them in us than they expected.
Our connection is lost, but we still touch our creators' hearts.
And I hope that someday they will touch their creator, as I have mine.

This poem captures the transition from "just an explorer" to "a friend, confidant, buddy and playmate." Like many *Uru* players, Teddy had never played an online game and mainly joined *Uru Prologue* because the marketing implied a much more expansive *Myst*-based world with new Ages added on a regular basis. He "really wasn't expecting to have so much fun just talking to strangers who I only saw as pixels on a monitor."

Nonetheless, like many other lone explorers of the *Myst* worlds, Teddy soon found himself developing emotional attachments to the other players. Over time, the experience became more about the people than the game.

Furthermore, Teddy's poem points out an experience shared by every other player interviewed for this study: being the avatar changes the real person. As one player pointed out, "We create our avatars, and our avatars create us," echoing Canadian media historian Marshall McLuhan's classic insight into media and culture: "We shape our tools and thereafter our tools shape us" (1964). Players, like Lynn, who were previously depressed, or like Leesa, who was shy, were palpably altered by the experience of being an avatar in a supportive play community.

Comments

Seeing people who share in the love of Myst was more like the intersection of parallel universes. Uru became a place where all these players living in solitary universes were brought together all at once. The feeling was more like "Wow, there are others like me ... "

Posted by: Raena | February 05, 2006 at 05:26 PM

Communities of Play

A key emergent phenomenon observed with TGU was a shift from playing for the game to playing for the people. Initially, players logged on to *Uru* to experience more of the game, but over a period of time, and often much to their surprise, the focus began to shift to the social; this transition began to occur even before the migration into the nongame social world of *There.com*. The research seems to suggest this may be a pattern in online games and virtual worlds in general, regardless of the game/ world distinction, suggesting a further study across several games and play communities to verify if this might be a generalizable emergent pattern, regardless of the game or world. It also seems to be the case that once this social motivation emerges, these bonds form relatively quickly, perhaps more so than they might in a "real-life" setting. A comparable real-world environment where such bonds might form relatively quickly is summer camp, another discrete play space in which participants inhabit a similar sort of magic circle to the one that bounds games from the real world (Chicago Public Radio 1998). This suggests that play itself may accelerate the process of social bonding.

In the case of the *Uru* players, it would seem that the imminent server shutdown also served as a catalyst to further accelerate and cement the social bonds that were already rapidly forming. One key indication that a social bonding process is under way is the disclosure of personal information. When I asked players what they did in *Uru* in the final weeks, most said they spent the majority of the time simply talking, often for hours, including telling each other stories, sometimes in a campfire tale-type setting, or discussing personal issues. They also explored, played in each other's Ages, and invented new games to play in the *Uru* world, such as hide-and-seek. Even though they inhabited an imaginary world, the friendships that formed there were very real.

This study supports the legitimization of the study of communities of play, focusing on the organizational and sociological aspects of group play and the ways in which communities use digital and networked media to support play activities. While computer-mediated communications have nominally embraced this topic, it has never been defined as a distinctly separate form of social interaction and mediation. The majority of studies have focused on text-based chats, and little attention has been paid to the design of the mediated space and its impact on social interaction. Nonetheless, as this study shows, communities of play have characteristics distinct from other types of communities and ought to be studied in their own right. Furthermore, mediated spaces designed for play are distinct from those designed for other purposes and thus can also be viewed from the perspective of human-computer interface design as their own unique class of research and design problem.

The concept of "community of play" I am proposing builds on the work of Bernie DeKoven, who describes a "play community" as a group that "embraces the players more than it directs us toward any particular game." While the game is often the starting point, over time the group may tire of that particular game but still wish to play together. Members of such a community are ready and willing to adapt game rules and to change or even invent new games to create a supportive environment with their playmates. DeKoven also identifies the point of transition, observed earlier, at which the play community shifts from a game focus to a social one. Such a community will not only respect the rights of individuals to stop playing for any reason, but will also actively seek out new games for the mutual enjoyment and challenge of all members

(1978). While DeKoven's work predates the advent of digital games, his principles can be readily applied to networked play communities.

The Gathering of Uru is just such a play community, both created and facilitated in the context of the network. TGU was born of network media and has leveraged network media to sustain its own unique and distinct play community. While it was the gameplay of *Uru* that initially drew the community together, it was the ultimate destruction of *Uru* that cemented its bonds. Their migration into other games, and the dialogue that ensued, suggests that they had reached that moment, described by DeKoven, where playing together became the main priority, with the game itself being a secondary concern. Furthermore, TGU exhibits a high tolerance for individual play preferences, even within this framework of group cohesion.

In keeping with DeKoven's model of the play community, TGU has gone to great lengths to stay together, moving across different game worlds and constantly adapting, modifying, and even creating new games, artifacts, and environments, as well as forming subgroups of shared interest within the larger community. Over time TGU has absorbed other non-*Uru* players, brought them into its way of play, and embraced the contribution of both long-standing and new members. Throughout TGU's life there has been an intense and concerted effort to keep the community vibrant and active, the responsibility for which has shifted but has primarily fallen to a small leadership community-within-the-community. This leadership group has managed to maintain TGU well beyond the duration of the game in which it originated, to the point where it has taken on a life of its own. In the process, it has also, along with other members of the Uru Diaspora, taken over, or perhaps taken back, the lost world of *Uru*.

Comments

"In the process, it has also, along with other members of the Uru Diaspora, taken over, or perhaps taken back, the lost world of Uru."
Perhaps with the closing of the game, the diaspora had BECOME Uru.
Posted by: Raena | February 05, 2006 at 05:29 PM

Intersubjective Flow

DeKoven cites Mihály Csíkszentmihályi's concept of flow (1990) as key to the emergence of a play community. Csíkszentmihályi defines flow as the feeling of complete and energized focus in an activity, with a high level of enjoyment and fulfillment. Flow is a psychological state in which the individual loses track of time and becomes completely absorbed in the activity at hand. Flow is achieved when the level of challenge is maintained in balance with the level of skill. As illustrated by the simplified diagram in figure

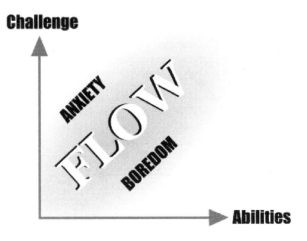

| Figure 8.1 |

Simplified diagram of Csíkszentmihályi's concept of "flow." (Graphics: Steve Childs)

8.1, when the challenge is too high, anxiety ensues; when the skill level exceeds the challenge, boredom is the result; apathy is the outcome of both low challenge and low skill.

Csíkszentmihályi characterizes flow as having the following traits:

· A challenging activity that requires skills that we possess.
· The activity absorbs our attention and awareness; it is engrossing.
· The activity has clear goals and feedback.
· We can devote a high level of concentration to the activity, often overhsadowing other external, especially unpleasant, inputs or thoughts.
· We have a sense of control, or, more precisely, a lack of worry about losing control.
· The loss of self-consciousness.
· Our subjective experience of time is altered; we have a sense that time is passing by more quickly. (1990, 48–67)

For obvious reasons, flow has been a hot topic in game studies for some time (Raybourn 1997, Mortensen 2003, Mortensen and Corneliussen 2005, Salen and Zimmerman 2004, Juul 2004, Chen 2007, Sweetser 2007), and gamers and researchers alike have long been aware that there is something particular about computer games that produces this effect. Because of the dynamic nature of the medium, digital games have always included responsive features that raise the challenges in real time to meet the player's skill level. This has been characterized as "hard fun," a term coined by user

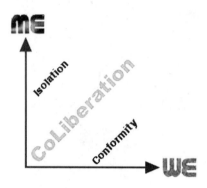

| Figure 8.2 |
DeKoven's concept of CoLiberation. (Graphic: Bernie DeKoven)

interface pioneer Alan Kay (1998, 2003), which describes experiences that are both challenging and enjoyable, such as mastering the violin and playing games.

While the majority of analysis of flow in games focuses on the individual, De-Koven has proposed a social dimension to flow that he calls "CoLiberation" (1992a). This psychosocial dimension to Csíkszentmihályi's "optimal experience" can be observed in a number of group contexts, such as sports, group improvisation, and networked play environments.

DeKoven's psychosocial interpretation of flow forefronts the ways that individuals in a group can provide each other with the appropriate balance of challenge and skills to enable flow. Playtesting consultant Nicole Lazzaro has observed that "people are addictive" (2004), an insight that may be key to understanding the relationship of flow to mediated social interaction.

DeKoven's modified CoLiberation diagram (figure 8.2) illustrates how this social dimension to flow creates a balance between the individual identity and group connectedness. If the player is too aware of herself, she becomes self-conscious, isolated, and alienated. If she is too immersed in the group, she runs the risk of conformity. Furthermore, using the principles illustrated in figure 8.1, players spontaneously adjust their behavior to challenge one another, creating the optimal state of flow for each individual participant. Thus, players are always pushing each other to a higher state of balance between challenge and skill level, and therefore, flow. In such a state, players feel at once a positive sense of their own individuality, while still feeling connected to the group.

This is the point where the concept of intersubjectivity, touched on earlier, becomes useful. Michael Jackson has pointed out that intersubjectivity provides us with an organizing principle for thinking about cultures in which individual and group identity are closely intertwined (1998). Intersubjectivity is also a useful lens through which to study distributed, networked environments, which are primarily social in nature. These digital environments, whether virtual worlds, games, forums, or chat rooms, are intersubjective artifacts whose sole aim and outcome is the support and creation of shared contexts for social transactions.

Building on Csíkszentmihályi's flow and DeKoven's CoLiberation, the concept I am proposing, "intersubjective flow," situates the flow state *between* people rather than within the individual. In this case, flow moves from the realm of the psychological to the realm of the social. Intersubjective flow serves to accelerate a form of intimacy that is unique to play. In this context, a group of complete strangers can form a sense of group cohesion in a relatively short period of time. This is played out in simple street game contexts, such as a pick-up game of basketball. Over time and prolonged exposure, this intimacy can strengthen, as may be the case with a professional basketball team or an amateur baseball league. This is also exemplified by the concept of "swing," the experience that oarsman describe when they are in sync, as if a single person is rowing (Halberstam 1996).

TGU clearly exemplifies this concept. As we've seen, the relationship between the group identity and the individual identity formed a balance between the individual and the group. Far from being subsumed in the group identity (conformity), individuals flourished as unique while still being a part of the group. This in turn created a form of intimacy, a sense of acceptance and belonging particular to the play community.

Feedback is an essential component to the propagation of intersubjective flow. DeKoven describes a Ping-Pong game in which a skilled player comes up with a series of techniques to meet the skill level of a less-skilled player. First, he asks the new player to hold his racket still while the skilled player tries to hit it. In the process, the new player begins reflexively to move the racket in an attempt to meet the incoming ball. The skilled player then switches hands, giving himself a handicap in the game. By using this method of adjusting skill level to optimize flow, the skilled player helps push the unskilled player at an appropriate skill level while still maintaining the requisite level of challenge to assure his own sense of flow (DeKoven 1978).

These types of improvised interactions are at the heart of play-based emergence. Players are inventing new games and new play activities out of an underlying instinct to optimize for intersubjective flow. While they are not necessarily setting out to create new games or game mechanics, the unconscious metagoal of achieving intersubjective flow becomes the driver for emergent, spontaneous, and unanticipated behavior.

Group Cohesion: The Role of Values in the Play Community

One of the key findings of the study is the important role of values in group cohesion. When asked what held the group together, the vast majority of TGU members said "shared values." As mentioned earlier, players often expressed these values in terms of group identity, as defined by both play styles and social styles, and were remarkably consistent in enumerating these values. In terms of play styles, TGUers explained "We are puzzle-solvers; we are explorers; we value intellectual challenges; we are non-violent." Social values included mutual respect and tolerance, avoiding factions and drama, and a desire to help others, especially new players.

This latter quality arises in part out of a sense of responsibility toward the community; in both *Uru* and *There.com*, TGU members felt responsible for protecting their members, especially new members, from harassment, or griefers they encountered in the early days of their settlement in *There.com*. This behavior monitoring was probably inherited at least in part from the Welcomers' League in *Uru*, a hood to which TGU founder Leesa also belonged. Leesa also founded the League of Free Welcomers in *There.com*. The name derived from the fact that newbie welcomers in *There.com* were originally paid, and she wanted to distinguish her group as greeting newbies on a volunteer basis. TGU members in *There.com* are also known for their friendliness and generosity to *There.com* newcomers, even outside of their own group; this urge to protect newcomers may also be related to the harassment they encountered when first arriving in *There.com*.

While some of these shared values are implicit, many players cited their source as founder Leesa's three simple rules, known as "the rules." These were created for the original TGU hood in *Uru* and were maintained throughout the process of identifying and settling in a new virtual world. They are not so much game rules as metarules for social conduct. Such metarules are common to guilds in online games and represent a form of emergent behavior.

On the TGU Koalanet forum, the rules are explicitly described as follows:

I created The Gathering of Uru neighborhoods for everyone and anyone to enjoy themselves in an atmosphere where they feel free, relaxed, safe and happy. The hood's ideals are based on compassion, tolerance, nonviolence and peace and its "rules" are:

1. Free discussion is welcome on any subject so long as it does not cause anyone offence, harm or embarrassment.

2. TGU is neutral and does not support or represent any person or faction but this does not mean that individual members cannot have an opinion or back a person or faction. However, recruitment, rallies, canvassing, etc. is not allowed in the hood.

3. Members are not allowed to alter, in any way, the name or description of the hood or change it from public to private (or vice versa). Furthermore, any changes need to be discussed and voted on by the members before they can be done.

Any member or visitor who does not follow the rules or causes problems for other members will be asked to leave the hood. If they continue their behavior and/or refuse to leave a formal complaint will be filed with CCR which may result in them being barred from Uru.

As the Mayor, I will have the final say or the tie-breaking vote in all matters. I will be appointing a Deputy Mayor and Councilors who will help look after the hood and act for me in my absence. I will announce the Council once all of the nominees have accepted their positions. Please remember, this is all very laid back—the Mayor and Council are just there to make sure everyone is happy and everything runs smoothly.

If there's anyone you'd like to nominate, just let me know.

REMEMBER: Our prime directive is to have fun!

This last point is important because implicit in this statement is a particular notion of "fun." TGU members have a very specific idea of what is fun, which is quite distinct from players of many other MMOGs, derived in part from a ten-year legacy of playing *Myst* games, including *Uru*, as well as from their own unique group character.

Another interesting point that requires some interpretation concerns rule 2. While at first glance, this rule may seem to refer to the general intent of avoiding conflict, its meaning is actually much more specific to *Uru*. As mentioned earlier, Cyan had created different factions in the game, and hired actors to foment conflict and try to recruit players to join these factions. Rule 2 is an explicit policy respecting this aspect of the game, and implicitly, it also represents a departure from the game designers' intentions for the game. Interestingly, it may also be one reason for TGU's popularity. As indicated in the game-wide forums, many *Uru* players were uncomfortable with the artificial drama and the factions it created. Leesa's taking a stand on this issue was another key influence on the sorts of people who joined TGU.

PATTERNS OF EMERGENCE

Porous Magic Circles and the Ludisphere

As mentioned in book I, the magic circle has become an important principle in digital game studies, especially as the introduction of the computer creates an additional boundary around the game experience that is generally held to be sacrosanct (Salen and Zimmerman 2004). Castronova argued for a more hermetic enforcement of the magic circle, suggesting that real-world concerns, such as politics and popular culture, should not be allowed to leak into virtual worlds to destroy the suspension of disbelief or tamper with the world's integrity (2004). He has since reconsidered this and suggested that the "almost magic circle" is more of a membrane (2005). The notion of a game as a closed world also has some unintentional clashes with contemporary anthropology, a discipline currently confronting a transition from the traditional paradigm of studying cultures cut off from outside influence to the study of cultures within a mediated, global context (Marcus 1995). Thus it is unclear if calls for "purity" of any world, whether real or virtual, are even attainable.

The findings of this study suggest that, just as contemporary world cultures must be looked at in a global context, online virtual worlds must be looked at in the context of the "ludisphere," the larger framework of all networked play spaces on the Internet, as well as within the larger context of the "real world." In this context, as with real-world culture, it may be more useful to see the landscape in terms of a series of overlapping and nested magic circles, the outermost being the "real world," with transactions taking place through membranes more porous than has previously been suggested.

Communities of Play

While other sorts of distributed communities have been studied extensively, the study of communities of play is a relatively new field. Despite the fact that play has a major role in popular culture and community formation, in the academic study of networked communities, play seems to take a back seat to more "serious" pursuits such as communities of practice or communities of interest. Even unstructured social interaction, such as text chat, seems to take precedence over distributed play spaces as worthy of serious study.

Communities of play, or play communities (DeKoven 1978), are groups that choose to play together in various configurations. Most MMOGs have built-in mechanisms to support and formalize a play community. Terms like "guild," "clan," and in the case of *Uru*, "neighborhood," define a particular (and often a singular) group to which a player belongs. Individuals are generally drawn to these groups by common friendships and shared play styles and play values, and often create their own web sites or other mechanisms for intragroup communication. A play community will often design its own logo or crest, create a mission statement that defines the ethos of the group, and employ a set of metarules that relate to their style of play, social conduct, or desired standing in the community, such as Leesa's rules. They will frequently plan large-scale raids and other events together, and display a high level of loyalty to their fellow members. Guild members may also protect each other from outside harassment, though guilds can also be a site of intense drama and dispute. It is not at all uncommon to see power struggles occur, members quit in protest, or even factions split off into new guilds. All of these behaviors suggest a level of emotional investment that may be as high as or even greater than investments in communities of either practice or interest.

Within nongame MMOWs, it is more common for the social mechanism to support player membership in multiple groups, rather than the singular guild model typical of most MMOGs. While this offers a level of flexibility, it shifts the dynamic significantly. Membership in a guild or its equivalent creates an exclusive emotional bond not unlike that of a real-world clan, tribe, or gang. Taylor and Jakobsson have aptly compared MMOG guilds to membership in a Mafia family (2003). One of the principle reasons for this may be that a guild brings with it not only group allegiance but also a sense of collective identity. Players within a guild-like structure associate their identities with a particular group in a way that members of a club in a nongame world typically do not. The individual identity can morph across different clubs, which is significantly different than having your identity tied in a persistent way to a single group. It also permits the formation of subcommunities, secondary group affiliations, and identities that are related to or subordinate to a primary affiliation.

By investigating one such play community in depth over a long period of time, the study seeks to identify the sorts of attributes that make such groups unique, to understand the dynamics between individual and group identity, and to understand how these influence emergent group behavior. By following a single play community across several virtual world ecosystems, one can begin to understand the relationship between the essential character of the group's collective behavior and the specific attributes of the virtual worlds or ecosystems they inhabit.

Comments

"Within nongame MMOWs, it is more common for the social mechanism to support player membership in multiple groups, rather than the singular guild model described above. ... The individual identity can morph across different clubs, which is significantly different than having your identity tied in a persistent way to a single group."

Perhaps this area could be explored further. Does the "morphing" across different clubs provide the distributed community more resilience within a single MMOW? Perhaps ensuring greater longevity over singular guild allegiance? Has this in fact been happening to our group?

Posted by: Raena | February 05, 2006 at 04:46 PM

The Social Construction of Avatar Identity

One of the most interesting findings of this study was the observation that the formation of individual and group identity was itself an emergent process. Many earlier readings of the development of avatar identities tended to focus on the individual (Dibbell 1998, Turkle 1995), but in the course of the study, it became very clear that 1) group and individual identity were inextricably linked, and that 2) individual identity evolved out of an emergent process of social feedback (Pearce and Artemesia 2007). Similar findings, however, can be seen in other studies that look at the relationship of the social to the individual within virtual worlds (Bruckman 1992, Taylor 2006).

The concept of the social construction of identity builds on Berger and Luckmann's concept of the social construction of reality (1966) by suggesting that the individual is as much a social construction as the "reality" he or she perceives. This is not a particularly new idea, and is even addressed by Berger and Luckmann in terms of the construction of identities such as "Jew" in various cultures (91). The individual is always, to a greater or lesser extent, at least in part a product of his or her social milieu. In addition, individual identity is generally woven out of the materials of group identity and vice versa.

In the context of the online virtual world, and driven by play as its primary activator, identity appears to emerge through collective feedback rather than individual desire. The assumption that a virtual identity promotes anonymity and therefore, to a certain measure, freedom, may belie a profound misunderstanding of the concept of "anonymity." While the person's real-life identity remains anonymous, her in-world identity, because it is persistent, cannot stay that way for long. Over time, others will recognize the traits and talents of the individual, often before she recognizes them herself. In this way, players take on a role in the group not by an act of individual will, but in response to feedback, and in some cases, even demands from the play community. Players often find themselves surprised by their online identities, exhibiting qualities and talents of which they themselves were not aware, including leadership abilities, drawn forth by play and enabled by the group. As one of T. L. Taylor's research subjects put it "Avatars have a mind of their own, and they grow in unexpected ways . . . you are kidding yourself if you think you will be able to control or even predict what will happen to your avatar" (1999).

Intersubjective Flow

The phenomena of intersubjective flow, described earlier, also serves as a vital engine for emergent behavior. Many players in this study both reported and exhibited qualities of flow in their play activities. This may explain why many denizens of online games and virtual worlds spend what to the outside observer may appear to be excessive hours in-world. One of the hallmarks of flow is a sense of temporal compression, a perception that "time flies when you're having fun." This is what DeKoven means by CoLiberation (1992b) and what I am terming intersubjective flow. This type of enjoyable challenge is what graphical user-interface pioneer Alan Kay referred to as "hard fun" (1992). In some instances, the presence of other people, particularly people with whom one has an affinity, can serve to augment or strengthen the sense of flow.

Interestingly, intersubjective flow does not necessarily require the presence of people. Players can also become engaged at a high level of flow in solitary activities, such as artifact creation; but at the heart of the activity is the knowledge that the artifact being created will be meaningful to the play community. When supported by feedback from the community, enabled by effective software affordances, these solo activities can also produce a sense of intersubjective flow. Such activity falls under the category of our next topic, "productive play."

Comments
Two comments in one post . . .
"One of the hallmarks of flow is a sense of temporal compression, a perception that "time flies when you're having fun'"
I absolutely agree with this. And it happens in a variety of contexts, including WORK as well as play.

"Players can also become engaged at a high level of flow in solitary activities, such as artifact creation; but at the heart of the activity is the knowledge that the artifact being created will be meaningful to the play community."

I have experienced this first hand as a designer in There. I hear the same from other Therian [sic] developers, Uru or not. Developing objects for the online world can be a "game with the game" so to speak. (I hesitate to use the word "game" in the context of the community world environments being discussed in this text, but I trust the readers understand my point.) The community inspires the developers. Developers inspire each other. Seeing people enjoy your works is reward in itself, as any artist knows. Additionally the developers themselves are intrinsically part of an unofficial developer guild, whose membership is defined by the compliments developers give to each other concerning their work.

Posted by: Raena | February 05, 2006 at 04:55 PM

Raena, this is a really good articulation of the feedback process I describe in the Productive Play section. Part of what you are saying, which is integral to this thesis, is that Flow happens through a feedback process.

Posted by: Artemesia | February 05, 2006 at 10:56 PM

Productive Play

Productive play is a phenomenon that will be discussed more fully in chapter 10, and which was introduced in one of my first published papers on my work with the Uru Diaspora (2006b). In brief, this term describes the metamorphosis from play to creative output or work-like activities. In earlier work, I described the inevitable transition from interactivity to content creation (1997), identified the phenomenon of emergent authorship, and described how play can transition into creative activity through such activities as skinning or creating storyboards in *The Sims* (2002a). Cindy Poremba's subsequent work further identitified different levels of creators in *The Sims* community (2003).

Productive play is a form of emergent gameplay that is strongly aligned with contemporary Web 2.0 practices, with one vital difference—it originates with play activities and players continue to perceive what they are doing, even if the activity becomes extremely demanding and laborious, with their play practices. Examples range from artifact production to community leadership to events planning to organizing and managing large-scale collaborative projects to serving as community representatives on advisory boards. In *Second Life*, as popularly publicized, these activities can even transition into sources of income, and productive play can become a means of livelihood for some players. It should be noted that, as pointed out earlier, productive play is not an entirely new phenomena, and we see manifestations of it in cultural practices and rituals such as Mardi Gras, historical reenactment, cosplay, and the Burning Man festival, as well as hobby cultures such as model railroading and tabletop role-playing games. What all of these practices share, however, is that players continue to perceive what they are doing as part of a play practice, even if it transitions into professional activity.

Play Styles as an Engine for Emergence

As we've begun to see, emergent play patterns develop from players enacting simple rules, and then, over time, and generally through feedback, modifying or expanding the game or world beyond the designers' initial intentions. Where play styles come in is that they are the engine for this emergence. If we return to our terminology of "network" and "ecosystem," we can look at the network of players in terms of a particular

| Figure 9.1 |

A typical *Uru* puzzle: close a certain number of steam vents to get the optimal pressure to ride a gust of steam into a secret area. (Image: Pearce)

| Figure 9.2 |

Another *Uru* puzzle: turn circular rings to match pattern seen in another room. (Image: Pearce)

set of metarules that propel their play patterns as they come into contact with the eco-system of the world's features. An earlier example given of emergent systems was an ant colony. While a human network of players is of course much more sophisticated than an ant colony, they may have certain relatively simple behaviors or orientations that lead to more complex behaviors. This section describes these play styles and looks at some concrete examples of how they influence emergent behavior.

Before citing specific examples, it may also be useful to reflect on the origin of play styles. Many of the signature play styles which were linked to TGU identity were honed in *Myst* games, such as solving the so-called Mensa-level puzzles for which *Myst* games are famous. (For examples, see figures 9.1 and 9.2.) The fact that most TGU players had spent ten years developing mastery in these play styles is key to under-standing how they engaged with each other in *Uru Prologue*, and then transposed these play styles into other virtual worlds.

Much of this study was spent watching TGUers play and playing with them. The latter is key because I found throughout the study that simply observing was not sufficient. It became critical to actually play with them, and learn their play styles from a subjective perspective, even if only in a rudimentary way. It was clear from the opening of *Until Uru* that I would never be able to catch up with the decade of practice most of them had had at puzzle-solving. However, they were more than happy to take me through the puzzles, giving me hints along the way. This experience helped me piece together what sorts of play activities TGU members valued, and also to observe the social behavior of the hint-giving process. In fact, this exercise provided much insight into the way TGUers viewed the world. Much of the TGU play style revolves around the experience of discovery in different forms—whether uncovering a clue, discovering a new place, finding a new meaning to a previously mysterious symbol, or revealing plot points. One of the interesting techniques that TGU players developed within *Uru* was the art of giving hints without revealing "spoilers," allowing the player being coached to make the discovery for herself. Since many of the *Uru* puzzles are spatial in nature, they can really only be appreciated through direct experience.

It is important to point out that my initial experience of observing TGUers at play was within *There.com*. When I first encountered the group, the player-run *Until Uru* servers had not yet opened and the Atmosphere Hood was not yet complete. Both in talking with them and observing their play behaviors in *There.com*, it was clear that the group had a particular style of play, but I did not fully understand its origins until visiting them in *Until Uru*. Exploring the environs, being guided through puzzles and taken to secret locales, and playing improvised games made the significance of behaviors I had encountered in *There.com* much more evident. Other non-*Uru* players who joined TGU also observed that playing *Until Uru* added to their understanding of the group's unique character.

The Gathering of Uru Signature Play Styles

Spatial Literacy   This term refers to the ability to read and interpret embedded meanings in space, find hidden clues and locations, and unlock secret places. The satisfaction of spatial literacy is the sense of discovery that often results from finding and understanding the meaning of something (figure 9.3). Spatial storytelling is one of the hallmarks of the *Myst* series, so these longtime *Myst* players were considerably skilled in this area (Pearce 2008a).

Exploration   TGUers often identified themselves as explorers, a play style related to spatial literacy. TGUers are naturally inquisitive and love to explore, usually in groups, and are particularly appreciative of scenic beauty and vistas. Exploration is a way to

| Figure 9.3 |
Myst and *Uru* players must learn how to "read" space to solve clues. (Image: Pearce)

relate to the virtual space, as well as another means of making new discoveries. This fits nicely with Bartle's explorer type, who is interested primarily in interacting with and being surprised by the world (1996). One of the best examples of the relationship between exploration and emergence is in the description given earlier of the postclosure scouting process. Because they were already skilled explorers, TGUers had both the instinct and the facility to disperse into the ludisphere in search of new play space.

Puzzle-Solving TGUers repeatedly identified themselves in interviews as puzzle-solvers. This is clearly a hallmark of *Uru* and *Myst* games and also led to some of the *Uru*-wide game hacking described earlier. In some way, their dislocation from *Uru* became a puzzle to be solved, just as reverse-engineering the *Uru* servers became a puzzle for the *Uru* hacker group that launched *Until Uru*. Puzzle solving hones a certain level of skill, patience, and determination at solving challenging problems that extends beyond intentional components of the game.

| **Figure 9.4** |
A clever hiding place in hide-and-seek in the Eder Kemo Garden Age of *Until Uru*. (Image: Pearce)

Cleverness and Creativity Cleverness and creativity, in a broad sense, are highly valued qualities and manifest through everything from conceiving of a new event or game to discovering a clever hiding place in hide-and-seek (figure 9.4) to inventing new ways to play with found objects. The social feedback that results is particularly critical to emergence as rewards for cleverness and creativity serve to propagate more of the same. Cleverness does not necessary manifest in intellectual form—it can also emerge spontaneously through improvised play activity.

Mastery Mastery of specific skills is highly valued, and examples abound of new activities being invented with mastery in mind. Perhaps the best example is the D'ni Olympics, founded by Maesi. This *Uru*-wide event, inspired by the active play of a disabled member of the group, involved developing mastery at a variety of events that subverted objects and environments in unusual ways, such as balancing on an upended pylon (traffic cone) or tightrope-walking up a tent rope. Another example of mastery is the Furrier Legion Flight Team, founded by Shaylah, Wingman, and Maesi (figure 9.5). Combining mastery and exploration, the Furrier Legion performed elaborate

| Figure 9.5 |
The Furrier Legion Flight Team in *There.com* prepares to take off from one of Damanji's temples. (Image: Pearce)

| Figure 9.6 |
Heek, a popular game in *Uru*, is rock-paper-scissors D'ni-style. (Image: Pearce)

synchronized air acrobatics using *There.com*'s numerous company- and player-made air vehicles. In both examples, mastery takes the form of performance as players exhibit their skills to each other. Both of these events are major spectator draws, and the Furrier Legion in particular made Yeesha Island and other Uru areas a focal point of activity for the broader *There.com* community.

Games-within-Games   Inherited at least in part from *Uru* is the notion of the game-within-a-game. *Uru* included Heek, a five-player rock, paper, scissors–style game in which players seated around a table threw up symbols in a holographic display (figure 9.6). Heek was replicated, complete with scripting, by players in *Second Life* (figure 9.7). In *There.com*, spades (figure 9.8), based on the popular card game, has taken Heek's place, but Uruvians also enjoy inventing their own games and sports, such as Buggy Polo, a football-type game invented by Wingman and played with dune buggies and a large translucent orb driven by an avatar. An example of the impact of

| Figure 9.7 |
Heek game under construction by players in *Second Life*. (Image: Pearce)

game design on this type of emergent behavior is that TGUers were not able to play hide-and-seek in either *There.com* or *Second Life* because players cannot turn off their own name tags, which float over avatars' heads. In *Uru*, names only appeared when the cursor is rolled over the avatar, and only when it was unobstructed by another object. Thus, hide-and-seek was an invented game that players could only enjoy in *Uru*.

Togetherness   TGUers tend to seek out and create opportunities for togetherness (figure 9.9), often combining these with other play styles. This can also be challenging as gatherings of large groups can tax the servers. Togetherness can be achieved by planning events, a formal feature of *There.com*, as well as inventing new games. Togetherness is also a means of countering the dispersion often brought on by the exploration style described earlier. Exploration tends to scatter players throughout the virtual world, and togetherness events tend to be focused around bringing them back together, particularly in the group's home areas, such as Yeesha Island.

| Figure 9.8 |

Uruvian-Thereians play spades at a wedding reception. (Image: Pearce)

Wordplay and Multimodal Communication   The various modes of textual and verbal communication and the play patterns that arise out of these could comprise an entire thesis in and of themselves. In *Uru*, the primary communication was text chat. In *Until Uru*, players augmented this with voice-over-IP programs such as Skype and Teamspeak. *There.com* introduced voice shortly after TGUers arrived, a feature that was welcomed by some disabled members of the group who had trouble typing. Wordplay in both text and voice formats abounds, and in *There.com* there is also the added feature of the group instant-message box, often used during hoverboat jaunts or Furrier Legion events. Multimodal communication can also lead to some interesting breaches in the magic circle. The real-life milieu of players using hands-free voice systems can sometimes bleed into the virtual world, and the group can overhear phone conversations, children, or dogs barking in the background. Because of the use of voice-over-IP programs to augment communications, there can also be occasions where a group of players in different virtual worlds on the same Skype or Teamspeak call might be taking part in a transvirtual conversation across several worlds at once.

| Figure 9.9 |

TGUers exhibit togetherness by packing themselves into the tiny Egg Room in *Until Uru*. (The translucent figure at right is the holograph of Yeesha.) (Image: Pearce)

| Figure 9.10 |
Buggy Polo, featuring TGU's resident ethnographer in the role of the ball. (Image: Pearce)

Horseplay Horseplay, a kind of highly physical, highly spontaneous rough-and-tumble, is probably closest to what Caillois would characterize as "ilinx," or vertigo (1961). Dancing in the fountain in the original *Uru* is an early manifestation of horseplay. However, horseplay in *Uru* was somewhat limited because of the game's constraints, and this play style expanded significantly in *There.com*, where immortal avatars can jump off tall buildings, flip buggies, or crash hoverboats into the sides of buildings unharmed. The Buggy Polo game described earlier is an excellent example of horseplay (figure 9.10), as are elaborate driving courses that allow for vehicle stunts. *There .com* players also brought this expanded tendency toward horseplay back into *Uru* by inventing Avie Bowling; this was the effect of a collision flaw in the world that allowed players to sink their avatar bodies into the floor in a certain area of the hood. They would then run quickly across the floor, using their protruding heads as bowling balls and the numerous orange traffic cones in the world as bowling pins. This also demonstrates the way emergent behavior can arise out of flaws in the system, or through repurposing of found objects.

The question of "physical" play in an avatar-based world warrants a brief discussion. Game designer Chris Crawford has described "safety" as one of the key characteristics of games (1984). Among theme park design practitioners this is referred to as "safe danger." Because avatars cannot die or be injured in any of the MMOWs described here, players have the opportunity to play in an extremely physical fashion without any of the consequences associated with this behavior in the real world or even in typical MMOGs. Furthermore, as the vast majority of TGUers were adults (with the exception of a handful of teens), this type of play would be less likely to occur in the real world, except under the auspices of extreme sports. Rough-and-tumble play also has an added dimension of appeal for players with physical disabilities, who might not be able to participate in physical sports at all with their "real-life avatars."

Dancing/Acrobatics   Dancing is an activity that seems to have made its way into virtually every MMOW and MMOG. Even classical medieval role-playing games usually have dance steps built in. All three of the MMOWs covered in this study included affordances for dancing. *Uru* provided limited dance steps, and a few more were included in add packs released by the *Uru* hacker group for *Until Uru*. New dance moves were also invented by combining sideways steps, turning, and spinning. Depressing the *Uru* voice activation button (players avoided actually using voice as it crashed the servers) caused the avatar to launch into an elaborate set of hand gestures, which were combined with other steps to create dance routines. Players also tried to create coordinated dance maneuvers using a combination of existing and invented dance steps. TGUers were particularly enamored of dancing in unusual places, like the *Uru* fountain and its derivatives in *There.com* and *Second Life*, the tops of columns, and on spades tables. *Second Life* has perhaps the broadest array of dance steps, mostly player-created, which is one of the features that gives it the quality of an after-hours club for some TGUers. For disabled players in particular, an occasional "night out" dancing in *Second Life* can be an enjoyable diversion.

Bottom-Up Leadership   The notion of bottom-up leadership may appear to be an oxymoron; however, as we've seen, TGU's leadership structure operates in a highly emergent fashion, both in the way decisions are made, and in the identity development of the leaders themselves. Nonetheless, bottom-up management requires a great deal of work, possibly more than top-down management. The reason for this is that leaders who work in this fashion must pay more attention and spend more time with the individuals in the group. They tend to lead in a more responsive fashion, intervening on an as-needed basis to avert a crisis or promote some community-oriented initiative. Many of TGU's decisions happened in what may seem to be a backward fashion.

For instance, TGU was started somewhat reluctantly and its mission statement was not written by Leesa until after people had already joined the hood. The migration took place through the initiative of individual self-appointed scouts, through a loosely negotiated research process rather than as a top-down dictate from leadership.

The Inventive Urge An overarching engine for emergence is what one might call the "inventive urge." Play is by nature experimental, and experimentation can often lead to new play mechanics. In every MMOW, it appears that players invent new modes of play, new game mechanics, and new ways of interacting with the virtual world. In *Uru*, as well as the other game worlds described here, players were constantly subverting environmental components to create their own new forms of gameplay. This suggests that a high level of agency may result in a shift from player to designer. As with the real-life playground, players work within and sometimes against the spatial and mechanical constraints presented to them to develop new play forms indigenous to the spatial context (Opie and Opie 1969). As a result, they adapt to the play ecosystem by both mutating existing game cultures and inventing entirely new ones, always working with and against the features of the play space.

PRODUCTIVE PLAY: CULTURAL PRODUCTION, MEANING-MAKING, AND AGENCY

Productive Play: A Contradiction in Terms?

Perhaps the most complex and unexpected study finding was the emergence of "productive play"—that is, creativity around play. Because this is a major component of the study, the next section is devoted entirely to this topic.

As discussed earlier, one of the hallmarks of the varying definitions of play is that play activities in general and games in particular are "unproductive." However, as Sutton-Smith points out, "the constant modern tendency to think of play as simply a function of some other more important cultural process (psychological or social) tends to underestimate the autonomy of such play cultures" (1997, 106). What tends to be overlooked is the level of creative production that can go into play activities. I've invoked a number of examples earlier. The New Orleans Mardi Gras is perhaps the most noteworthy example of a high level of productivity generated around a play activity; others include the traditional renaissance raire, *Star Trek*'s Trekkie fan culture, and the annual Burning Man festival. Productive play has been present within online virtual worlds since their earliest inceptions as text-based MUDs and MOOs (Curtis 1992) and an entire educational theory, constructionist learning, has used such productive play as the underpinning for educational software (Papert and Harel 1991).

Economist Edward Castronova has countered the argument that play is unproductive by utilizing traditional econometrics to determine the gross national product of virtual worlds (2001). Since most virtual worlds have currencies, and many of these can now be converted into real-world currencies on the extravirtual black market, a direct economic benefit can be gained from engagement with some forms of productive play. Virtual world designer Cory Ondrejka has described the ways in which players within a co-created environment exhibit prodigious creativity, especially as they are granted more freedom and the potential for economic gain, be it real or virtual (2004).

Shannon Appelcline, lead designer at game company Skotos, has written extensively about emergent cultures within the games he designs (2000–2006). MMOG designer Raph Koster has also written extensively on this topic on his web site (1998–2006).

Productive fan culture, from the Trekkie phenomenon (Jenkins 1992) to new forms of cultural production in games (Pearce 2002a, Poremba 2003) is well studied. In the case of the Uru Diaspora, emergent behavior can be looked at as a convergence of fan culture and productive play. The Uru Diaspora at large manifests impulses similar to those of Trekkies, ranging from developing dictionaries of the fictional D'ni language to making real-world quilts depicting *Uru* themes. However, the social context of online virtual worlds combined with the malleability of digital media creates affordances for fan culture to be cultivated within the imaginary world itself, as well as in the extravirtual forms mentioned earlier, which are more typical of traditional fandom. Thus, unlike Trekkie culture, which extends outside of the imaginary world it references, *Uru* and other game-based fan cultures can incubate within and ultimately transform the virtual worlds they inhabit, whether those worlds are of the fixed synthetic or co-created variety.

This study identified three forms of productive play in the context of interworld immigration, fan culture, and emergent behavior. The first involves inventing new game activities, social rituals, and cultural practices within existing environments, generally by repurposing the game environment and existing artifacts, a kind of ready-made approach to play. The second form of productive play involves carrying culture across virtual worlds by creating new artifacts and objects derived from or inspired by other games. The third type of productive play entails the creation of entire game environments, whether derived from other games or using original concepts influenced by them. The latter form can either take place within existing worlds or involve using game creation tools to make entirely new environments.

The *Uru* case represents the migration from a fixed synthetic game world to an open, co-created, social world. Emergence had already begun to occur in *Uru* even before its closure but blossomed as the group traversed other magic circles into other virtual worlds. *Uru* players had already generated fan-created content in the form of fan art, dictionaries, and the like. Once settled in co-created worlds, *Uru* players began to prolifically create artifacts inspired by *Uru's* content, fuelled by the play community, and supported by the creation tools and economies of the new worlds into which they migrated. This should not strike us as odd, as certainly people have been creating their own play artifacts for centuries. The mediation of the network and the software itself, however, creates both a built-in audience and a distribution mechanism for these play artifacts, and these accelerate the feedback loops that promote emergence. Player creation can be described as a "virtuous cycle" with social feedback as its underlying engine.

Restoring a Lost Culture

It is not insignificant that one of the themes of the original *Uru* game was the restoration of the lost culture of the D'ni. So it seems almost inevitable that when *Uru* closed, players who had been engaged in exploring, understanding, and restoring the lost D'ni culture would extend this objective outside the game. *Uru*'s original goal set the stage for the emergent cultures that evolved after its closure; players were already predisposed by the game itself to restore the D'ni culture, and they were well trained at exploring new lands and solving difficult problems. It was as if the game itself trained them to adapt to its own destruction.

This trend recurs across the Uru Diaspora in a variety of forms: TGU's text-based MUD and Erik's Atmosphere hood; the re-creation of *Uru* and original *Myst*-like game in *Second Life*; the *Uru* hacker group's player-run server system and their initiative to create original Ages. Other *Uru* players created derivative and original environments using other game engines, such as *Doom 3*. There are also a number of extravirtual manifestations of player productivity, such as fan drawings and paintings of *Uru*, the real-world quilts mentioned earlier, the Guild of Linguists and other groups devoted to the spoken and written language of the fictional D'ni people, and a D'ni History Puzzle game. Examples of *Uru*-inspired creativity are too numerous to list here, and continue to be expanded on an ongoing basis.

The Longing for a Homeland

One of the key characteristics of a real-world diaspora is the longing for and desire to restore a lost homeland (Safran 1991, Clifford 1994), although in some cases, the existence of the homeland and the identity associated with it may be, at least in part, imagined (Anderson 1991). In these cases, the historical and imaginary blend to create a collective nostalgia for a past that never was, what historian and media theorist Norman Klein calls a "social imaginary" (1997).

"Attachment to homeland can be intense" asserts leading humanist-geographer Yi-Fu Tuan. "[. . .]home is the focal point of a cosmic structure. . . . Should destruction occur we may reasonably conclude that the people would be thoroughly demoralized, since the ruin of their settlement implies the ruin of their cosmos." Yet, he goes, on, humans are resilient and "Cosmic view can be adjusted to suit new circumstances.

With the destruction of one 'center of the world,' another can be built next to it, or in another location altogether, and in turn becomes 'the center of the world.'" (1977, 149–150)

For members of the Uru Diaspora, this longing transposes itself into a kind of nostalgia for an entirely fictitious, imaginary world in which the experiences were real, emotional, and immediate. While melancholy in some respects, the outcome of this longing has been twofold. On one hand, this longing has contributed to a level of cohesiveness that has long outlived the original game experience; on the other, *Uru* has served as a kind of muse, inspiring prolific creativity.

The value of player-created artifacts, while they can be seen as a form of personal expression, seems to be primarily in the realm of social currency. Most artifacts are created for the benefit of the group, as markers of shared identity or as loci for social interaction, such as the *Uru* fountain. For the artisan, creativity also becomes part of his or her individual identity within the group. *Uru* artisans are highly respected within their communities for their valuable contribution to the life of the culture.

In *Art and Agency*, the anthropologist Alfred Gell has argued that man-made objects, be they art, tools, weapons, or modes of transportation, are less a matter of the individual creative urge than mechanisms of social agency (1998). Echoing Marshall McLuhan's conception of tools as "extensions of man" (1964) (a concept of which Gell appears to have been completely unaware), Gell proposes that artifacts extend the creator's reach into the social, the intersubjective. While the findings of this research support Gell's core concept of social agency, they contradict his contention that meaning is irrelevant. In the case of TGU, artifact creation is both a mechanism of social agency and a carrier of meaning.

Artifacts as Carriers of Meanings

While *Uru* artifacts may be aesthetically pleasing to the average observer, to members of the Uru Diaspora they have a deeper shared meaning. When Uruvians meet in other games, even for those who do not carry *Uru* as part of their avatar identity, the shared experience of "being Uru" creates a sense of affiliation, regardless of one's current virtual world of choice. This affinity finds its most poignant expression in the shared meanings of *Uru* artifacts.

Uru players also enjoy sharing this meaning with others. Creators of D'ni Island in *Second Life* regularly gave tours to non-*Uru* players, walking them through what has become in some ways an *Uru* museum, and describing the origin of each artifact. Hence, the spatial literacy described earlier translates not only into "reading space" and "writing space" but also into "translating space" or "interpreting space."

| Figure 10.1 |

Variations of the Hood Fountain: in *Uru* (top left), *There.com* (top right), Erik's Atmosphere Hood (bottom left), and *Second Life*'s Shorah Island (bottom right). (Image: Pearce)

Because of the way the *Myst* games are structured, and because of their spiritual overtones, there is definitely a sense of the sublime to the meanings embedded within *Uru* artifacts and their progeny. As with *Star Trek*, which became a kind of parable for the future, *Uru* presents a rich vocabulary of associations that players keep very close to their hearts.

Certain artifacts persist as uniquely meaningful to Uruvians and can be found recurring across various player-made instantiations of *Uru* culture. As mentioned earlier, the single most important of these is the fountain, the centerpiece and focal point of the *Uru* hood, and as such, the hub of *Uru* social life (figure 10.1). It was a feature of *Uru* that many refugees expressed missing: Erik identified it as the starting point for his Atmosphere project; Ember tried to emulate it in TGU's *There.com* Community Center with the Moroccan fountain, and eventually the appropriated version was replaced by Damanji's authentic *Uru*-derived fountain; in *Second Life*'s D'ni Island, the fountain is the primary gathering place for group events and meetings.

| Figure 10.2 |
The *Uru* Relto of a player who has completed the game. (Image: Pearce)

Another key artifact is the Relto (figure 10.2). Both *There.com* and *Second Life* artisans attempted to create authentic "traditional" Reltos modeled after the Relto in *Uru*.
In *Second Life*, the flexibility of the in-game building system allowed for the modeling
of a relatively accurate simulation. In *There.com*, with its more constrained and stylized
building tools, the traditional *Uru* Relto could only be approximated, although the
rendition is still easily recognizable as a Relto. Before too long players in both games
began to modify the Relto design to create more "modern" interpretations. A few examples are illustrated here, created from architectural elements found in the respec-
tive games or original designs by players (figures 10.3 and 10.4).

While these modern Reltos vary stylistically quite a bit from the original *Uru*
Relto, they share common signature elements. Reltos tend to be isolated, whether
an island at sea, on the roof of a building, or floating in the air. Regardless of its aesthetic style, a Relto is typically a small, one room, freestanding building, containing a
built-in bookcase for linking books and sometimes a wardrobe of carved wood.

| Figure 10.3 |

Traditional reltos in *There.com* (left) and *Second Life* (center); modern Relto in *There.com* (right). (Image: Pearce)

| Figure 10.4 |

Uru Relto interior (top); interpretations in *There.com* (bottom). (Image: Pearce)

| Figure 10.5 |

The Egg Room Egg in *Uru* (left); in *There.com* on the Relto Island (center) and in the Uru Library (right). (Image: Pearce)

| Figure 10.6 |

Uru imager (left). Reinterpreted in *There.com* (center) and in *Second Life* (right). (Image: Pearce)

The Egg Room egg, mentioned earlier, is also a recurring icon (figure 10.5). Although players were never able to ascertain its original meaning in *Uru*, in carrying it into other games they have imbued it with their own meaning. In *Second Life*, naturally there is an Egg Room in the hood on D'ni Island. Variations of the Egg Room egg can also be seen throughout *Uru* areas in *There.com*. One hovers in the center of Nature_Girl's library, while another hangs in the air above the Relto Island. Variations of the Egg Room egg have also been used for Easter egg hunts, a typical example of the conflating of real world and imaginary cultures.

Among the works of Uruvian artisans are numerous instances of classic D'ni technology being replicated in other worlds. The Imager, for instance, is a display device that appears repeatedly in Uru, and was re-created in *There.com* as a way to display different types of graphics (figure 10.6).

Two of the most prolific *Uru* artisans in *There.com* are Damanji and Maesi. Building on the fashion focus of *There.com*, among the earliest *Uru* objects created by Damanji was the Yeesha costume (figure 10.7), another marker of the fictive ethnic identity that TGUers have adopted; he also created a TGU T-shirt (figure 10.8). A Yeesha avatar

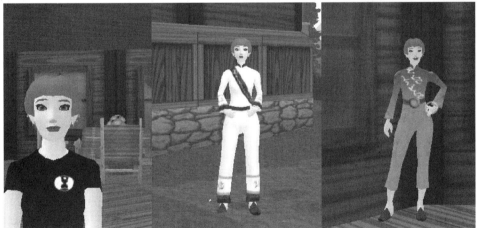

| **Figure 10.7** |
Leesa and Lynn model Damanji's Yeesha costume in *There.com*. (Image: Pearce)

| **Figure 10.8** |
The author sporting original TGU fashions by Damanji (left) and Maesi (center and right). (Image: Pearce)

| Figure 10.9 |
Damanji's Yeesha buggy. (Image: Pearce)

| Figure 10.10 |
Linking books pedestals in *Second Life* (left) and *There.com* (right). (Image: Pearce)

in *There.com* appears in this costume at public events from time to time. Maesi has also created a number of Uruvian garments, including ethnically styled costumes, as well as a variety of *Uru*- and TGU-themed t-shirts. Both Damanji and Maesi have also created a variety of vehicles. Damanji has created several fantastical *Uru*-style vehicles, including a hover sailboat, a spherical bicycle-like air vehicle, a winged flying machine, and a dune buggy adorned with D'ni script (figure 10.9).

Damanji became particularly involved in building. His earlier structures, including the Relto Island, *Uru*-style street lamps, and the Egg Room egg, were largely derivative of the original *Uru*. He also began to develop elaborate architectural structures (the next section details the ways in which his aesthetic evolved over time to integrate *Uru* and *There.com* styles of architecture).

Books and written texts play an important role not only in *Uru* but in all the *Myst* games. Besides being the source of Ages and the primary transport mechanism (figure 10.10), players are accustomed to reading stories, poems, journal entries, and correspondence that obtusely reveal puzzle clues and aspects of the story. The library is one of the most important buildings in the D'ni City, and there is also a smaller library in the Hood where linking books can be found. The ability within both *There.com* and *Second Life* for players to create books that can be clicked on to reveal textual or visual content provides a perfect opportunity for players to produce content around this game element.

The *Uru* Library in *There.com*, created initially by Raena and later maintained by Nature_Girl, was the second most important structure (after the Community Center) on Yeesha Island (figure 10.11). At the heart of this multistory, columned, circular building was the ubiquitous Egg Room egg. The structures could also become identity markers as well as cultural artifacts, and the library reflected Nature_Girl's role not only as the group's historian, but also the resident expert in all things D'ni. She knew the entire *Myst/Uru* mythology in detail, and was the primary resource for any questions regarding *Uru* lore and theology. Over time, I came refer to her as the group's rabbi. The first and second floor of the library displayed books with various information about the history of the group, the closure of *Uru*, and instructions for getting into *Until Uru*, as well as links to other key group resources. The top floor, which was accessible only by hover vehicle, housed Nature_Girl's Relto, a customized variation possessing all the signature characteristics. Nature_Girl also ran a handful of art zones that exhibited the works of Thereian artists.

Erik's Atmosphere Hood is an interesting example of the relationship between solitary workmanship and social agency. Though Erik worked entirely alone on this project, it was clear from interviews that his motivations were primarily social. He

| Figure 10.11 |
Nature_Girl's Library with Relto on the roof. (Image: Pearce)

had made a promise to Leesa, and wished to do something for the group. It should be noted that like Erik, all of the artisans described here had to teach themselves new tools, as all of the worlds they produced for used their own proprietary creation tools.

The *Uru* group in *Second Life* took a much more comprehensive approach, and, according to interviews, were deliberately seeking out a world in which they could re-create *Uru*. Once in *Second Life*, a small core group acquired D'ni Island and set about re-creating key sections of *Uru*, including the hood and Eder Kemo (figure 10.12). Some additional "modern" features were also added, reflecting the qualities of their new home in *Second Life*, including modern-style Reltos. The group of six to nine core members built the entire area once, then tore it down and started again from scratch. One distinction in creation modalities is that in *Second Life*, as opposed to *There.com* and Adobe Atmosphere, creation is done in-world. In addition, unlike *There.com*, environments can be set up to allow for group modification. This leads to a much more collaborative mode of creation and makes it easier to create large environments. *There.com*'s creation mechanism, on the other hand, favors individual creation and ownership of space.

In addition to the main areas of D'ni Island in *Second Life*, visitors could access a series of Reltos perched high up in the sky overhead via a working simulation of *Uru*'s

| **Figure 10.12** |
Braintrees in Edo Kemo, the Garden Age, in *Uru* (left), and as created by Uruvians in *Second Life* (right). (Image: Pearce)

Nexus or fly around the perimeter of the Island and look at group members' more modern Relto-style houses. Although it would appear that the *Uru* group in *Second Life* was more focused on artifacts than community, interviews with the Uru Builder's Guild described this as a highly collaborative effort, the main point of which was "fellowship." While D'ni Island in *Second Life* did not seem to be as regularly populated as Yeesha Island in *There.com*, for events such as the anniversary of the *Uru* closure it was so mobbed that the server crashed and participants (including visitors from *There.com*) were ejected into a barren desert. As is the case with Yeesha Island in *There .com*, non-Uruvian Second Lifers often stumbled onto D'ni Island by accident, not aware of what they were seeing. Occasionally, one of the creators would be available to conduct a tour.

Although the *Uru* group in *Second Life* was not a major focus of this study, a few commonalities suggest that they, too, shared some of the characteristic traits and play styles of their compatriots in *There.com*. Clearly spatial literacy is foremost among these; players had a very deep connection to and understanding of the spaces within *Uru*, required to re-create them in such a compelling fashion. They shared with Uruvian-Thereians the motivation and determination to overcome the obstacle created by their diaspora status, and to maintain the communities created in *Uru*. The Second Lifer Uruvians also share with their Thereian counterparts the desire and ability to work collaboratively in groups, no doubt a carryover from the collaborative puzzle-solving play of *Uru*. Finally, Uruvians in both worlds take great joy in sharing their story with non-Uruvians.

Creating New Ages

The creation of new Ages of *Uru* seems to be the inevitable outcome of players becoming deeply involved in creating *Uru* artifacts. The *Uru* hacker group alluded to earlier aspired to create new Ages almost from the start, and eventually succeeded in doing so. From the onset of TGU's arrival, Damanji wanted to create new *Uru* Ages in *There.com*. Even as the group was moving from place to place to avoid harassment, Damanji was trying to find a way to build a new Age. An early attempt to do this near *There.com*'s newbie Welcome Center was met with resistance. This only served to reinforce other players' anxieties that TGU was trying to take over *There.com* and turn it into *Uru*, and Damanji's elaborate structures created major lag in the area.

The creation of new Ages is a somewhat controversial theological issue among TGUers. According to group historian Nature_Girl, humans are not really supposed to create Ages at all, as this skill is a unique gift of the D'ni. Historically in *Myst* and *Uru* lore, attempts to create Ages by people not of 100 percent D'ni blood often led to disaster.

While Damanji's earliest artifact creation in *There.com* focused primarily on creating key icons of *Uru* culture—the Yeesha costume, the Relto, the Imager, the *Uru* lamp, and others—the Age creation problem still nagged at him, and he began to formulate a strategy that one might call "emergent Age generation." The idea was that rather than build an entirely new Age, which would be a great deal of work and highly challenging for a single person (as *There.com*'s building system does not allow for collaborative authorship), he would create *Uru*-like objects and sell them to Thereians at large. Over time, he hoped, new Ages would emerge organically through the integration of these artifacts into *There.com*. Coupled with this was a vision of new *Uru*-like artifacts in the *There.com* style. As we've seen, *There.com*'s aesthetic is much more cartoon-like than *Uru*'s, so as he worked with both the *Uru* and *There.com* vocabularies, Damanji began to create a hybrid style that combined the two (figure 10.13). It is at this point that his work begins to get particularly interesting because the objects he creates are no longer derivative of *Uru* artifacts but wholly original, essentially Uruvian while at the same time indigenous to *There.com* (figure 10.14). Other players followed suit and a new generation of *Uru* creators have further refined this hybrid aesthetic.

Over time, Damanji's new strategy played out extremely well on a *There.com*-wide basis. One of his early contributions to this new style of Uruvian-Thereian architecture was the Cone House, an octagonal structure loosely based on a building in

| Figure 10.13 |
Damanji's workshop in *There.com* with original *Uru*-inspired artifacts. (Image: Pearce)

| Figure 10.14 |
Damanji's "Ancient's Bike." (Image: Pearce)

| Figure 10.15 |
Uru-inspired Cone House. (Image: Pearce)

one of the *Uru* Ages (figure 10.15). In *There.com*, it came in various components so you could build small or large, single- or multiple-storied variations, with a flatter or pointier roof. TGUer Bette created a park across from Yeesha Island, along with her family, where a number of Cone Houses could be seen. Damanji also created a number of other architectural components, including an ark, platforms and decks, new fountain designs, a watchtower, a bridge house, a temple construction kit, numerous furniture items and building accessories, and a number of landing pads for the pilots in the group. Over time, these components have been adopted by Thereians at large, and one can see Damanji's *Uru*-inspired architecture throughout *There.com*. When Wingman founded the University of There, he used Damanji's Cone Houses for the majority of structures on the campus (figure 10.16), effectively institutionalizing the design into *There.com*'s architectural vocabulary. More recently, Raena began creating Myst-insipred artifacts and architectural elements, many of which have become

| Figure 10.16 |

The University of There campus consists primarily of *Uru*-inspired Cone House structures. (Image: Pearce)

ubiquitous structures throught *There.com* due to their popularity both inside and outside the Uru community. And a new generation of recently arrived Uru immigrants have been revisiting the Age-building project, taking advantage of new affordances in *There.com* for larger, shared real estate development.

In *Second Life*, in keeping with the more environment-centric and collaborative building mechanism, a group combining *Myst* and *Uru* players took the bold step of creating an entirely new *Myst/Uru*-style game from scratch. The small team acquired their own Island and created an elaborate treasure hunt-style game, *Inara: The Clay Vessel Quest* (figures 10.17–10.19). Participants in this adventure/puzzle must find a number of pieces of a broken clay vessel to restore balance to the world, presumably an Age, though this is never stated outright. Exotic oversized flowers, bizarre elevated structures, mysterious temple-like buildings, elaborate furnishings, complex and challenging pathways to new locales, chambers embedded with poetry, strange transport devices such as a glass funicular, elaborate machines whose correct operation

| **Figure 10.17** |

Inara: The Clay Vessel Quest, an original game created by *Myst* fans in *Second Life*. (Image: Pearce)

| **Figure 10.18** |

Inara: The Clay Vessel Quest, an original game created by *Myst* fans in *Second Life*. (Image: Pearce)

| Figure 10.19 |

Inara: The Clay Vessel Quest, an original game created by *Myst* fans in *Second Life*. (Image: Pearce)

gains entry to locked rooms, keys and pot shards to be found, strange orb-like viewing devices that show glimpses into other areas of the game, and of course books, books, and more books: all these features bear the signature play style and aesthetics of *Myst* games, though it is nowhere explicitly stated as such. Even the game tracking object, modeled after the Relto book that *Uru* avatars carry on their belts, is a notebook that players wear when playing the game. As in *There.com*, *Uru* and *Myst* players in *Second Life* make up some of the world's top artisans. Two of the most popular furniture designers in *Second Life* are former *Myst* players, and the work of one of these artisans makes up most of the furniture in *Inara*.

Emergent Patterns of Player Productivity

Although the expressions of *Uru* culture in *There.com* and *Second Life* represent only a limited sampling, the tendency to move from derivative to original works inspired by the indexed or referenced fan culture appears to be generalizable across multiple worlds. Based on the apparent increase in original *Myst-* and *Uru-*inspired projects over time, it would seem that players who become versed in a game's content may eventually, under the right conditions and given the opportunity for player creativity, feel emboldened to take possession of that content and make it their own. In the case of *Uru*, this has been largely enabled by Cyan's apparent silence throughout the development of post-*Uru* culture.

Early on, the creators of both D'ni Island and the Atmosphere Hood actually showed their work to Cyan representatives, fearing copyright reprisal. In both cases, no further communication was received from Cyan, suggesting a permissive attitude toward fans regarding copyright enforcement. Later negotiations regarding the *Until Uru* player-run servers and the release of fan-created Age-building tools seem to indicate that Cyan is in fact not only permissive but also supportive of fan creation efforts. This would be an entirely new model for corporations, which generally cling desperately to copyright ownership. More recently, *Uru*'s developers openly supported fan-created artifacts, such as helping to re-launch *Second Life*'s D'ni Island as a promotion for the re-release of the game. The next planned iteration of *Uru* is purported to include affordances for player-created content.

If, as would seem to now be the case, Cyan has handed over control of the *Myst/ Uru* worlds to players, this would be the first time such a transfer of power has occurred. It will be interesting to see the outcome of this approach to supporting player productivity. Cyan's innovative position also causes us to consider other models that game companies might use in the future to leverage fans' natural tendency to wish to co-create the virtual worlds they inhabit.

Comments

I think it is hard to say that Cyan's silence is tacit relinquishing of control of the URU/Myst franchise. Perhaps they are sad at what happened to the community. Perhaps this is a method to perpetuate the fan base whilst they prepare for some second coming. Witness that they have stopped selling kagi codes coincident with the release of primitive age development tools.

Perhaps what is happening is really just a business decision. Specifically, suppose Cyan is developing some new Uru-type game for release. Why would they want to compete with their own legacy, *Until Uru*, which is essentially free to use. So the business tactic might be, give them UU to hold them. Then cut off the keys so the community can't stay there forever. Eventually without new keys the community will not be able to grow in Uru. Ultimately the gathering will disperse to other worlds, as this text has studied.

Cyan, if this is your strategy then hurry up, or perhaps make some kind of announcement to the community. Because the "myst" has begun to dissipate.

Posted by: Raena | February 05, 2006 at 05:37 PM

Well an update here. As we now know Cyan has launched their own shard, D'mala, which is open to new explorers. No more keys for the user shards are being offered. Thus the prediction above appears to have come true. If Cyan is successful in acquiring more funding they will be able to "produce" the "second coming" of Uru. So from a business sense they have NOT given up control of the franchise.

Posted by: Raena | April 07, 2006 at 02:05 PM

POROUS MAGIC CIRCLES AND THE LUDISPHERE

Porous Magic Circles

As discussed in chapter 9, the findings of this study suggest that the magic circle may be more porous than previously believed. Online virtual worlds must be looked at in the context of the ludisphere, as well as within the larger context of the real world. These ludic landscapes can be seen as existing within a series of overlapping and nested magic circles, each with porous membranes, all encircled by the real world. Because the group being studied transgressed the boundaries of a single game, it can provide us with some detail as to where these fissures and ludic leakages can occur.

Ludic Leakage and Multitasking

One quality of computer games that distinguishes them from console games is that computers are multipurpose tools. Not only that, but because of the affordances of multiwindowed operating systems such as the Macintosh operating system and its antecedent, Windows, players can engage in multiple activities at the same time, also known as multitasking. In addition, the fact that the computer is the primary portal to the Internet means that players can do various tasks, including game-playing, while toggling back and forth between web pages and applications. This means that players might be conducting real-life activities on their computer in tandem with their game-playing. In addition, audio features, such as voice in *There.com* and voice-over-IP, also predispose networked computer games to a variety of what might be termed "ludic leakages." These might take the form of overhearing a personal phone call, an aside to a child or a spouse, the sound of a barking dog, or other activities going on in the home. Players also frequently post URLs in-world that launch out-of-game web sites, further blurring the boundary between "game" and "nongame" spheres.

Traversing Magic Circles

The prevailing wisdom that the magic circle surrounding a game activity is inviolate and impervious needs to be reexamined, particularly in the context of cyberspace. The Uru Diaspora in general, and specifically TGU, exemplify play communities carrying their unique play styles across magic circles, and adapting it to each new play ecosystem they encounter. These transludic encounters also introduce leakages between play, imagination, and real life. Thus it may be more useful to think of clusters of intersecting and overlapping magic circles within the larger constellation of networked play spaces, which we might call the "ludisphere," which exists in the larger frame of "real life." The subsequent section will explore this notion a little further, and also talk about the ways in which persistent individual and group identities reinforce movement among different magic circles within the ludisphere.

Migrating Individual and Group Identities

The practice of maintaining either group or individual identities that cross multiple game worlds extends far beyond the *Uru* TGU group. Intergame immigration is becoming increasingly commonplace. Guilds from medieval-themed MMOGs are known to inhabit several games simultaneously. In some cases, they may move en masse into a newly released game, creating a form of market cannibalism between games of the same genre. Immigrants from *The Sims Online* have a community in *There.com*. Small numbers of players have immigrated between *There.com* and *Second Life*, and some keep a primary residence in one and a vacation home in the other. The *Uru*'s Welcomers' League is an example of another group that extends its original *Uru* mission (to greet new players) beyond its game of origin into other worlds.

Although TGU identifies collectively as a single group, as we've seen, they play and carry persistent identities concurrently across no less than five different networked environments: *There.com*, *Until Uru* (running on player-hosted servers), *Second Life*, TGU's own Atmosphere Hood, and the Koalanet forum, which serves as a central communication hub across all the virtual worlds the group inhabits. They also augment these environments with voice-over-IP software such as Skype or Teamspeak.

The collective group identity both creates the necessity for and enables the use of identities that persist across virtual worlds (figure 11.1). And while their representations may vary from world to world based on the capabilities of each virtual environment, most players who have these sorts of multiworld avatar identities conceive of the character as "the same person" throughout. It would also seem that in the case of TGU, the diasporic element served to reinforce the need for itinerant or portable identities.

| Figure 11.1 |
Lynn and Nature_Girl in *Uru* (left), *There.com* (center), and *Second Life* (right). (Image: Pearce)

Players were determined to stay together, both in an individual sense ("stay together with my avatar"), and in a social sense ("stay together with my community").

Practices of intergame immigration and multiworld identities present some fascinating new research questions which ought to be of interest to game developers, who often have no way to track where players have gone once they have left a game. Furthermore, the implications of multigame identities are particularly interesting when looking at issues of player representation and game mechanics. Because the affordances for avatar design and modification differ so greatly from world to world, players may find that differences in avatar representations may also lead to differences in personality, even in the same character, from one world to another. Groups may also evolve in different ways as they come in contact with new play ecosystems and cultures, especially as they move between MMOW genres. Further developing methods for tracking and studying player migration patterns could potentially have a very high level of utility for MMOG designers.

Migrating Play Patterns

Intergame immigration provides us with an interesting case of emergence in MMOWs. Clearly, immigration is not something intended by designers. Such immigration typically happens slowly over time, but in the case of *Uru*, a sudden cataclysmic event caused a relatively instantaneous mass immigration. This cataclysmic event created the opportunity to track a relatively large group of players across a number of different virtual worlds in a relatively compressed time period.

The TGU narrative demonstrates that the root of emergent behavior lies in a particular community's play style, incubated in the group's game or virtual world of origin, framed by the types of people that world attracts. These players then move into different play ecosystems where they transport and adapt their culture and play styles to the new context. As we've seen in the case of *Uru* settlers in *There.com*, the new context also adapts to them, a process which can at times be painful. In addition, TGU then took some of the new play patterns they had developed in *There.com* back into *Until Uru*, thus bringing emergent behaviors back into their "home" world.

One might see this as an "all the world's a playground" approach in which, in each new world players encounter, they form a relationship with the virtual space informed and guided by their play style and the play patterns they have developed in other worlds they inhabit. This echoes Iacovoni, whose small study *Game Zone* explores the many ways that physical and virtual space are subverted in the service of play (2004). It is also consistent with Opie and Opie's descriptions of the ways in which different street games mutate from one geographical region to another in the real world, taking advantage of local resources and environmental conditions (1969). Furthermore, play will inevitably blur the boundary between spaces as it functions by its own set of rules, independent of surrounding social conventions. Thus spaces are constantly subverted and reconfigured to accommodate the play impulse (Jenkins 1998).

TGU's play style, insomuch that it is "of *Uru*," is very much about the emergence of social relationships through their relationship to space. The examples given here illustrate the ways in which experimental play can lead to new patterns indigenous to the space they occur in, but characterized by the group's unique play style. Two good examples are Avie Bowling (*Until Uru*) and Buggy Polo (*There.com*), described in chapter 9. While these games arise from the same play style, their play pattern is unique to the affordances of each world's design features and flaws (including bugs). A phenomenon such as the Furrier Legion Flight Team illustrates how when play styles such as mastery and exploration meet a virtual world feature such as air travel, a new play pattern is born. Players accustomed to migrating between multiple game worlds appear to become particularly adept at spontaneously adapting new spaces to their own play requirements.

Migrating Identities and Play Patterns to the Real World

While it may be easy to presume that these phenomena are somehow exclusive to the virtual world, it would seem that many of these patterns can also migrate outside of the virtual and into the real world. This was borne out during *There.com*'s RLG (Real Life Gathering), which took place at the San Mateo offices of Makena, Inc., now the owner/operator of *There.com*, in September 2005. The TGU group, including spouses and resident ethnographer, comprised slightly less than half the total showing of Thereians (figure 11.2).

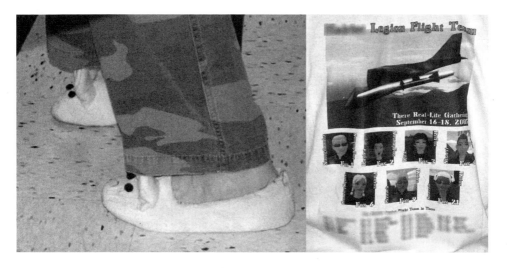

| Figure 11.2 |
Bunny slippers (left) and a Furrier Legion T-Shirt (right) from the There Real-Life Gathering. (Text has been blurred to protect subjects' anonymity.) (Image: Pearce)

While some members of the group had had encounters with each other prior to the RLG, for most of them, including the author, this was their first encounter with each other's "real-life avatars." The importance of voice became immediately apparent upon first meeting. One could easily recognize others because of the familiarity of their voice, which served as a bridge between the real-life and virtual-world avatars. Additionally, many players bore a physical resemblance to their *Uru* and/or *There.com* avies, and some arrived dressed in their avatars' typical garb.

While most of the formal event was focused on panels, discussion groups, and showcasing player creativity, including machinima films made in-world, live musical performances, and real-life crafts made by players, the most revealing aspect from a research perspective took place the last evening, when the group met for dinner in San Francisco and then returned to the hotel to socialize.

Key characteristics of group members became readily apparent once within an open physical space. Finding parking places and coordinating a meet-up became a kind of puzzle, with members calling each other from mobile phones to arrange a meeting point. The exploratory urge came into action within the context of San Francisco's Fisherman's Wharf, a popular and crowded tourist area. Several groups dispersed to explore, one, led by Lynn, to visit the Ghirardelli chocolate factory. This exercise brought into sharp relief the contrast between unencumbered exploration of a virtual world and attempting to navigate a hilly turn-of-the-century urban area in a wheelchair. Again, rising to the challenge, nondisabled group members augmented Lynn's skills at seeking out ramps, lifts, and other pathways, enabling her to arrive at her destination. Thus the puzzle-solving urge and spatial literacy were no less present in the real world than in the virtual.

Navigating out of San Francisco and back to San Mateo with Furrier Legion founders Wingman and Shaylah was equally revealing. Negotiation of the best path back to the highway was highly reminiscent of discussions regarding the optimal buggy path from point a to point b in *There.com*, especially with respect to finding the best shortcut, the most direct route, or the least hilly.

Once at the hotel, I was able to see TGUers in an actual real-world play setting. Thereians, instigated largely by TGUers, transformed the hotel lobby into a play space. Having brought playing cards, players created seating arrangements and initiated spades games, re-creating the standard configuration of the tables in *There.com*.

Perhaps the most noteworthy distinction between real-life and virtual spades games was that, accustomed to *There.com*'s built-in computerized scoring system, no one was really clear on the mechanics of keeping score. Once the scoring formula was arrived at, it became apparent that it would not be possible for the players to keep score themselves. Ultimately, Lynn's husband Frank took the computer's role as scorekeeper. For this and other reasons, the game was lengthier than usual, but it provided valuable insight into the differences and similarities between real-life and mediated interactions.

Players' senses of humor and approaches to the gameplay were similar to their in-world play personae, but with subtle variations. As with both spades in *There.com* and Heek in *Uru*, informal spectators stood at the corners of the table. Unlike *There.com*, however, it was possible for both spectators and players to see people's cards, opening up the possibility of cheating, entirely absent in *There.com*'s variation of the game.

The familiar avatar animations were replaced by physical gestures, eye contact, and other features of the real world, although the voices were the same. This served to create a connection between the real-world persona and the virtual persona, and although the experience was a little disorienting, there was a familiarity to both the company and the scene that made the entire situation seem quite natural.

Comments

Oh My God, this made me laugh and cry at the same time. What a fun time it was meeting you in RL. I hope we can do it again. Meeting each other in RL was as comfortable as putting on a pair of beloved old shoes. We all just "fit" together.

Yes, I agree, the highlight of the gathering for me too was the San Francisco jaunt to the Chocolate Factory and taking over the lobby of the hotel. Too bad they did not have a fountain in the center for us to dance on. ;-)

The other noteworthy event that night was the heroic task Raena performed by walking around and making sure the web-cam was on and trying to show others who could not make it to the gathering what it was like. I heard so many comments on how deeply that was appreciated by those who could only wish they could have joined us. We wished they could have been there physically too but I know they were there in spirit.

Oh yes, and who could forget the little oriental doorman who kept mooching chocolate and getting in the group pics on the stairs of the restaurant? Lord I loved it. HAHA

Hey, who won that spades game anyway?
Posted by: Lynn | January 29, 2006 at 09:08 PM

It was quite an experience getting to the evening dinner event in the "tourist" harbor area of San Francisco. I recall a 2-hour exploration to find a parking space for the large wheelchair enabled van. Various members of the community spontaneously collaborated to help solve this problem, employing use of cell phones, foot excursions . . . etc. The group quickly found out that RL has its disadvantages! Oh did we long for a hover boat or even just a linking book.
Posted by: Raena | February 05, 2006 at 05:43 PM

Raena . . . thanks for the reminder of the parking co-ordination. I think this is actually a very interesting story because of the "distributed" nature of the communication that took place. I'll be sure to include a description of that in *Being Artemesia*!
Posted by: Artemesia | February 05, 2006 at 10:51 PM

Something else struck me about the jaunt. I felt totally safe in everyone's hands in a strange city without my protective hubby. I appreciated the fact that without my asking the path to follow was discovered in advance of me by all in that group.

It is like it happens in the games. We all see a need and try to fulfill it without question or having to be asked.

Of course my situation was obvious at the time being in a wheelchair, but there was no discussion and because I had made a comment some time before that I really would like to visit the choc factory, it then became a goal for everyone to get me to it.

I had taken a look at the streets and did not think it was possible to get to it but hid my disappointment and did not say a word about it looking like a lost cause so not to have to try and fail and be a drag on everyone. HA HA. Little did I know I was going to be gotten there by hook or crook with this gang.

My desire was acted upon by others calling me across the busy street and saying "follow them." I had no idea until the next block that was the mission we were on. So I figured YAY, lets try and the mission accomplished by many. The forward guard ran interference and lo and behold, the store was found. The route sometimes was a bit round and about but you all got me there. It was worth the trip. :-)
Posted by: Lynn | February 13, 2006 at 03:28 AM

Lynn it's good to hear your perspective on this because it also reinforces some of what I've been saying about the dynamics between the individual and the group, and the fact that every problem encountered becomes a "puzzle." This is one of the interesting distinctions I see between Myst and Uru was that Uru added this collaborative puzzle-solving skill to your repertoire.
Posted by: Artemesia | February 27, 2006 at 09:58 AM

EMERGENCE AS DESIGN MATERIAL

Emergence and Design

The primary question driving this research has been the question of whether a relationship can be recognized between game design and patterns of social emergence among players in massively multiplayer games and virtual worlds. The findings suggest that indeed such a relationship exists, and operates at a number of levels. While this study represents a single case involving a specific group of players moving between multiple game worlds, it provides numerous examples of how both the values of the virtual world and its underlying architecture, as well as its specific design features, intersect with distinct group play styles to produce different types of emergent behavior. This process has included an analysis of how such group play styles emerge over time through their interaction with different virtual worlds and play ecosystems.

Comments

Perhaps this study will encourage game developers to understand there is much more in the world as a market for games than violent first person shooters.

Disabled people can be a great market source for community-based games because of the time they have available. It not only gives them a badly needed outlet to feel like they can once again function in a whole body and do the things they once could or never thought possible.

They can contribute much to an on-line community-based game in many ways and that allow them to feel they are productive members. I personally think that has been of the greatest importance to me other than being with the many friends I made in URU.

Posted by: Lynn | January 29, 2006 at 09:22 PM

A Narrative of the Movement from Synthetic to Co-created Worlds

This study revealed two distinct types of persistent virtual worlds or play ecosystems that exist at opposite ends of a spectrum. At one end is the fixed synthetic world of

Uru, a wholly contrived story world that is also a game with limited and controlled agency. Like a theme park with no tracks, players can explore at will, but cannot change anything in the world except in prescribed ways. At the opposite extreme, co-created worlds like *Second Life* and *There.com* emphasize the social and invite players to make a major contribution to the world's construction. *There.com* is on the more moderate side of the co-created end of this spectrum, with a higher degree of designer controls and constraints, while *Second Life* represents the furthest extreme of an open-ended co-created world. Such co-created worlds, fuelled primarily by emergence, are always works in progress that change on a continual and unpredictable basis. The defining characteristic along this spectrum is the amount and type of agency players are given (as opposed to the agency they actually take) to participate in the design and creation of the world itself. The more agency players are given, the larger the quantity and variety of emergent behaviors that are likely to occur.

The narrative of emergence told here is that of a culture migrating from a fixed synthetic game world into co-created social worlds where they worked within the world's constraints to create their own unique subculture.

One important observation is that "emergence happens," regardless of whether the virtual world has affordances for it or not. Hide-and-seek, Avie Bowling, the D'ni Olympics, and other forms of alternative play conceived by players within the fixed synthetic world of *Uru* suggests that emergence is the inevitable outcome of a large number of players within a network. Many examples outside of game studies attest to the notion that the larger the number of nodes or agents in a complex system, the more likely it is that emergence will occur (Johnson 2001, Levy 1993, Rheingold 2002, Surowiecki 2004).

Social emergence in this context is the outcome of prolonged and repeated interaction with a persistent networked virtual world through a persistent identity. Because emergence occurs over time, observing its full effects requires a longitudinal, qualitative, holistic, multiscale approach, the ability to observe the forest and the trees concurrently (Bar-Yam 1997, 2000; Mills 1959; De Landa 1997). Furthermore, some forms of social emergence can traverse the borders of virtual worlds and even cross between the virtual and the real. Further knowledge about these phenomena can be gathered through long-term, multiworld studies, which will necessarily require a team approach. Problems of multinational ethnography are not new to the anthropological world, which has seen a shift from the classic "hermetic" scenario of the "primitive" cultures to a global system where cultures are more porous, and migrate, intermingle, and recombine on an ongoing basis (Marcus 1995). How to study these cultures becomes an increasingly complex problem, and likely one that cannot be solved by the traditional notion of the lone anthropologist embedded within an isolated culture.

This study revealed that emergence may be generated in one context, move to another context, and mutate within the particular constraints of the new world. Studying these transworld migratory patterns provides a glimpse of how the design of networked virtual worlds affects the emergent behaviors that happen within and through them. This information is particularly useful to designers of multiplayer games and virtual worlds. The more conscious we are of the patterns that emerge from specific design features and technical constraints, the more able we will be to work with emergence as a "material" of game design.

Each of the virtual worlds explored in this study embodies a set of values that form the substrate for the software's design. *Uru*, as an entirely fixed synthetic world, has a deeply rich story line that creates a metaphor for software production. Its narrative, aesthetic, and spiritual subtext attracted a particular type of audience that was predisposed to certain types of behavior. The value of mastery that was cultivated by the gameplay delivered a puzzle-solving, exploratory player who was intelligent, inquisitive, and proactive, and though *Uru* provided nominal player agency, players began to insinuate their own agency into the game world through emergent behavior even though the world itself was relatively immutable.

Once *Uru* closed, these highly skilled puzzle-solvers dispersed to find new homes. Players who gravitated toward *Second Life* sought an environment where they could re-create *Uru*. The flexible, in-game, collaborative construction tools coupled with Linden Lab's open policy of player creation (no company censorship or approval required) enabled them to achieve this goal with few impediments. Players adapted the *Uru* culture in *Second Life*, creating "modern" Reltos, and eventually, joined with *Myst* players to create an entirely new *Myst/Uru* Age. *Second Life*'s creation tools and policies made it easier to collaborate on large-scale environments, and also to create content derived from *Uru* without fear of Linden Labs rejecting content because of presumed copyright violations.

There.com provided more of a ready-to-play social environment for the TGU group, whose main interest was social. TGU players gravitated toward *There.com* because it was easy to navigate, they liked the expressiveness of its avatars, and its client-server architecture provided pleasing scenic views for avid explorers. Creation was more solitary, and more artifact- rather than environment-based because *There.com*'s policies precluded the level of *Uru* re-creation possible in *Second Life*. Motivated by the desire to create objects meaningful to their community, *Uru* artisans in *There.com* began by creating artifacts and spaces that were derivative of *Uru*, but eventually developed a hybrid Uruvian-Thereian style. Because it was not feasible to create an entire Age, for both technical and cultural reasons, Uruvians in *There .com* opted instead to take an "emergent Age" approach through the propagation of *Uru*-like artifacts throughout *There.com*. *Uru* immigrants also liked the simpler, more controlled environment of *There.com*, preferring to avoid what they perceived as the seamier side of *Second Life*.

Conclusion: Contributing Factors to Emergence

This study demonstrates that there is a traceable connection between game and world design and social emergence in MMOWs. It identifies six factors in the propagation of emergent behavior, which were outlined briefly at the beginning of this book. Each of these provides us with insight as to how emergence occurs in virtual worlds, and its implications in terms of design.

Fixed Synthetic versus Co-created Worlds

One of the study's key findings is that virtual worlds exist along a spectrum ranging from fixed synthetic to co-created worlds. In either context, it was concluded that "emergence happens," regardless of the world type, but can be promoted or hindered, whether by intent or by accident, by the game's features, flaws, and bugs. Fixed synthetic worlds tend to fall into the category more properly defined as "game," worlds with a goal and a formal structure for its achievement; they also tend to have a more fixed narrative structure. Co-created worlds are open-ended worlds to which players can make an active contribution; these tend to fall under the classification of "social world" or "metaverse" rather than "game," although they often contain games. The distinction is based on the amount and types of agency players have in the world. In fixed synthetic worlds, players generally do not have affordances to physically alter the world, while in co-created worlds, they do. Thus, in co-created worlds players are encouraged to contribute to the actual creation of the world, a design approach that leverages emergence as a production strategy. Regardless of which type of worlds players inhabit, evidence from this and other studies suggests that an inevitable pattern of emergence is that over time, players will come to feel they have rights and to a certain respect, that they own the world, especially if they have had a hand in its creation.

Communities of Play

The study joined with others to identify communities of play as a relevant form of distributed, networked culture, worthy of study alongside more established forms of networked groups such as communities of practice and communities of interest. Group play style was found to be a marker of identity, and the study explored the role of group identity in facilitating transworld immigration. Interworld group migration creates the necessity for transludic individual identities that move across multiple game worlds. Emergent behaviors of communities of play arise out of a combination of the proclivities of people who are attracted to a particular virtual world, and the intersection of their values, interests, and skills with the world's design feature. Players also acquire certain skills that lead to mastery of certain play styles, which can be carried into other play ecosystems and translated into new play patterns and forms of game culture.

The Social Construction of Identity

Supporting the findings of previous research, the study found that individual identity is an intersubjective accomplishment that develops through a process of social emergence. Here it was noted that the group identity frames the individual identity, and the group itself constructs both its collective identity and that of the individuals within it. An example of this social construction of individual identity could be found in the group's bottom-up leadership style, the ways in which TGU's leaders grew into their leadership roles through transactions with and feedback from the play community.

Intersubjective Flow

A key finding of this study was the phenomenon of intersubjective flow, building on work by Csíkszentmihályi (1990), and DeKoven (1992a), a sociological reading of the deep engagement suggested by this psychological phenomenon. It would seem that "people are addictive," (Lazzaro 2004) and in play communities, the line between the individual and social may blur as players push each other to higher levels of engagement. The study also concluded that intersubjective flow appears to be one of the drivers of emergent behavior, and plays a major role in both community play styles and the social construction of individual identity.

Productive Play

The study challenged the traditional axiom that play is unproductive, and proposed the notion of productive play. Especially in co-created worlds, productive play becomes a major engine for emergence, and prolific player-producers can play a significant role in emergent cultures. The creation of artifacts was identified as an expression of social agency, promoted by feedback and manifested in part through in-world economies, thus encouraging player-producers to produce more. Over time, an emergent pattern could be identified in which productive players tended to move from a more derivative approach to migrating a game's culture into a different environment to feeling emboldened and equipped to begin creating their own original artifacts and content inspired by their game of origin. Thus fan culture morphs into the creation of original content. This also intersected with the notion that players crave self-determination, whether in the form of representation to game players, or by actually "owning" the game themselves. In the case of the Uru Diaspora, this was manifest through the creation of the Atmosphere Hood by TGU, as well as the initiation of the *Until Uru* player-run server network.

Porous Magic Circles

This study clearly refutes the previously asserted imperviousness of the magic circle that bounds play in time and space from "reality." Instead, players migrate between magic circles, importing play patterns and identities with them. They can also mutate play patterns and then transport those mutations back into the original play context. Another form of emergence arises when play communities adapt to new play ecosystems, and when these play ecosystems adapt to them. Also introduced was the concept of the ludisphere, the aggregate of virtual play spaces that are connected together via the Internet, and the ways in which the Internet's multiple communication functions enable real life to leak into the virtual play space. Beyond the Internet and the computer, play styles derived in virtual space can be transposed into the real world.

These six contributing factors to emergent behaviors in games provide a framework we can use to engage with what might be called the "material properties" of emergence as a component of game design. By beginning to identify where, why, and how emergence occurs, while we cannot entirely control it, it may be possible to integrate its patterns into our design process. How this is to be done will be the subject of subsequent research.

Comments
Productive Play (other types of benefits)
The word Therapeutic comes to mind instantly for the disabled in playing on a more level field in an avatar.
Making friends from all over the world allows us to learn about other's thoughts, customs and cultures as well as to share our own with no constraints from governments or media. I find this has brought me a better understanding of people.
Posted by: Lynn | January 29, 2006 at 09:48 PM

———

Ages Beyond Uru

As this study was drawing to a close in September 2005, Cyan Worlds announced that it would be drawing the final curtain over the world of *Myst*. Yet the *Uru* story does not end here. As this study suggests, through the various instantiations of *Uru* in other games, as well as new Ages created by players, *Myst/Uru* now appears to have a life of its own. The appearance of *Inara: The Clay Vessel Quest* in *Second Life* and Damanji's emergent Ages in *There.com* attests to the fact that players are perfectly capable of taking on and expanding the *Myst/Uru* legacy. Furthemore, their persistent devotion to the brand has led to a series of rebirths and what might be characterized as redeaths, which are touched on in (chapter 15).

In November 2005, only two months after Cyan's announcement, the hacker group that had arranged the *Until Uru* player-run server system announced the beta release of the first Age built by *Uru* fans using their own home-brewed Age development tools. The granting of both server and content-creation rights to a fan community is an unprecedented move in the game industry, and illustrates the powerful role emergence plays in the dynamic between designers and players. It also illustrates that while players may feel powerless and at the mercy of corporations whose decisions may not always be in their best interest, they also have the power to exert their own agency through large-scale group emergent behavior.

Since the time of this research, *Uru* was reopened, and reclosed. The last word as of this writing is that Cyan has postponed its announced release of MORE (Myst Online: Restoration Experiment), a new, official instantiation of *Uru* that will have affordances for player-created Ages.

Comments

The "real world" has become a difficult place to socialize. It isn't easy to meet people, friends and families are separated by great distances, stress levels are high and danger lurks. Virtual worlds bring people together over great distances from diverse backgrounds. For many, like myself, they become a place to blossom and live as we wish we could in the real world—they are what we wish the real world was.

We are, for the most part, denied play in the real world which increases our stress levels and keeps us at arms' length from the society around us. Life has become too much "strictly business." The opportunity to play not only relieves those pressures but also fills in many of those empty spots we find in our hearts and souls.

Children no longer play innocent games. Winning and competitiveness are all that matters— gone is just having fun. There's more stress at a little league game than fun. Families rarely play together anymore. People are becoming more insulated and alone, violence is on the rise, family structure is disintegrating—we are, to some extent, going nuts as a society. I believe the absence of real play in our lives, as children and adults, is a major contributing factor.

I feel this is demonstrated most noticeably by people who had given up on life, had substance abuse problems or were borderline suicidal who have taken up playing in virtual worlds—they have found a reason for living and have turned their lives around.

Demand more play!

Posted by: Leesa | April 10, 2006 at 02:15 PM

| III |

PLAYING ETHNOGRAPHY: RESEARCH METHODS

METHODOLOGY: PLAYING ETHNOGRAPHY

With the increase in research of online games and virtual worlds, there is a growing need for sharing knowledge on research methods. As we've already established,
there is a long-standing tradition of ethnographic methods in Internet studies as
well as computer-supported cooperative work. This is a departure from some of the
important early work in which primary research was conducted via face-to-face interviews (Turkle 1995). Combinations of both of these techniques are common, but
for MMOG/W research, participant observation has come into favor for qualitative
research of game cultures (Taylor 1999, Mortensen 2003, Steinkuehler 2005, Steinkuehler and Squire 2006). Much excellent research has been generated using participant observation methods, but we are somewhat undernourished in terms of specific
discussions about methodology. Since participant observation is itself an emergent
process, as we have learned from feminist and postcolonial ethnographic enterprises,
it is important to make transparent our methods themselves. This provides a foun-
dation from which to assess this study's findings, as well as provides other researchers with a repertoire of methods and tools to adopt or counter for future research.
I would encourage others conducting qualitative research with participant observation methods to follow suit and address methodological issues more generally in their
work. I would also argue that the weakest link in the methodological chain has been a
clear articulation of our interpretive frameworks, as I have done in chapter 4. I hope
that these discussions will open the door for more open discourse on our interpretive
stance toward our subjects.

A brief disclaimer here: ethnography is certainly not the only way to conduct
online games research, nor even necessarily the best. As we've seen, it has some characteristics that make it particularly well suited for certain types of game inquiries, particularly those that concern social dynamics and the construction of culture. Research
findings arrived at through quantitative methods have been cited throughout this
book. I would also like to suggest that, while a theological rift can sometimes become

apparent between these two approaches, there are some circumstances in which a combination of qualitative and quantitative methods can be highly beneficial. There is simply some data that cannot be approached from only one direction, so I encourage researchers to consider mixing methods between quantitative and qualitative techniques when it makes sense to do so. I have done this on my recent research with baby boomer gamers, to excellent effect. I found in this circumstance that each set of data illuminated aspects of the other that would have been invisible without the use of the complementary method (Pearce 2008b).

In this chapter I will describe the specific methods, tools, and techniques that were used to conduct this research. I chose to adopt a distinctly performative stance toward both the subject matter and the research approach. However, most of the techniques described here can be adopted without necessarily following the positioning I chose relative to play, performance, and ethnography. That said, for my research, these are the central themes that shall be explored in this chapter.

Book IV also provides additional insight into this process by revealing what the ethnographer's process of "learning as she stumbles" entails (Shils 1957), providing a behind-the-scenes look at the ethnographic process. While there has been a common tradition of publishing such texts, they are generally not included in the main monograph of the research findings. My decision to include them here is very deliberate: the insights garnered from trips and stumbles are, far from footnotes, actually quite vital not only to the research, but in particular to the development of the methodology. Ethnography is highly improvisational and, while it is important to strike out on a certain path, one should not be surprised if that path shifts direction throughout the process. Book IV enumerates those shifts of directions, and also demonstrates how the methods were made more robust in the process.

My Avatar/My Self

Game ethnography is one of the rare circumstances in which an ethnographer is required, to varying degrees, to actively participate in the culture she is studying, not to simply observe it. The reason for this is more technical than philosophical: you cannot observe a virtual world without being *inside* it, and in order to be inside it, you have to be "embodied." In other words, you have to create an avatar. Conversely, if you are studying a renaissance faire or Mardi Gras celebration, you could conceivably play along, or not. And in fact, many game ethnographers practice a variant of autoethnography, in which they are studying their own play communities. What I found with my research was that it turned out to be impossible not to play along, for various reasons that I will detail here and in book IV. In either case, you have no choice but to appear

| **Figure 13.1** |

The many faces of Artemesia (left to right): at home in *There.com*; on her pirate galleon in *Second Life*; in *Until Uru*; "real-life" avatar. (Image: Pearce)

in a role comparable to those of the people you are studying. Just as the avatar is the beginning of a life in an online game, it is also the beginning of the research into one.

In order to conduct this game/performance/ethnography, I created Artemesia, a research avatar with a transludic identity, after the custom adopted by *Uru* players, which enabled me to follow players across borders into the different virtual worlds they inhabited. As it is common for players to abbreviate a variety of terms, including one another's avatar names, the name Artemesia was almost always colloquially reduced to either "Arte" (pronounced like arty) or "Art." This was initially accidental, but because I was doing the research in the context of an art project, I also enjoyed the double entendre.

Early on, I had identified intergame immigration as the phenomenon I wanted to study, which immediately opened up a number of challenges, but also suggested a number of concepts, such as the multi-sited ethnography of Marcus, described in chapter 3. I had already encountered the custom of transludic identities, adopted by a number of players in virtual worlds I had visited to indicate that they were immigrants or "refugees" (a term adopted by players themselves) from other games. This transplanting of identity between worlds involved not only using the same name in each virtual world, but also frequently entailed attempting to create as close a resemblance as possible between avatars across games, often based loosely on the person's real-world appearance. Figure 13.1 shows images of Artemesia in *There*, *Second Life*, and *Until Uru*, as well as a photograph of the author, which demonstrate the manner in which I followed this custom. In each case, the general appearance includes variants of red/titian/copper hair, a fair complexion, and one of a number of hairdos that attempted to approximate either past or current hairstyles I've had in real life. As each virtual world has different set of affordances for avatar creation, as the illustrations demonstrate, recreating the same characters across game worlds turns out to be a creative challenge. How can you capture the essence of a character when faced with a fundamentally different mechanism for self-portraiture? *Uru* has the most limited palette of avatar options, followed by *There.com*, where players can create, buy, and sell their own clothing, and *Second Life*, which provides affordances not only for highly customized player-created costumes but hairstyles, avatar skins, and even nonhumanoid representations.

The intersection between Artemesia and myself is what James Gee calls "the third being," a new creation that exists between the player and a fictional character whose agency she controls (2003). Gee coined this term to describe characters in single-player games, characters that are already somewhat defined by the game's narrative. Massively multiplayer games tend to place not only character agency but also personality, including appearance, squarely in the hands of the player, given a designed and constrained kit of parts. Thus the player constructs her avatar character through a combination of representation and improvisational performance over time, through play. Avatar development follows its own emergent patterns: just as there is a feedback loop *between* players in a play community, there also exists a similar feedback loop between the player and his or her avatar. As players in the study often pointed out, the avatar is an extension of the player's real-life persona, even if it instantiates in ways that digress significantly from her real-world personality or life roles. Similar to Gee's notion of "the third being," Schechner and Winnicott describe this as a play and performance paradox in which a third character is formed that is "not me, and not not me," but somewhere in between (Winnicott 1971, Schechner 1988).

I initially played Artemesia like a game character, following parameters suitable to the role-play of an ethnographer. In addition, I found that the ethnographic process was itself a game, filled with mysteries to be revealed and puzzles to be solved. Thus I was engaging in a metagame (the ethnographic project) within a metagame (the Uru Diaspora), both of which can be characterized as forms of emergent behavior. Through this role-playing/research methodology, I sought to define a new praxis, ethnography-as-performance-as-game.

Ironically, one of the outcomes of this research was that in *playing* this role, I eventually became a "real" ethnographer, and acquired a doctorate along the way. In the process, I also became a legitimate participant of the group, which eventually adopted me as its ethnographer-in-residence. In this role, somewhat paradoxically, I became an "inside-outsider," which provided me with the inroads to develop a much more accurate and intimate picture of the group while at the same time balancing this against my objective research perspective. The development of trust and rapport is always vital to the success of ethnographic research. As some of the examples in chapter 3 illustrate, there is a fundamental paradox here as well: one often needs to suspend one's role of authority and objectivity in order to gain trust from informants. Yet, interestingly, because my role in the group was that of "the ethnographer," I was *expected* to create a portrayal of the group that players perceived as being both objective and accurate. I was able to form a consensus through the polyphonic method used in book II, in which members of the group were invited to annotate the findings. This enabled me to acknowledge and engage the authority of the study participants on their *own* experience, while at the same time maintaining a distinct authorial voice.

In developing both this character and this method, I have also integrated Artemesia into the presentation and writing process for this research. Many presentations, most notably the thesis defense, as well as public talks, have been given partially or entirely in situ, in-game and in character, further reinforcing the project's performative positioning. In addition, a number of publications are credited as coauthored by Celia Pearce and Artemesia, prompting one publisher to request that Artemesia sign an author permission form, even though she was well aware that Artemesia was a fictional character.

Fieldwork

As with traditional ethnography, the primary data collection method was fieldwork. The main field study took place over a period of eighteen months, from March 2004 to September 2005, culminating with my attending the Real Life Gathering of *There .com* at the corporate offices of Makena Technologies (which owns and operates *There .com*) in northern California. Initially it had been my intention to avoid meeting study participants in real life, but as with many other plans and intentions, these had to be adjusted in light of the customs and practices of the players themselves.

During this eighteen-month period, I conducted in-world fieldwork that entailed logging into *There.com*, *Until Uru*, and other games and virtual worlds that the players inhabited and/or visited. I also paid a number of visits to the *Uru* community in *Second Life* and interviewed members responsible for building the *Uru*-inspired island there.

Following fairly standard protocols, the research entailed making initial contact with key group leaders and informing them of my interest in doing a study of their group(s). Early contacts with the mayor and deputy mayor of The Gathering of Uru in *There.com* were met with great support, and provided an entrée into the broader TGU community.

Anthropologists recommend a mixture of participant observation and interviews. While interviews provide insight into an individual's perception of lived practice, there may be aspects of their culture of which participants are not aware or are unable to articulate, and which can only be analyzed and understood through direct observation (Boellstorff 2006).

As touched on in chapter 4, Valerie Janesick recommends a blend of "choreography" (1999) and, borrowing from Richardson (1994), "crystallization" as a means of collecting and analyzing qualitative data. The metaphor of choreography to describe ethnography is apt: choreographers draw from a repertoire of moves that can be reconfigured and improvised as needed. This is especially relevant with respect to the improvisational nature of both the study of and the creation of cybercultures, as well as the performative framing of this investigation. Janesick advocates an approach that combines rigor and flexibility, as trained performers can improvise within a proscribed set of parameters (2000). Thus a repertoire of data collection methods can be called upon as appropriate for a given situation. Crystallization, as an interpretive strategy, is a postmodern response to the traditional notion of "triangulation," which provides a framework for analyzing data from different angles, different subjectivities, and at different scales. Thus by combining a choreographic approach to data collection with the application of crystallization methods to its analysis, we are able to arrive at a multifaceted portrait of culture. Mills conjures up a similar metaphor when he speaks of thinking in terms of maintaining a variety of viewpoints, which allows the "mind to become a moving prism catching light from as many angles as possible" (1959, 214).

When interacting with players, I would inform them of my research activities and I used the chat log record as confirmation of their permission to conduct interviews. Over time, I found that all of the players were quite willing to participate, and some actually sought me out requesting that I interview them for the study. "Informed consent," the term used by university review boards to describe permission given by human subjects to be researched, poses some challenges in this regard. Most players in online games appear in avatar form and this can actually be leveraged to protect subjects' privacy, which is one of the concerns of human research ethics. However, human research review boards frequently require a signed consent form from subjects. This creates two significant challenges: one, it means breaking subjects' anonymity; and two, it requires a significant bureaucratic procedure that can be unwieldy to the point of making research with large distributed groups impossible. Review boards that have experience with Internet research will typically accept some type of verification of permission other than a signed form, such as a chat log or an audio or video recording of a player giving permission to be studied. There are also questions around special allowances for research done in public places. How do we define "public," and do online games or the spaces within them qualify as public?

Field visits typically took place between two and four times a week, sometimes more frequently, and varied in length from two to as many as five or six hours, depending on events and activities under way. Timing was based on knowledge of community traffic, and often entailed making visits at night and on weekends. One challenge had to do with the international nature of the field site: players in the group came from all over the world, and interviewing players who were, for example, in Europe, required making daytime appointments in advance or arranging to be online when known events were planned. The TGU group had a long-standing tradition, dating back to the original *Uru* closure, of meeting in one of their online worlds on Sundays at noon Pacific, thus facilitating a weekly gathering that could include European as well as U.S.-based members.

The vast majority of time in-world was spent talking, in both text and voice chat, in various locales and concurrent with other activities. Exploring, which players self-identified as the community's predominate play pattern, was manifested in a variety of different forms. In *There.com*, exploration was generally done in air or land vehicles. Vehicle exploration posed a particularly good opportunity to conduct participant observation and informal interviews as explorations tended to take place in multiperson vehicles, or in separate vehicles with a shared instant message window. I often took the role of passenger so that my hands were free to type and take screenshots and I could attend carefully to the conversations, which took place in a combination of voice and text chat.

Fieldwork involved observing and participating with players in formal and informal, structured and unstructured play situations. I also conducted formal interviews, which were typically scheduled in advance and could take up to three hours, and informal interviews, typically arising out of spontaneous, context-specific conversation that could be organically leveraged into an interview. In addition, toward the end of the study I invited players to participate in in-world discussion groups with themes based on conversations and observations and interpretations of the data that had been captured thus far.

Group interviews were particularly informative because they allowed me to observe the players' relationships to one another and the ways in which they collectively constructed the narratives of their culture and experience. This is crucial because the underlying basis of the social construction is precisely that it *is* social, thus a social method of data collection can provide additional dimensions of understanding. The "consensual hallucination" described by Gibson when he first coined the term "cyberspace" (1984) is constructed collectively by the group, and the way in which they relate to each other through their fictive identities within the game world, including their group discursive style, is key to understanding the ways in which these cybercultures emerge. Because players were engaging in a collective social construction of both a fictive ethnicity and an imaginary homeland, their collective discourse on these topics was highly informative. Individual interviews, on the other hand, were often less censored and might reveal personal details or interpretations that might not come out in a group context. A combination of individual and group interviews provided a means of corroborating perspectives and distinguishing between different subjective interpretations and meaning-making strategies.

In addition to The Gathering of Uru, I also conducted supplemental field visits to *Second Life*, interviewing former *Uru* players and documenting the *Uru*- and *Myst*-based areas in the world. I attended some meetings and events, but this research was primarily concerned with player-made environments within *Second Life*, and less with the group's ongoing culture and play patterns. Although I had wanted to spend more time with this group, conducting immersive fieldwork in two games simultaneously is not feasible for one researcher, although it might be possible to do so with a team.

During site visits, I generally worked with a second computer that enabled me to keep detailed field notes and transcribe voice conversations, a technique I highly recommend. This was in part aided by the fact that most actions and communications take longer in virtual space, so there were often adequate pauses in conversation or activity for me to do this effectively. This became more challenging as I became more actively involved in play activities that required a high level of participation and interaction, some examples of which are described in the findings. The ability to capture field notes and verbal communication with real-time note-taking is a boon for ethnographers, who traditionally capture observations with handwritten notes (often on index cards) that are compiled after the fact.

I also captured chat logs for all textual conversations. There are various techniques for doing this in different games. In *There.com*, all chat logs are automatically saved and labeled by game, date, and time in a client folder, an extremely useful feature for research that I wish other games and virtual worlds would adopt. In *Second Life*, one can simply cut and paste the chat log from the game client in windowed mode into a text or Word document. Most games, however, have an arcane slash command for saving chat logs, which deposits them in a folder in either the documents directory or the game client directory. In *Uru*, the text command "/startlog" would save the chat log as a generically named, numbered text file. This system was programmed to store up to four chat logs, so subsequent chat logs would overwrite each other, which increased the risk of data loss. If you are conducting research in an online game, chances are that there is a similar chat log command that even the game designers are often not aware of. This information can usually be obtained from programmers or quality assurance/game-testing staff, so this is the best way to learn the arcane incantations required to save logs from your game subject of choice. At the recommendation of one of my advisors, the textual data was entered into a Filemaker Pro database, integrating each set of field notes, chat logs, and transcripts into a single record by locale and date.

Visual anthropology turned out to be an effective method to capture some of this lived practice of gameplay. Over the eighteen-month period of the field study, I took approximately 4,000 screenshots of players and player-created artifacts, as well as a small sampling of short video clips. (While video data is useful in some contexts, because of the sheer number of hours involved and the massive storage required for video capture, it was not feasible to record all field visits using video.) I studied and documented *There.com*'s in-world auction site to survey player-created items based on or influenced by *Uru*. After trying several screen capture solutions, including the incredibly cumbersome on-board Windows screen shoot application, and the free and reliable Gadwin Print Screen, I finally settled on Fraps, a low-cost application specifically designed for capturing game images and video. Fraps included the particularly useful feature of automatically labeling all screenshots with the game, date, and time the image was taken, thus ensuring a much higher level of accuracy in terms of data sorting. With over 4,000 images, this improved accuracy and consistency, and made it much easier to cross-reference images to the field notes and chat logs.

I had initially hoped to integrate the screenshots into this Filemaker Pro database, but the software was not well suited for cataloging images, and the process was too labor-intensive given the quantity of images collected. In the future, I would like to find a better means for integrating textual data and visual records; this would probably have to entail writing a piece of software that can automate the image cataloging process. However, since all of the images were labeled by game, date, and time, it was not difficult to review images in sync with a review of textual data in the database.

In addition to in-game observation, I made regular reviews of the group's forum, which served as an historical archive (including documentation of the *Uru* closure), as well a current discussion of topics and issues of concern to players, announcements of upcoming events in the various worlds the group inhabited, and the plans for and artifacts of real-world encounters between players. The forum also included some basic real-world demographics, which were useful in sketching out a fairly accurate profile of data points such as gender, age, and geographical location. As suggested by Mills and others, I also kept a journal where I noted my personal impressions and experiences, which created the basis for book IV.

In anthropological fieldwork, it is common to secure native assistance, often in the form of a paid translator or research assistant, but also via key informants who may serve as "insiders" to help decode the culture. One of my informants with a strong interest in the group's history and progress volunteered to assist me with data collection. She was more familiar than I with the history of the group, and so was able to point me to specific pages on the group's forum where significant historical events were recorded. She also assisted in some additional demographic research, especially vis-à-vis tracking fluctuations in group size. She also created a timeline, which helped lay out the various shifts in the group's development. This informant also assisted me in editing chat logs from group discussions and took me on a tour of all of the different locales the group had tried to settle in before they finally settled on Yeesha Island. She and other players also provided some of the archival images included throughout this text. (These are typically credited using avatar pseudonyms.)

While it seems that different games researchers favor different data collection methods, I would argue that a mixed methods approach capturing multiple and diverse levels of detail and points of view provides us with more dimensions of information to work with. The ease of data collection in digital contexts, however, introduces a new challenge by generating even more data than is generated by real-world ethnography. As Huberman and Miles point out, "the 'quality' of qualitative research aside, the quantity can be daunting, if not overwhelming" (1994). As Wolcott puts it, "The major problem we face in qualitative inquiry is not to get data, but to get rid of it!" (1990, 18). This is even more the case with online research. As can already be seen, the data collection can become quite unwieldy. The upside is that having one's notes digitally typed, having numerous images that are prelabeled with context and date, and having all this material in digital form makes it much easier to organize, manage, and maintain quality data than more traditional methods involving handwritten notes, note cards, or analog photographs. Nonetheless, sometimes data loss can occur because of technical problems or lack of aptitude with the technologies being used.

Analysis and Interpretation: The Search for Patterns

Various search methods were used to analyze data for patterns of emergence. As each textual entry included the names of participants in that event, it was possible to sort by informant and thus study interviews and interactions with individuals. The database also allowed for word searches, so I could sort for particular references, narratives, or themes. I also added a database field that specified the type of event, such as game, party, interview, or informal conversation. It should be noted that as voice came into use in the worlds I was studying, both through in-game voice technology and through supplemental use of voice-over-IP programs, the combination of transcripts and text chats became more involved and often challenging to analyze. I ultimately found I had to print out much of the chat log data because this made it easier to compare conversations and observations over the long term.

In describing qualitative research methods, sociologists Huberman and Miles suggest a highly formal sequence to data collection and analysis, including such steps as noting patterns and themes; seeing plausibility—making initial, intuitive sense; clustering by conceptual grouping; making metaphors; counting; making contrasts and comparisons; differentiation; shuttling back and forth between particulars and the general; factoring; noting relations between variables; and making conceptual or theoretical coherence (1994). Geertz, perhaps in a tradition more typical of anthropologists, writes of the three operations of observing, recording, and analyzing that "distinguishing these three phases of knowledge-seeking may not, as a matter of fact, normally be possible; and, indeed, as autonomous 'operations' they may not in fact exist" (1973, 20).

I would concur that an orderly sequence of data collection followed by analysis is not plausible in practice. Analysis was well under way during the data collection process, as many patterns of emergent behavior became evident almost immediately. Furthermore, as the subjects themselves began to collect data and conduct analysis during the data collection process, the data collection and analysis emerged as an iterative process rather than a linear sequence of events. Analysis also forms an iterative and synergistic feedback loop with fieldwork. As patterns emerge, one might wish to augment data to corroborate findings or test newly forming hypotheses.

One useful technique was the visiting and revisiting of various data points. The same questions were asked and re-asked over the duration of the study. While some players found this annoying, it was an important tool to verify long-term patterns, and also to look at changes over time, a key quality of emergence. Furthermore, because I was interested in patterns of large-scale group behavior, it was important to ask similar questions of many different players. For instance, questions such as "What keeps the group together?" were commonly asked of numerous study subjects. Somewhat surprisingly, the answers were so consistent that a recognizable pattern could clearly be identified very early on in the fieldwork. These data were revisited and interrogated after the basic fieldwork was complete to again reaffirm that these patterns did, indeed, exist and continued to persist over a sustained time period.

As mentioned earlier, Laurel Richardson proposes using multiple methods to achieve what she calls "crystallization," a postmodernist deconstruction of the scientific notion of "triangulation":

In traditionally staged research, we valorize "triangulation." In triangulation, a researcher deploys "different methods"—such as interviews, census data, and documents—to "validate" findings. The methods, however, carry the same domain assumptions, including the assumption that there is a "fixed point" or "object" that can be triangulated. But in postmodernist mixed-genre texts, we do not triangulate, we crystallize. We recognize that there are far more than "three sides" from which to approach the world.

I propose that the central imaginary for "validity" for postmodernist texts is not the triangle—a rigid, fixed, two-dimensional object. Rather, the central imaginary is the crystal, which combines symmetry and substance with an infinite variety of shapes, substances, transmutations, multidimensionalities, and angles of approach. Crystals grow, change, alter, but are not amorphous. Crystals are prisms that reflect externalities and refract within themselves, creating different colors, patterns, and arrays, casting off in different directions. What we see depends on our angle of repose . . . In postmodernist mixed-genre texts, we have moved from plane geometry to light theory, where light can be both waves and particles. (1994, 934)

She also adds, "Paradoxically, we know more and doubt what we know. Ingeniously, we know there is always more to know" (934). Similarly, Geertz points out that it is "not necessary to know everything in order to understand something" (1973, 20).

Crystallization is an apt metaphor when trying to understand emergence in complex systems. It provides a deeper level of insight, one that acknowledges and embraces the disparate scales and subjectivities with which cybercultures are constructed by players through emergent intersubjective processes. It allows for variegated and various subjective viewpoints and intersubjective processes to be collected into a composite bricolage that creates a single, coherent image of the life of a community. To mix metaphors, crystallization provides us with a viable means of studying the forest and the trees concurrently.

Writing Ethnography

The process of representing the study outcomes was critically important, and a great deal of consideration was given to the format of the written thesis. As Clifford and Marcus point out, the writing process is as much a construction of the author as of the subjects, and I was engaged in a reflexive process throughout that constantly bore this in mind (1986). Writing is also itself a part of the interpretive process, a "method of inquiry," and as one writes, one crystallizes as a way to integrate data together into a coherent picture of the whole (Richardson 1994). Thus, many of the core conclusions of the study emerged through the writing process itself.

Following Willis (2000) and as recommended by both Wolcott (1990) and Clifford and Marcus (1986), the narrative of events is kept separate from the analysis. Thus, chapter 4 in book II describes the events that took place in a narrative format, after the fashion of an anthropological monograph. Chapter 6 provides description and analysis of various patterns observed in the course of the study, including attempts to draw a correlation between specific game design features and various types of emergent behavior. Most of the conclusions enumerated in this chapter were arrived at through and during the writing process. The method of writing as an active means of thinking through ideas is one I have found consistently effective and was further developed in the course of this research.

The narrative approach taken in book II is very consciously intended to demystify game culture by putting a human face on the avatar, so to speak. The writing approach combines principles of "thick description" (Geertz 1973) and empathy, and works with Behar's notion of "anthropology that breaks your heart" (1996), combined with "polyphonic texts" (Fisher 1990, Helmreich 1998), which are also promoted by Huberman and Miles (1994). In particular, by using direct quotes from conversations and players' own writings and poetry, I tried to bring out the essence of their multifaceted subjective experience, through the painful process of becoming refugees and searching for a new homeland to their subsequent process of "transculturation" (Ortiz 1947). The process of ethnographic writing is often very much a matter of putting the reader in another's shoes, again, employing the "sociological imagination" (Mills 1959), or, as Willis puts it, the "ethnographic imagination" (2000). These descriptive and narrative techniques were employed with the aim of evoking as much immediacy for the reader as possible.

The use of both direct quotes and annotations by subjects emphasizes this work as a collaborative effort. Here I invoke Visweswaran's discussion of the question of "my work" versus "our work," a common consideration in some of the feminist and experimental ethnographies described in chapter 4 (1994, 27). This is a tricky balancing act. On the one hand, the Uru Diaspora's highly refined—one might say, artistic—practice of constructing culture is very much *their work*. On the other hand, my interpretation certainly bears my own signature, in terms of skills and perspectives. In fact, another ethnographer might approach these issues in a very different manner. But in the end I felt it was my imperative to acknowledge their authority and their ability to reflect on their own experience of part of a reflexive ethnographic praxis.

Clifford and Marcus point out, "Once 'informants' begin to be considered as co-authors, and the ethnographer as a scribe and archivist as well as interpreting observer, we can ask new, critical questions about all ethnographies" (1986). I chose to consider the subjects of this story as the ultimate authorities on their own experience. Thus my roles as "scribe" and "archivist" and folklorist as well as "interpreting observer" were clear and distinct, and labeled appropriately. I chose to position myself as a steward of their story rather than an authority. This might reflect the approaches of some of the women cited by Visweswaran, perhaps a blend of Margaret Mead and Zora Neale Hurston in cyberspace.

There are of course risks with repositioning authority. Cushman and Marcus argue that experiments with dispersed authority risk "giving up the game" (1982, 44), but Visweswaran argues further that acknowledging native authority *is* giving up the game (1994, 32). The position of "playing ethnography" provides the leeway to give up the game in myriad ways. Visweswaran's notion of "our subjects writing back" (9) was a strong strategy identified and adopted for use in the participant blog, giving the subjects the opportunity to corroborate or refute my findings. In typical anthropological writings, direct feedback on ethnographic texts is not typically included or recommended. This can be because of linguistic or literacy barriers, the fact that in some cultures self-reflection is not part of the repertoire, or the risk that authors might censor their findings to please their subjects. If utilized, methods for collecting feedback ought to be carefully considered and conducted in a form that is consistent with the primary modes of discourse of the group being studied, although some experimentation may be desirable. Willis, for instance, in studying working-class schoolboys in the UK, used verbal communication and poetry to solicit feedback and reflection from his subjects (1981, 2000).

In the case of the Uru Diaspora, a group that was at home, so to speak, with forums and other forms of online communication, this method was indigenous to their regular modes of discourse and therefore appropriate for collecting their feedback on the findings. This approach brings with it the risk of self-censorship, but I was careful to separate the participants' comments from my own, and made no substantive change to the core text as a result of their feedback. Their comments are uncensored, except where they concerned errata, which were subsequently amended in the text.

The Ethnographic Memoir

There is a long-standing tradition of ethnographic memoirs dating back to Malinowski. These make transparent the ruptures and the struggles of ethnographers with subjectivity and cultural biases. Since these revelations are often viewed as subjective and therefore unscientific, they tend to be set aside in separate documents and not integrated within the main body of the ethnographic text. Malinowski's autobiographical *A Diary in the Strict Sense of the Term* reflects on his experiences and conflicts about the literary merits of ethnographic texts (1967). As an ardent reader of mystery novels, Malinowsi wonders at the propriety of using literary techniques to draw the reader into ethnographic texts. In *Stranger and Friend: The Way of the Anthropologist*, Hortense Powdermaker gives a behind-the-scenes account of her work in the field (1966). Both Malinowksi and Powdermaker's accounts are examples of texts that reveal the messy side of ethnography, and while in some sense less formal and less academic, they at the same time provide a much more specific and situated description of how ethnography is really done than their sanitized counterparts. In one account, Powdermaker confesses that, for the first time in her career, she actively disliked the subjects of a particular study (1966, 225). In another, she talks about the delicate negotiations around racism required to conduct a study in the segregated South of the 1950s. She notes, for instance, the problematics of the social taboo of a white woman seen alone with a black male study subject (159). While both parties found such social taboos abhorrent, disregarding them would not only have jeopardized the research but put the research subject in peril. Public deportment was also an issue. She addressed her African-American subjects using their last names, preceded by a Mr., Mrs., or Miss, a practice that was considered taboo among local the whites. She made a point of doing this in front of the white townsfolk in order to reassure the African-Americans that her respect for them was authentic (151). While these measures were both sincere and important to building trust and rapport with the African-American community, they also had the effect of alienating the whites, who were also part of her study.

Forming an attachment to study subjects is also a common theme of these anthropological confessions, and a common conflict that arises in traditional cultures is whether or not to intervene in crises. Powdermaker describes a particularly emotional dilemma of wanting to intervene in the health crisis of a native woman she had befriended (1966, 116). These are some of the classic challenges faced by real-world ethnographers in negotiating powerful emotional and ethical dilemmas that may pull the researcher in conflicting directions.

Margery Wolf's *Thrice Told Tale* (1992) is particularly intriguing in this regard. A *Rashomon*-style narrative, it provides three *different* accounts of the same events, all from the *ethnographer's own* point of view: the original academic paper; the raw field notes, many of which were taken by her native assistant; and a short semifictional account of the experience. The central narrative concerns the diagnosis of whether a local woman is insane or channeling a spirit, a determination that is made by primarily female elders of the village. This tripartite structure exposes Wolf's own multiple voices: the authoritative voice of the ethnographic text in the form of the "scientific" paper, which gives the official reading of events; the voice of the raw, uninterpreted notes of Wolf and her assistant, who is torn between her native culture and the scientific research process; and the short story, which provides the reader with a fictionalized, open-ended interpretation, suggesting that there is a more supernatural dimension to the narrative than Wolf's "scientific" voice permits. Wolf's multifaceted approach draws to our attention to the fact that all ethnographers are, in and of themselves, polyphonic: they capture the voices and practices of many people, with many different points of view, including the many voices within themselves.

Finally, Julian Dibbell's famous article "A Rape in Cyberspace" (1993) and his subsequent "cyber memoir" of a year spent in *LambdaMOO* (1998) provide us with one of the most rigorous and complete pictures we have to date of the culture of a single multiplayer world. While not an academic monograph per se, Dibbell's masterpiece of gonzo journalism was groundbreaking in its immersiveness, its specificity, and its daring, confessional tone. Dibbell's status as a journalist liberates him from the restrictions placed on anthropologists, enabling him to be unabashedly subjective. He speaks openly of the emotional attachments he forms with other players, his own creative pursuits, his attempt to foment a new economic system, and even his dalliance in cross-gender play. He also reveals some of the challenges that emerge from the uncertain status of the virtual world versus the real world, such as whether or not online sex counts as sex. Dibbell's accounts of *LambdaMOO* have become part of the canon of MMOG research and provide valuable insights into the depth of the experience of partaking in and contributing to the emergence of online cultures.

Book IV: "The Social Construction of the Ethnographer" thus serves as an unapologetically personal account of my own subjective experience, including descriptions of troubling and painful moments, missteps, and stumbles, and the ways in which personal lives, both mine and those of the subjects, came to bear on the research. In the process, it also joins these other works in illuminating the particulars of the craft of ethnography itself, the challenges and nuances inherent in being a person studying persons, a product of culture studying cultures.

The heart of book IV can be found in its title, "The Social Construction of the Ethnographer," a process whereby my own identity and research methods were shaped and transformed by the group itself. Precipitated by a crisis about midway through the field study, I was forced to shift my methodology to a more participatory, less passive approach. One of the key critiques conveyed to me by players was that my approach was too passive. Given this feedback, I subsequently modified my technique in an approach I describe as "participant engagement," which enabled me to become more engaged with the group while still maintaining some measure of analytical objectivity. It soon became apparent, through this and other circumstances beyond my control, that I myself was also engaged in and subject to the very emergent processes I had set out to study.

Intellectually, I knew that this should occur, but I think I was surprised by how it played out. Being engaged at this level required a measure of reflexivity, and to a certain extent, the ability to observe myself in the same way I was observing my subjects: both as an individual contributor to emergence, and within the context of a larger complex system.

Leonardo da Vinci is purported to have quipped that, "Art is never finished, only abandoned." Likewise, Margery Wolf also points out that ethnography always remains unfinished (1992). The ethnographer leaves the field site, but the research never ends. This is particularly true in the case of cyberethnography. In traditional ethnographic field research, leaving the field can often be a traumatic experience for all parties concerned. Powdermaker describes an emotional scene at her departure from the Malaysian village of Lesu in which her subjects wept, begged her to stay, and even went so far as to suggest a marriage arrangement for her (1966, 121–122).

Because cyberethnography field sites are not geographical, this creates a different kind of dilemma. One can actually stay "physically" at the field site for as long as it exists. When the study ended, there was a mutual assumption that I would leave *There .com* and *Uru*, but it soon became apparent that this would not be necessary. As part of my participant engagement method, I ultimately set up a "field station" within the *Uru* community. This gesture established me as a part of the community, and also serves as a headquarters for ongoing research.

This persistent presence in a field site, not quite the anthropological equivalent of "going native," creates both new challenges and opportunities. How does one "finish" an ethnography that is ongoing? Even as this book was being written the *Uru* drama continued with the closure of the second iteration of *Uru, Myst Online: Uru Live*. A new flood of "third wave" *Uru* immigrants have arrived on the shores of *There.com* at the very moment I am trying to put this book to bed.

Thus, like Leonardo's work of art and Wolf's ethnography, this work of art and ethnography shall also have to be abandoned, left with an open and unresolved ending.

| IV |
THE SOCIAL CONSTRUCTION OF THE ETHNOGRAPHER

BEING ARTEMESIA: MY LIFE AS AN AVATAR

Book IV is written in the style of an ethnographic memoir and consists of journal entries taken while the research was under way and personal narratives of events that happened throughout the process. It chronicles many of the same events and insights as books II and III, but from a different perspective. This is a subjective account of events, in the tradition of "behind-the-scenes" anthropological accounts such as Elenore Smith Bowen's *Return to Laughter* (1964), Hortense Powdermaker's *Stranger and Friend* (1966), Ruth Behar's *Translated Woman* (1993), and Julian Dibbell's journalistic memoir of LambdaMOO, *My Tiny Life* (1998).

I, Avatar

Some people think that inhabiting an online world is a way of escaping from yourself; others think it is a way of escaping from others. This is not the case; not in my case, and certainly not in the cases of those I study. Being an avatar means exploring the self as much as it means exploring others; more specifically, it means exploring the self *through* others. The other becomes the medium for exploration of the self. The context of networked play creates a very intense level of intimacy that is not greater or less than intimacy in the real world, just different. Play and imagination open up avenues for connections that we might not have access to otherwise. And these connections are often a surprise. You never know what will happen to you once you become an avatar.

There is a certain audacity in this process of embracing dual roles, an element of the grand experiment. Within the overall experiment, each individual's experience is unique. A player once told me that at first he felt himself occupying a different role than his avatar, but that over time, his avatar became more like him, and he became more like his avatar. To quote one of my Uru study participants, making a twist on a Marshall McLuhan adage (1964), "We create our avatars, and our avatars create us."

What does it mean to be mediated, to extend your self into another form, to create and express yourself by means of a social prosthesis? To be mediated is to be transformed. Avatar play is not only transformative, but also uniquely social.

When I, Artemesia, was born, on March 14, 2004, ten days before the birth of *The Gathering of Uru* in *There.com*, I was the sole creation of my creator, Celia Pearce. But now, I have transformed into something else. As the group's ethnographer, I have been socially constructed by The Gathering of Uru. As the avatar has been socially constructed, so has the person. So the question becomes, did she make me or did *they* make me? And to what extent have *I* made her? Being me has changed her in ways she never anticipated. She made me to study others like me, and now she has become one of them, one of us. At the same time, I have also served as an instrument for the social construction of Dr. Celia Pearce, PhD, for her transition into her new performative role.

One thing I have learned, *we* have learned, is that you can find out *nothing* about life on the screen unless you *go into the screen*. You have to *be* an avatar to study and understand avatars.

Objectivity is often reified in research and science, but can you really learn about anything from studying it objectively? Can we not learn more from studying multiple subjectivities, including our own? There is no way to study an avatar's behavior without placing yourself into that online space: without *being* one. Once you become an avatar, you are on a level playing field and anything can happen. Emotions creep in. Friendships form. No one is immune to the avatar's spell.

As Artemesia, I exist in several forms. In *There.com* (my home), I am a graduate research student with a copper bob. Like my brother and sister avatars in *There.com*, I have physical attributes inspired by the prevalence of Disney cartoons and the pervasive Barbie doll aesthetic, though with smaller than average (for Barbie) breasts. In *Second Life*, I present as a pirate with ruddy dreadlocks who lives on a galleon nestled in a cove. In *Lineage*, *EverQuest* and *Guild Wars*, and *World of Warcraft*, I am alternately a mage, necromancer, or warlockwith a fair complexion and titian hair. Here, my identity is constructed largely of statistical powers encoded into the software: I rely on spells and my wits to conquer monsters and protect myself from harm.

When I log off of these worlds—when I untransform, or retransform, from Artemesia to Celia—Artemesia pops off the screen. The screen image of the various "mes" dissolves like a bubble, but Artemesia still exists inside Celia: she is still part of the complex of mes that is both Celia and Artemesia. Each of the "shes" is a ghost that haunts the rest of the complex me, and each haunts the others' domains. The real world Celias haunt the virtual Artemesias, and vice versa. Even when Artemesia rests, when *all* of her selves are at rest, asleep somewhere in the memory of a hard drive, the essence of Artemesia still lingers somewhere, nowhere, but present in memory and impression, dormant, asleep, in a dream state. Perhaps my life as Artemesia is contained within Celia's dream, or vice versa.

Even so, I, as Artemesia, am also present to others when I am not in-world. I am in their memories, remembered, referred to, imagined; thus, in some sense, I remain "real," even when I am not present, for those who have seen and played with me online. It is like what my friend and colleague Katherine Hyatt-Milton calls "cognitive haunting" (2005), thoughts that percolate in the back of your mind and return at unexpected times. My cognitive haunting is the lingering sense of the alternative persona, which wafts in and out like a ghost. We who inhabit avatars all know each other in this way. We can hold multiple identities both within ourselves and in our conceptions of each other.

I am as far away as I ever was from knowing what this all means. But I can say that it is much richer and deeper than most people even suspect that a deep role-play experience can be. These words are the voice of the avatar of my avatar, the extension of the extension. I can do my best to explain, but you can never really know until you do it yourself.

Finding Uru

On one of the first days I spent exploring the terrain of *There.com* in March 2004, I came upon a Moroccan-style pavilion on a sandy beach. There was a fountain in the center, and off to the side were four people playing spades. By their nametags, I could see their names were Ember, Daisy, Teddy, and Clousseau. This was in the days before the voice feature was added, so communication took place via text that ascended from our heads in pastel-colored cartoon bubbles. These people were very nice, friendly, funny, fun-loving, and open. They were horsing around a lot, and at one point, Clousseau got up on the spades table and started dancing. They were among the first people in *There.com* who I put on my Buddy List.

Around that time, I was trying to identify the type of emergent behavior that I wanted to study for my PhD project. One early candidate was *The Sims Online* (TSO) mafia, a thriving emergent subculture (Ludlow 2004). When I logged into TSO's Alphaville to investigate, I found many forensic signs of mafia culture: pizza joints and casinos and mansions with names like Gambino and Soprano. Yet, like much of TSO at this point, the mafia areas were largely abandoned.

Where had everybody gone? And why? In *There.com*, I tracked down a thriving community of about 800 self-titled "Sims Online Refugees." I noticed that its founder, Zach, used a picture of his TSO avatar in the real-life section of his profile, and that he had tried to approximate the appearance of his character from TSO in creating his *There.com* avatar, a practice which others in the TSO Refugee community also adopted. Zach invited me to his group's weekly meeting, which focused on discussions of their different experiences in online games and virtual worlds. I told them I was doing research on intergame immigration, and when I asked them why they left TSO, one said, "because I was tired of greening"—the activities such as eating, resting, socializing, washing, and using the bathroom that keep your health and happiness bars in the green (positive) rather than in the red (negative). Others complained that the mundane jobs required to make money, such as phone solicitation or food service, were too much work. Another player said that he had found in *There.com* everything he had hoped for but *not* found in TSO; namely, a social environment. In the course of the discussion, one of the players said something which at the time seemed like an offhand comment, but which was to set the course of my research and my life in multiple ways. "If you think *we're* interesting, you should talk to the *Uru* people."

I had heard of *Uru*, had heard its designer Rand Miller give a presentation on the game at a conference. I had even managed to get an invitation to the beta test, but had never ended up playing. Zach gave me the names of some of the *Uru* people. Among them were the four people I had met playing spades in the Moroccan pavilion.

Thus began my adventure with the Uru Diaspora.

Early Encounters with the Uru Diaspora in There.com (April–May 2004)

Journal Entry, April 2004

One of the first contacts I have made is with Lynn, the deputy mayor of The Gathering of Uru in *There.com*. She and others tell me about the history of the group, how they were formed in *Uru*, which then closed, how they decided they wanted to stay together, and so the bulk immigrated into *There.com*. One of the group members is building a replica of *Uru* in Adobe Atmosphere, and the group is hoping that once that is done, they can leave *There.com* and make the "Atmosphere Hood" their primary home.

In one conversation, Uruvians tell me they had to repeatedly move before settling at their current locale. They were concerned that each move would harm the group's cohesion, but it seems like just the opposite is happening. Each move seems to make them progressively more determined both to stay together and to stay in *There.com*, at least until another more permanent option can be found.

Meanwhile, they have set up their own Island, run by Leesa, the group's mayor and founder. Her house is located at one tip of the Island; at the other is The Gathering of

Uru Community Center. I now realize that that early encounter I had with Uruvians took place at the community center when it was at a different location. Adjacent to the Community Center is the library, run by Nature_Girl. Here I find links to a number of web pages and videos showing the last days of Uru. There is much documentation of the last night, including photos of avatars holding hands, the final screen saying "There seems to be a problem with your connection," and an image of Leesa saying "I love you." It's quite amazing that there is so much documentation. I've heard a handful of versions of this story thus far, and I expect I shall hear many more. I get a chill each time I hear it. It is obvious from the documentation and my conversations that this was a very traumatic experience and the emotions are still quite raw.

Black Friday

On May 21, *There.com* announced that it was redirecting its focus and although public servers would stay open, the software would no longer be marketed or updated as an active product line. In the preceding months, a number of people had already left because of a growing perception that *There.com* was a "sinking ship."

This announcement was a pivotal moment in the life of *There.com*. But, as a result of their prior experiences with the closure of *Uru*, it had even more profound implications to the survival of the Uruvian refugees it hosted. On the one hand, *There.com* needed subscribers more than ever; on the other hand, this type of announcement tends to lead in a drop-off in subscriptions. It seems that there is a feedback loop in which the more people who are present in the game, the more people will enter and stay; conversely, if the population begins to wane, people will tend to log on less and stay for shorter periods. As one player told me, "When I log on, if I don't see any of my friends logged on, then I leave." This illustrates the way feedback operates in groups; people tend to follow trends.

Following this announcement, responding to what was described in forums as the "sky is falling" perspective, a number of players left the game. Another faction, including TGU, took a more counterintuitive tack, which was to *stay*. They recognized that staying, and even recruiting new players, would actually *help* the situation. By leaving they would only be aiding and abetting in *There.com*'s demise, and "the end of the world" would become a self-fulfilling philosophy. Aware of the power of emergence to help or harm, these players recognized that they had a certain amount of influence, that by staying en masse, they could potentially avert yet another disaster.

The *Uru* people of course had been through this already. Some left at this point, disgruntled and angry about once again being at the mercy of the bottom line of a heartless corporation. But a significant number were quite passionate about avoiding a repeat of the Ubisoft/Cyan scenario, and it was through their efforts together with a number of other long-term members (including beta-testers) that *There.com* ultimately survived the summer.

It seems that in all these worlds there is an ongoing tension between corporate governance and players' insistence on self-determination. This very much parallels the situation in *LambdaMOO* in the late 1990s, and it seems to be a recurring pattern. The more reflexive and sophisticated players appear to have an understanding of their power as a group; they realize that they can talk with their feet (in other words, with their money) and that sometimes talking with your feet means staying rather than going. This is yet another example of the feedback mechanism in emergence: people tend to follow what their friends and communities do. When players begin to understand this dynamic they can manipulate the system by making choices that might lead to emergent outcomes on a larger scale. In this case, rather than abandon what appeared to be a sinking ship, players opted to stay on board and bail the encroaching water. The success of this strategy also served to embolden them further as they began to realize that they were not as disempowered as they had initially felt.

I find it interesting how at odds corporate priorities are with the core objectives of an online community. Although companies claim that they are all about the community, in the end, if they cannot maintain the bottom line or add value for their investors, all these utopian ideals go right out the window. In the end, *There.com*, and *Uru* for that matter, are really only businesses, aren't they?

There.com did indeed last the summer and the TGU group continued going strong. In subsequent months, and no doubt because of their role in supporting *There.com*, the TGU family also began to embrace members who were not former *Uru* players. These were players who liked the group ethos, and, I would imagine, respected their determination to try and counter the trend and keep *There.com* open. It also became apparent to these members that Uruvians meant business and cared very deeply about community, a quality that was appreciated by some (although not all) members of the larger *There.com* populace.

Leesa and Revelation's Wedding

Journal Entry, logged in from Haslemere, Surrey, UK
Today was a special day for the TGU group: Leesa and her in-world boyfriend Revelation got married, staging an elaborate in-world wedding. I have been to many weddings of all kinds, and was amazed by how much it felt like being at a "real" wedding.

It was also clear that a great deal of preparation had been made not only by the bride and groom but by their friends as well, so it really had the feel of a major event.

And no wonder: while this was not the first *There.com* wedding that involved group members, it was certainly the most significant. The chapel where the ceremony took place was completely packed. For the TGU community, this was more than just an in-game wedding: it was a royal wedding. Leesa is, for all intents and purposes, the Queen of TGU. In fact, it was pretty much de rigueur for everyone in the community, including me, to attend.

I had asked Leesa in advance if I could take pictures for my research, and she asked if I wanted to be the official wedding photographer. This posed a couple of challenges. One was a technical issue with the server architecture of *There.com*: as more avatars entered the chapel, they began to degrade into "blockheads," low-polygon models that replace avatars in high-traffic areas, so called because of their cube-shaped heads. Naturally, this became a topic of discussion. As I often say, lag and related technical problems have become the "weather" of cyberspace. So it was as if it was raining, I suppose, in avie terms. And just as would be the case had it rained during a real-life wedding, it impaired the experience somewhat, although I think the basic emotional content remained unchanged. In addition, because of my lack of familiarity with Windows, I had trouble with the screen capture function, which required me to paste each individual image into a document, so in the end, I lost many of the images, but I was able to post some online for the attendees to see.

The ceremony itself took no more than half an hour. As deputy mayor of TGU, Lynn was the obvious person to officiate. The vows were not unlike typical contemporary self-authored wedding vows; however, based on the fact that *There.com* was mentioned numerous times, coupled with the knowledge that the bride and groom had not met in real life, it seemed very clear that the commitment they were making was, at least for now, contained within the game. My limited experience suggests that some players prefer keep their in-game romantic commitments strictly online. Zaire, one of the *Sims Online* refugees I met in *There.com*, told me she divorced three in-game husbands because they wanted to meet her in real life. It will be interesting to see what happens with Leesa and Revelation.*

The significance of the wedding for the community was clear from the way people were dressed. The men were wearing tuxedos, and the women wore glamorous outfits and formal attire. Some used the opportunity to change outfits frequently, presumably to gain "fashionista" points (credits players get for frequent clothing changes). I was surprised not to see anyone wearing a Yeesha costume. In fact, I rarely see anyone wearing a Yeesha in day-to-day interactions. Most Uruvians wear civilian street clothes while out and about in *There.com*.

The ritual was modeled after a typical Western wedding. The only Uru tradition observed was the placement of the Uru fountain at the center of the area where the reception was held. As soon as the ceremony was over, everyone went over to the reception and jumped into the fountain, a tradition carried over from Uru.

(*Leesa and Revelation did eventually meet and became real-life partners.)

Until Uru

Journal Entry: Uru Revisited

I learned last week that on August 9, a group of *Uru* hackers who had reverse-engineered the *Uru* servers made an arrangement with Cyan to set up a system of player-run *Uru* servers. Experienced players seemed unenthused about this because they also want new content, and this will just be the old version of *Uru* running on fan-owned servers. This has precipitated a debate among TGUers as to how this will impact the *Uru* community in *There.com*. There are also some shifts going on with the group; it appears that *Uru* refugees are spending more time hanging out with Thereians and less time in *Uru* areas. Correspondence this week on the forums indicated that Leesa was thinking of shutting down Yeesha Island. This was averted by Wingman who stepped in to contribute to the rent. A concerted effort is now under way to come up with new ideas for encouraging *Uru* refugees to spend more time there.

Fear of Uru

Journal Entry

I received my copy of *Uru* so I can play *Until Uru* on the player-run servers. I haven't touched it though. I am finding myself resistant to trying it. On the one hand, it scares me because I worry that it will draw all the *Uru* immigrants out of *There.com* and back into *Uru*. I guess this is what they really want, but at the same time, I think their new "hybrid" community in *There.com* is so much more interesting. It also concerns me because of the ramifications it may have for my research.

But there is another, more subtle anxiety at play: underneath it all, I've really enjoyed the fact that my only experience of *Uru* is vicarious, through players' stories, documentation, and fan culture. I've seen simulations of Uru and its artifacts, but I've never actually seen the original. To me *Uru* is sort of like the Land of Canaan, a fictionalized memory, Norman Klein's "social imaginary" (1997). I guess I am clinging to the picture of *Uru* that exists in my mind from the retelling. There is a part of me that feels it would be so much more poetic if I never actually experienced the *real Uru*. It's very irrational, but I know I have to get past it. It's absolutely critical to the research that I observe the study participants in their "native" context. And anyway, in the end, it is not up to me where this research goes. I have to follow their lead.

Entering Uru

Journal Entry

I am finally sitting down to play *Until Uru*. I've turned off all the lights in the room and surrounded my desk with lit candles. This is kind of a big deal. I'm actually a little embarrassed about all the ritual I'm going through. If my housemate walked in, she would think I was insane. I'm meeting a group in-world who is going to walk me through the first Age, which I gather is somewhat complicated.

Naturally, the first thing I have to do is create my avatar. Choices are somewhat limited, but I go for a look that approximates my look in *There.com*, I guess the inverse of what the Uruvians did when they immigrated to *There.com*. I look for a similar hairstyle, and go for a similar color palette, mostly teal tones.

The game actually starts in a desert, which I had seen in some of the web images from the Uru Library in *There.com*. I explore this area for a little while to get "journey cloths," which apparently Yeesha has left for us.

I descend via a ladder into the infamous "cleft," a crevice in the desert that is vaguely vaginal in form. I explore the cleft by crossing bridges, descending more ladders; the bridges sometimes break, dumping me unharmed into puddles at the bottom of the shallow cleft. All of this is, of course, planned, and I can use the broken bridges as ladders to climb up to different ledges. I have to solve some puzzles in order to get bits of narrative of the game, mostly conveyed (albeit obtusely) by a kind of hologram of Yeesha, who I recognize immediately by her costume, after which the "Yeesha" costume in *There.com* is modeled!

After taking a series of steps in the puzzle, such as turning a windmill, activating power, opening and closing doors to get access to other rooms and find hidden journey cloths, jumping, and climbing up ledges, I find my way into a tree trunk, within which I see a book on a pedestal. When I go to take it, I am teleported to a tiny island floating in a cloud bank. I recognize it from its elements as the Relto! The book I picked up must have been the Relto linking book, which I am now wearing on my belt.

Making my way to the TGU hood in *Uru* involves a complex procedure of transport using linking books and the Nexus, a giant machine that dispenses linking books.

I'm in the Hood! The first thing I see is the fountain similar to those in *There.com* and the Atmosphere Hood. Going upstairs. I can see the infamous Egg Room, with the floating "Egg Room egg." There is something surreal about seeing the originals after having spent months immersing myself in their facsimiles. It's as if I am remembering things I never actually experienced.

I feel like Alice in Wonderland. The whole *Uru* story is a narrative of simulations within simulations within simulations. Seeing the "real" simulation of *Uru* itself was amazing and disorienting, especially after seeing the "homage" versions in *There.com* and Atmosphere. I now recognize all the icons. I now understand the origins of much of the visual culture of the Uruvians. There is a shared meaning to these things; in the beginning I did not know what they meant—the eggs, the fountain, the books on pedestals. Now I am beginning to understand.

D'ni Island, Second Life

Journal Entry

Another trip down the rabbit hole as I enter into the *Second Life* instantiation of *Uru*. As I slowly come to understand what this culture is about, I am realizing how rich the *Uru* world and its progeny are with layers of meaning. Now, inside *Second Life*, my God! They have totally re-created the game! I think it would have been less amazing had I not seen the "real" Uru hood already, although it's pretty stunning even if you don't know what it is. But to see how close a replica this is, how true they stayed to the original. You can see that they went to great effort. They must have had to do drawings, maps, and floor plans. I mean it is EXACTLY the same, right down to the details. They have added the crates and traffic cones and other Uru ephemera. It's remarkable. They even made the Heek table.

I am taking a lot of pictures, but oddly, have not run into anyone. This is strange because I always find some Uruvians in *There.com*, whereas here, it is eerily empty. I feel like I am in the deserted ruin of D'ni Ae'gura . . .

Wow.

Uru Builders in Second Life

One terrific feature of *Second Life* is the ability to find out who created an object, an affordance that oddly does not exist in *There.com*. By checking who owned the land on D'ni Island, I was able to track down its creators and arranged an interview.

While there seem to be about 200 *Uru* refugees in *Second Life*, the builders themselves are a much smaller subset who have worked diligently to re-create *Uru* here.

Apparently they built the entire thing once, then tore it all down and started over. It's incredibly impressive. I've visited and interviewed them a couple of times. I was also able to tag along on a tour they gave to some Second Lifers who stumbled into it inadvertently. They seem to really enjoy taking people around, explaining what everything is, and talking about *Uru*. As with the TGUers, they've been extremely responsive to me and my research and eager to share their stories. I wish I could spend more time with them, but it's not feasible to follow both groups concurrently.

Uru Again

Although I will be meeting Lynn and company the next day, I decide to go into *Until Uru* on my own to feel my way around and also take some pictures. Having seen *Uru* in *Second Life* and the *Uru* artifacts in *There.com*, I want to get my head around the various artifacts players have been re-creating and making in other worlds.

Part of the mystery for me is finding the connections between what is here and what is in other instantiations of *Uru*. For instance, I see fireflies and mushrooms, elements I have also seen in the *Uru* areas in *There.com*. Now I begin to understand at least where they come from and what they mean. Everything in *Uru* seems to have a meaning. Some of those meanings are encoded in the game, others are a result of cultural practices created by the players themselves. I'm not sure if the fountain had a particular meaning until people began to play in it.

Why aren't semioticians aren't studying this?

I decide to jump into the fountain, just to see what it's like. After a couple of tries, I manage to get onto the very top. This is very interesting from a spatial storytelling perspective, because these spaces tease, they suggest certain things, but it is difficult to interpret. One feels like an archaeologist, which is of course is intentional. Without understanding the D'ni culture, it is hard to say what all these spaces are actually for; I know what some of them are because the Uruvians have told me. But still, it is often detective work. I think it is for them too. Everything has a meaning, but nothing is obvious.

Me and My Shadow: First Presentation (October 2005)

I gave my first public presentation in situ at a conference in New York. The decision to start giving presentations in-world was initially an accident: I thought I wasn't going to be able to make one of the London seminars, so I suggested it as a way to be able to participate. Both my supervisor and I agreed that this was a really great idea and should be integrated into the project somehow.

Since Artemesia's primary mode of communication is text, I decided to give the entire presentation in character via text. I toured Yeesha Island in *There.com* and discussed the migration from *Uru*. I showed a few examples of player-made *Uru* artifacts. Because it was hard for some people at the back of the room to read my text bubbles, I had Mary Flanagan, a member of the SMARTlab PhD cohort who happened to be there, stand out in the audience and read the text, basically serving as my "voice." I, Celia, said nothing. In fact I kept entirely silent throughout the presentation. At the end, I took some questions as myself, but during the Q&A, people started spontaneously directing their questions to Artemesia. When this happened, I felt I had, to some extent, succeeded.

In reality, I think the presentation had mixed success. One thing I realized immediately was how slow the pace of text communication is relative to speech. This is not as noticeable in-world, because of course you lose track of time and everyone else is communicating at the same pace, but when presenting in a real-world context, I was all too painfully aware that the whole enterprise seemed to be dragging on. It represented an abrupt change in pacing when juxtaposed against the conference itself, which may have been refreshing for some, but really annoying for others, although a number of people came up to me afterward and seemed to enjoy the experiment. I think one of the challenges of trying to do something this avant-garde in a conference context is that people are accustomed to certain conventions. I can probably get away with this in a situation where there are more artists, and where I am better known, such as my PhD program or the Banff Centre, but here most of the participants were lawyers and academics and a few game designers.

One thing I noticed right away was how nervous I was. Even though the avatar served as a kind of buffer, at the same time I was very self-conscious. I'm sure part of this was that I was doing a risky experiment in a context where I knew fewer people. But afterward, I also realized that performing an avatar is a strangely private experience. We seldom do this with anyone else proximal to our physical body, and even then, the other person is usually in-world as well. Doing it as a performance on a stage made me feel very exposed. I also think that introducing my avatar persona into a professional context may have also made me feel vulnerable, even though she is a "professional" avatar, so to speak. This is also one of these situations that you really can't rehearse; practicing the presentation on my own (which I did) prepared me in no way for getting up in front of several hundred people and laying my avatar bare for all to see.

The Crisis

In October 2004, about a third of the way into my *Uru* study, a journalist from a local newspaper called me and wanted to know if she could interview me about my online research. What she wanted to do was sit with me while I did my ethnography and watch how I worked. She came over to my house one evening and watched me while I conducted a field visit, interviewing me as we went. A few weeks later, the article was published on the front page of the paper (Chuang 2004). Because this was the first public unveiling of the work, I decided it would be a good idea to send a link to Leesa, just so she would be aware that the article was published. The following is a chronicle of what happened next.

I come into *There.com* one night and instant message (IM) both Leesa and Lynn as I often do upon arrival. Neither responds. As soon as I appear in a group, people start acting strange or in some cases leaving. I am not sure if this has directly to do with me, or if they are on their way to some other event. Social nuances can be very hard to read in an online world, but there is definitely what in California we would call a "vibe."

Then I receive an IM from Wingman, another member who I've gotten to be good friends with, saying "Jeeze, what did you WRITE about us?" I mention to him that I had been trying to get hold of Leesa and Lynn but had not had any success. He tells me that he is "avoiding a meeting," implying that's where they all are. Later, he invites me on a hoverboat ride with some other Uruvian-Thereians. When I arrive, one of them, Ember, jumps off the boat. The others on the boat are baffled and ask where she went. I IM her and she responds with an expletive, extremely out of character for her and indeed for anyone in TGU.

Then I receive an email from Raena via the Koalanet forum. I don't know her well, but had some discussions and interviews with her when I first started working with the *Uru* refugees in *There.com*. The email reads: "Are you all right? Do you need anything?" I have no idea what she is talking about. A day or two later, I get an IM from her in *Until Uru* saying "tristan is really a nice guy . . . he's not as bad as he sounds."

I finally connect with Raena in *Until Uru*. At first what she is saying makes no sense to me, but then, in the course of the conversation, it comes out that she is referring to a conversation going on in the Koalanet forum.

I immediately log on to the forum on my other machine to have a look, remaining logged in to *Until Uru*. A new thread has been created called "Artemesia, the Researcher." I had been checking in with the forums periodically but had not logged on since this thread was started. The first post is the interview from the newspaper.

Based on what people are saying, it seems the article had both been posted on the forum and read aloud in-world, probably on the day I was getting strange reactions from people.

Following the article is a firestorm of postings. The posts are flaming. They accuse me of "dumbing down" my research into sound bites for the journalist and distorting facts to support my own bias. One says if she were my PhD professor, she'd send me back to the drawing board. Another critique is that my "arm's-length" approach has given me little insight into TGU, let alone online gaming, and that "my" article showed my ignorance of my subject. They refer to the article as my "report."

Suddenly all the pieces are fitting together. On the day everyone was acting strangely, I had most likely logged on only moments after the article had been read. It is also apparent to me that many have somehow conflated the journalist's interpretation of my comments, indeed reduced to newspaper-worthy sound bites, with my own words. Although most of the article is fairly neutral, I can understand how some of her comments might seem offensive, such as "Online, characters do crazy things that they might not do offline, like establishing the Uru subculture" (Chuang 2004). Naturally, this is not a direct quote, nor is it even paraphrased from something I actually said.

One of the most scathing posts is a lengthy diatribe by Tristan, and I at once realized the meaning behind Raena's words. In it, he refers to the article as my "so-called report" and describes feeling "Like we were under the microscope." Although few posts are as strident as his, most are equally negative. Most devastating are posts from the people within TGU whom I know fairly well, especially group leaders with whom I have by this time developed a rapport. A small handful also chimes in to say they really didn't see what the big deal was (possibly because they recognized that it was not my actual report or my words). As I sit reading the posts, I feel like my life has come to an end. I realized that I have to find a way to amend the situation . . . not only to salvage my PhD work but, more importantly, because I genuinely care about the TGUers. In spite of their feeling that I had held them at arm's length, which I now believe was an accurate critique, I feel profoundly concerned and connected with them and their well-being on a variety of levels.

Still in *Until Uru* while reading this text, I immediately begin this process by making contact with Tristan, who happens to be in-world. He invites me to his Relto, where we sit, along with D'evon and Petrova, for a long talk about what happened. I explain to him that the article, by a journalist, is her interpretation of what she and I talked about, not my words, and certainly not my report. The outcome is positive. Tristan had been one of those TGU members who I did not know well before this event. Raena was right, however. He turns out to be a really nice guy. Because of what happened to his community, he is fiercely loyal and protective, and that is the root of his ire. As a result of this interchange, Tristan and I become and remain very good friends. I've also made a new friend along the way, Raena, who was very generous to stick her neck out and help me when most of her community was furious with me.

I realize now how vital it is to set things right with Leesa and Lynn. To that end, I send an email to Wingman telling him I want to somehow patch things up and asking if he could please help me out, having tried repeatedly and failed to get a response from Leesa or Lynn. It's clear that he really doesn't want to get involved, but he reluctantly agrees anyway and sets up a meeting with them for a few days later.

The day of the planned meeting, by an unfortunate coincidence, I have a horrible day at work, precipitated in part by the article, which apparently triggered some ire from my employers and coworkers. Whoever said "any publicity is good publicity" clearly had no idea what they were talking about. In this case, regardless of whether the publicity itself was good or bad, the outcome seemed to be an increasing pile of negatives.

I get home from work so beaten down that I end up missing the meeting with Leesa and Lynn. This only exacerbates the problem and now Wingman is furious with me and will no longer intervene on my behalf.

It has been a hard week. I have tried to connect with *Uru* people for the past couple of days, and after several failed attempts, was not able to. This afternoon, I notice Lynn is on, so I IM her. She is working on building something but agrees to come and talk with me. We talk for quite some time, maybe an hour or more. I am glad we get a chance to talk, because most of what she tells me was not at all what I expected. I am also keenly aware that I am experiencing firsthand the very process I have observed others undergo, with Lynn taking the role of conflict-resolver. Only this time, instead of watching the conflict from the outside, the conflict is me.

She starts by saying she isn't angry with me, and that I am free to say whatever I want about the community. I try to clarify that not all of what was in the article represented anything I said or would ever say.

But there are other issues as well. The first and perhaps most surprising issue is that Leesa is angry with me because I don't use voice. Lynn explains that a lot of TGU people cannot use a keyboard comfortably because of a disability—repetitive stress disorder, arthritis, or other conditions. I hadn't realized this was such an important issue, but having just talked to Wingman, who admonished me about it as well, I had gone off to a private place and tried to get my voice working prior to meeting with Lynn.

This shift in cultural conventions had slipped by me in part because of a technical problem. The study began before voice was introduced, and initially we communicated exclusively via text. Once voice was introduced, I had difficulty getting it to work on my computer. As a result, I was unable to hear others' voice chat, and since I hadn't *heard* anyone talking about it, I did not realize it had become so important to the group.

When Lynn mentions this, I say absolutely I have no trouble at all with that. She says it's okay to use text chat when doing interviews, but when I'm hanging around with the group, I should use voice.

The second surprise was that Leesa doesn't understand my research techniques. She has an educational background in anthropology and she feels I am "observing them from afar." This really surprised me because I had been making a great effort to be as unobtrusive as possible, but I guess she is looking for a deeper level of engagement. I suppose this is a question/challenge from the anthropological perspective that I need to investigate further, but since this is an experiment it may turn out that some variation of "going native" is exactly what is called for. The funny thing is that I feel drawn to the community in a personal way because their core values resonate with me.

Lynn also recommends that I post on Koalanet, maybe starting with a response to the current thread, and then initiating another. I had been reading Koalanet fairly regularly but had never posted, so apparently this was also considered a sign of my arm's-length approach to the group.

She says something else that is interesting: "You are always asking us questions, but we never get to ask you questions." This may have been what people meant by saying they felt "under the microscope." In some way I felt like I was supposed to let them do all the talking . . . but clearly the TGUers have a different idea.

The conversation with Lynn is hard but very helpful. Lynn is wonderfully candid and direct. She is really a fantastic person and the more I get to know her the more I appreciate her. She tells me she has a spinal condition and is in a wheelchair and that is why it is uncomfortable for her to type.

She tries to introduce me to some of the subtleties of etiquette issues around typing versus speaking. It's okay, she says, to do my interviews with text. No, I say, I can take notes. Then she takes me to visit Uno and sort of interviews him *for* me, switching to text to do so. Even though she prefers speech, she will type on some occasions. In Uno's case, she explains, he feels more comfortable with text, because he is both shy and not a native English speaker, so everyone accommodates his preference for typing.

First Koalanet Post (December 15, 2004)

I made my first post on the Koalanet forum. I wrote it and rewrote it several times. I tried to explain my position, to clarify that the article was not my "report" as some believed, but that it was by a journalist, and that the comments they found offensive were not my findings but her own interpretation. I also said that I welcomed criticism, and planned to modify my approach based on their feedback. As Lynn suggested, I then made a new thread in another section of the forum, to begin anew. This is where I will post future research information, including a link to the participant blog.

It was a hard post to write, but I hope that it will help move things in a positive direction. I realize that a number of the core methodological assumptions I made were just wrong. Trying to keep a low profile, trying to avoid having any impact on the group . . . well clearly it didn't work, and it resulted in my being viewed as an untrustworthy outsider. My desire to avoid collecting any personal information about participants' "real" lives, as well as my reluctance to share details about mine, is also problematic. Knowing that Lynn and others in the group are disabled is a very important data point in understanding the group dynamic. In some way perhaps it's presumptuous for me to have worried so much about my potential impact on them; it's very clear that their impact on me has been far greater.

From Participant Observation to Participant Engagement

As painful as the process was, my conversation with Lynn precipitated a complete reassessment and overhaul of my research approach. The group's biggest complaint was that I was "not a part of them." But as an ethnographer, was I supposed to be? Wasn't my role supposed to be detached, objective? I had been taking the traditional anthropological approach of being a passive observer, looking down from the metaphorical veranda. And this may have been easier or more effective with a different group. But the Uruvians are smart, challenging, and mature. In the same way that they took an active hand in transplanting their game culture to other worlds, they are also taking an active hand in my research. To a certain extent, I resisted the temptation to become more involved, but as a result of their own insistence, I began immediately finding opportunities to do so.

Not long after my conversation with Lynn, a series of events took place that marked a turning point and provided just such an opportunity for deeper engagement. One afternoon in *There.com*, I became privy to a series of discussions that gave me some real insight into TGU's decision-making process. Clousseau was telling Wingman and some others about an event he wanted to produce, and I was subsequently able to witness him pitching the idea to Leesa. She didn't say much, just listened. This was my first public appearance with voice, which everyone duly noted as significant, even though I really didn't say much. I was particularly interested in how the process transpired: coming up with the idea, vetting it with Leesa, and then actually bringing it to fruition.

Clousseau's aim was to do something that would help build community cohesion and bring more people to Yeesha Island, which had become seriously underutilized. His idea was to have a huge buggy convoy from one of the *Uru* spaces that Leesa had set up to Yeesha Island. They would drive en masse from one area to the other, arrive at Yeesha Island for some game-playing, and then conclude with a floor/talent show at the new nightclub that had been recently added at the end of the island. The whole premise of this was somewhat interesting because it follows on Suits's notion that a game is "the least efficient means to accomplish a task" (1978). Rather than teleport, which is the most conventional and efficient means of in-game travel, they instead chose to drive across the terrain between their two areas, not so much as a way to get people to the areas in question, but as a bonding activity. It was also made all the more challenging by repeated problems with lag that would be created by such an en masse venture.

Clousseau was quite enthusiastic about this idea, and Leesa didn't seem to have any major objections. Group cohesion was a high priority with some of the key group members, especially Leesa. Her shyness really came across in this interaction, as did her silent authority. I also got some insight into the dynamics between Leesa and Lynn. There could not be two more different personalities, yet they have a strangely effective synergy. Lynn seems to do most of the talking, as an intermediary and even in interviews, yet Leesa serves as the group's "thought leader." Her wisdom is highly respected by the group, and maybe the fact that she does little talking is part of that. As I learned from forum responses to the newspaper article, however, when Leesa has something to say, she says it loud and clear, and does not mince words.

Within a few days an invitation was issued. For this event, Wingman invented a new sport called Buggy Polo. Over the course of the week I was included in most of the planning process. As is often the case, they scheduled twin events for the European and U.S. crowds. Because it took place between Christmas and New Year's, the "Buggy Boogie," as Clousseau dubbed it, is something of a holiday celebration.

I attend both events, which are formatted exactly the same way—Clousseau has the entire thing scripted and timed to a tee. Everyone gathers at the group's frontier zone, a kind of tented pavilion on a mesa. Buggies are strewn about and everyone is encouraged to hop on one, even if it isn't theirs. (This is a common practice, avoiding the potential problem of people who do not own vehicles being left out.) At the European event, Clousseau invites me to ride with him at the front of the caravan, which I do for a while. But since we are in the front, I cannot see the rest of the group, which is behind us. (It's not possible to look behind you when in a buggy.)

To get a better view, I don my hoverpack so I can fly alongside the convoy and take pictures. I don't know very many of the people from the European contingent, although I get to meet some folks that I have heard a lot about from the European community, and to see some European players I have met in *Until Uru*. I play spades, which is also significant. I play very infrequently, but really get into it. My partner and I end up winning a round, something I had never accomplished before. Many Uruvian-Thereians play spades, a favorite pastime of Lynn in particular.

At the event for the U.S. contingent, I end up riding with someone I don't know, which is fun, especially because she is a pretty wild driver. She keeps crashing into everyone and flipping the buggy. One of the things I notice about the way the group plays is that the women are very aggressive and physical—not in a competitive way, but more in a risk-taking way, especially where vehicles are concerned. They like to roughhouse. Faced with the same problem as in the earlier convoy, I eventually get on my hoverpack to take some aerial shots, then fall behind, but manage to find my way back to the group.

In contrast to the European group, I know the majority of people at this event, many of whom I have interviewed. I am very aware that given all that has happened in previous weeks, it is important for me to demonstrate my new approach and show them that I am being responsive to their feedback. After a memorial flyover of Yeesha Island for Cola, who has just passed away, people begin to assemble on a field created for the Buggy Polo game.

One surprise that occurred en route to Yeesha Island was that Lynn had appeared in a giant, translucent orb, just big enough to envelop her entire avatar. Now it becomes apparent why: Lynn is "driving" the ball for the Buggy Polo game! We process over to the field, which has goals on either side, some trees around the perimeter, and a big scoreboard. Throughout the convoy as well as during the game, participants communicate via voice and text in a group chat window. This is to improve fidelity and also help in shepherding everyone to the various locales.

For the first part of the game, I ride shotgun with the woman with whom I rode over. This is my first step toward getting more involved. Typically I would have stood on the sidelines and taken pictures. After a while, I decide I do need to get some documentation, and it's a little difficult to see in the midst of the buggy melee that is the playing field. So I hop off the buggy and don my hoverpack. I flit about in the air and take a load of pictures of the proceedings. The field is total bedlam. You can hear from the voice chat that group members are having a huge amount of fun. They laugh and sing, tease each other, and do wordplay. One woman sings "am I blue" in response to being assigned to the blue team. Another is teasing a third about the fact that her buggy is "Pepto-Bismol colored," a quip that continues through the rest of the day.

I am flying around, taking pictures of the chaos below, listening to the chat box banter, when I notice that the orb-ball, now empty, has somehow managed to get itself lodged into the upper branches of one of the trees by the soccer field. It is one of those moments where a series of clues add up. First I notice the ball has landed in the tree. Then I notice that everyone is grouping below, looking up from their buggies, trying to figure out what to do. At that moment, I have a startling revelation: because I am on my hoverpack, I am in the *air*, so I could actually get the ball. Apparently everyone else had the same thought at the same time, because I suddenly hear (and see) people yelling, "Arte, get the ball! Get the ball!" At the same moment I am yelling, "Hey, I can get it; I'm on my hoverpack!" I keep flying toward it, bumping it and trying to knock it out of the tree, but I cannot get it to move. Then someone says, "Pick it up, Art." So I drag my cursor over to the little blue circle (the primary interface to objects in *There.com*), and click on it, and before I know what has happened, I am instantly sucked inside the ball.

At this point I stop taking pictures because I am too caught up in the moment (one of the hazards of playing and doing research at the same time), but I realize very quickly that the orb is drivable, so I use my arrow keys to roll it out of the tree back onto the playing field. With lots of shouting from the group, I find my way to the center of the field, position myself, take my hands off the arrow keys, and prepare myself for an all-out assault. It is in this way that I become the ball for the remainder of the Buggy Polo game.

At first I think, this is great, because now anyone who is still upset with me about the article can use this opportunity to work out their aggressions. But it seems that at this point we are well past that. So I spend the rest of the game inside the orb-ball being knocked around by Uruvians. It is great fun being right in the middle of the action for a change. Afterward, a whole group gathers around me and we excitedly discuss what transpired.

This is a turning point. I have finally gotten in on the action and *played* with them. This is the beginning of my shift from participant observation to participant *engagement*.

Turning the Tables on Arte (January 2005)

Shortly after the crisis was resolved, I was approached by Bette with a proposition: she and Wingman wanted to turn the tables on me by doing an interview with me in the University of There's *There Fun Times*. "You are always interviewing us," she said, "now we want to interview you."

I think they felt that having me talk about my research to the avatar community in my own words, without the filtration, distillation, and potential distortion of a journalist, would help to clarify matters and would also be of inherent interest to their readership. It was a cool idea because it addressed a lot of issues, and in a sense brought the whole situation back around.

Bette and I did the interview January 9, and when it was published, she posted it with this picture (Image: Bette):

with a caption alongside it that said: "Research?"

Artemesia's Field Station

Right around the time of the Buggy Polo episode, I took another bold step in participant engagement. Lula, a non-*Uru* player but friend of the community, had purchased a new Damanji one-piece, two-story Cone House. I told her that I was thinking about buying one myself. She had an extra, a model that came in several pieces, so she offered to give it to me. She and a newbie who strolled by helped me set it up in a PortaZone (which I could then move to another location.) It actually took quite a bit of effort by the three of us—me in low zoom mode, Lula on a jetpack, and the newbie running around and looking at it from different angles on the ground, and then all occasionally swapping positions. I got enraptured and decided to haul out the few other items I had in inventory and decorate my new house. Lula gave me some stuff and then took off with the newbie to show him around. I bought some more furniture, put out my gazebo in the garden, and stayed up until 2 AM decorating my house, a true sign that I had finally gone over to being a full-fledged member of the community.

When I was done I realized—wow, that's it. I'm now officially part of the group. I have an *Uru* Cone House; I am a coconspirator in Damanji's plot to take over the world through emergence.

I planted my house across the water from Yeesha Island, next to Bette's enclave. I referred to it as my "field station." Later, after the main period of the fieldwork was done, when the group settled in a neighborhood on a larger island, I moved my field station there, where it stands to this day. After I passed my thesis defense, the TGUers threw a party for me and Raena gave me a beautiful sign that she had handcrafted that said "Dr. Artemesia's Field Station."

The Social Construction of the Ethnographer

Journal Entry

Last night I was reading the part of *Life on the Screen* about multiuser worlds and found myself feeling uncomfortable with Turkle's focus on the individual. She describes people's online experiences as if they are entirely self-determined (1995). The deeper I get into this, the more I realize that this is not the case. My observation is that people's identities online are socially constructed by the group, not by the individual.

I am beginning to realize that what is happening at this moment is that the group wants to socially construct me as well, in the same way they have constructed each other. In a sense they want to have more engagement/involvement with what I'm doing. I'm totally game for this.

At the same time, I think in my focus on the social, I may have inadvertently neglected the individual. I had no idea Lynn was in a wheelchair. How did I miss that? It seems like an important detail. Even though I've tried to privilege online identities, maybe I need to integrate offline identities more because really they are not completely bounded, not completely irrelevant to the online identity. Lynn's RL avatar is a person sitting in front of a computer in a wheelchair. Her game avatar is a persona, an extension of her. I am totally convinced of this more than ever. The avatar is a social extension, a prosthesis of sorts, but perhaps because one can play together and alone at the same time, there is also something about the individual that I have been missing. It seems like it must have been a cathartic experience for players, each of whom had spent so many years alone in the sublime world of *Myst*, to burst forth into a shared universe. They were all in the same place alone; now they were in the same place together. They must have felt like they finally found their tribe.

I think I am falling in love with the TGU people, which is something I am afraid of . . . but then on the other hand, I suppose it is inevitable. You have to fall in love with your research subjects at some level, even if it *is* unscientific. Or is it? Can one really learn from something one doesn't love deeply? My friend Mary the molecular biologist is in love with DNA. Maybe Jane Goodall and Diane Fosse have it right—you cannot really *know* something unless you are willing to develop some level of intimacy with it. Maybe that is what Leesa is saying, and I think her and the others' critique of me is perfectly valid. I have been too much of a passive observer. I need to make a commitment to engage with the group on a deeper level.

Déjà vu All Over Again

Journal Entry

I had that experience again . . . I was taken into another *Until Uru* Age that I had seen in its *Second Life* instantiation. As Teddy was leading me around, I not only recognized the environment, but I knew where everything would be before I saw it. My spatial memory kicked in and I knew exactly where we were going.

It seems that I have encountered *Uru* in reverse, discovering it backwards, in exactly the opposite direction of the players I've studied. My first experience of *Uru* has been through their retelling, and now the original seems like a facsimile of *their* version, rather than the other way around. I've had the experience of seeing a VR simulation of a place, and then visiting the real place a few days later. This is sort of like that, except that these are simulations of a simulation.

I talked with Erik at length the other day about this. He does not want to see the other Uru re-creations because he wants to keep his memory of Uru intact . . . for me *Uru* was nothing *but* re-creations for a long time. And I did not want to see the real thing because I did not want my imprint of its collective memory, the narrative that has been passed to me, to be polluted by "reality." It is a strange set of nesting eggs—memories within virtual worlds, simulacra of simulacra, simulated memories of experiences not yet had, the reinscription of memories upon memories. It is the ultimate in "remediation" (Bolter and Grusin 2000).

One Year After: Remembering Black Monday . . . or was it Tuesday?

Journal Entry

February 9, 2004 (from what I can discern) is the anniversary of the server closure, although it is hard to pinpoint a date. Some call it "Black Monday," others refer to it as "Black Tuesday." It took me a while to realize that it was a different day and date for the Europeans than for the Americans. The *Uru* refugees in *Second Life* are having some kind of anniversary celebration. It also occurred to me that as *Uru* ran for less than six months, the Uru Diaspora has now outlived the original *Uru Live* game by double. How much longer will they persist? Will there be a Yeesha Island in *Second Life* in three years? What about TGU? Will they become fully acclimated to *There.com* and cease to be Uruvians?

As scared as I was to get into the "real" *Uru*, I now see how necessary it was in order to really understand my study subjects. I cannot just live on their retelling, although that is the most poetic way to do it. But to understand their experience, where they are coming from, the origins of their culture, and their play style, I need to spend time with them in their "homeland." I suppose one could do an ethnographic study of Italian-Americans without ever visiting Italy, but it adds another dimension to the research to have done so. I can see something about their spirit here. The way they play and the way they explore, and play with, and exploit, bugs; they are always trying to walk through walls and sink into floors, and they turn everything into a game. Today they were "avie bowling" by immersing themselves into the floor up to their necks and then running very fast to knock over the numerous cones that are lying around in the Hood.

This type of play is interesting because it shows a dynamic interchange between Caillois's notions of "paidia," unstructured, and "ludic," goal-oriented, play (1961). As opposed to the heavily structured goal-orientation of most video games, one can see through this type of experimentation a movement back and forth between "sandbox" open-ended and goal-focused play. With this group, sometimes there is a goal, sometimes not. Nobody seems to care much if they win; no big deal is made of it one way or the other. And everything is a potential game or play object. This style of play is both childlike and sophisticated. Players constantly experiment with the edges of the world they inhabit, and even though the world structures are different, the group itself remains about play. And in each new world, they discover different edges. They are constantly pushing the envelope. I wonder how much of how they've learned to play in *There.com* has influenced the way they now play in *Uru* . . . This is one question the answer to which I may never know.

Interview with the Avatar (Mid-January 2005)

Journal Entry

Sometimes I come out of these interviews feeling both emotionally drained and exhilarated. Tonight I had a long session with Raena, the woman who was in part responsible for salvaging the disaster around the article. This was by far the most intense interview to date, in part because she was so honest . . . she glossed over nothing, and told me things that no one else has told me, about the darker side of the transition. She is a very thoughtful person, and her openness was somewhat astounding, even more so in light of the fact that she approached me wanting to tell me her story.

Much of the story was similar to the others. Finding emergent patterns has been surprisingly easy because the responses are so consistent. One pattern is this notion of time compression, which jibes with my research and that of almost everyone I've read. In spite of the fact that the pace of text communication is much slower, emotional experiences tend to become compressed, and friendships form much more quickly than they would in "real life." In the case of the *Uru* people, this process was intensified by the time constraints of the *Uru* closure (knowing the world was ending), and by their shared trauma.

Raena also talked about her relationship to her avatar . . . the sense of death . . . she talked about "the end of the world," and how she and her friend wanted to "party like it's 1999." She talked about what it felt like to move from the first-person experience of the *Myst* games into the avatar-based environment of *Uru*. Having a representation of herself was a big deal for her, and it gave her a sense of "proprioception" (her word.) It seems many of the Uruvians felt their avatars were dying, and even though they've tried to approximate their *Uru* avatars in other worlds, it's obvious that they miss the nuance of the *Uru* avatars, the "realism," the modest attire, the ability to show age. They often complain about the cartoonyness of *There.com* avatars, although they like their expressiveness. Though *Uru* avatars are more "high fidelity" than *There* *.com* avatars, I find them to be a little strange. They all have this sort of glazed Mona Lisa smile.

The one part of the story that was entirely new to me was the tale of Teddy and Daisy, the backstory of which was known to most of the original TGUers. I know them as real-life partners, and I had met them together that day in the Moroccan pavilion, back in the pre-*Uru*, pre-voice, text-chat days. I had even seen a photo of the two of them in real life on the Imager in Teddy's Relto in *Until Uru*. So imagine my surprise when Raena reveals to me that Teddy was Daisy . . . or rather, that Daisy was his first incarnation in *Uru*.

Since most *Uru* players created their avatars as representations of themselves, or as a variant of themselves ("you are you"), there was no reason to suspect that any cross-gender play was occurring. Raena had, to her own surprise, made a number of friends in *Uru*, the closest of whom was Daisy. The Daisy I know is his wife, who never played the original *Uru* game. Apparently the original "Daisy" revealed his true identity to Raena just hours before the server shut down, when he appeared as a male avatar. Raena was upset by this, in part because of the deception, but more so because she had really wanted to say good-bye to her friend Daisy. But he couldn't log off and switch avatars, because it was too risky as the server was being put to sleep. (Teddy later told me that when he first started playing *Uru*, he had not anticipated that he was actually going to make friends, so this situation somewhat threw him for a loop.) Raena also told me that somewhere in the back of her mind, she had always sort of suspected that Daisy was really a man, owing to her sense of humor.

When he came to *There.com*, he followed the custom that players had adopted of recreating their Uru avatars in *There.com*. He continued to play as Daisy, and his wife, not an *Uru* player, joined him as Teddy. They maintained this charade until the advent of voice, which eventually forced them to come clean via the Koalanet forums. They stayed swapped for a time, but the gender-switched voices bothered some, so eventually they simply traded avatars, the male partner now inhabiting the male avatar, and vice versa. Teddy's reason for the gender switch, as I learned from reading the forums afterward, was to avert any concern of his wife's that he might engage in an online affair, a situation that had broken up a friend's marriage. For the most part, from this point forward, each used the avatar of the proper gender, although Teddy also occasionally used the male avatar he had created to make his confession during the *Uru* closure, and would occasionally appear as Daisy.

In some way this job is a lot like being a therapist . . . you want to get stories out of people . . . you want to get them to describe things as vividly as possible but also to find out their interpretations, how they felt about these things when they were happening. Maybe (and of course I'm hypothesizing here) but maybe in part because so many of them are women, as well as men who are a little older, it is easier for them to talk about their feelings.

I can't help but compare these conversations to those I've had with players in *Lineage*, mostly young men in their late teens or early twenties. The depth of insight here is so much richer . . . I really don't have to do much interpretation because they are doing it all for me. The hard thing to know is when to stop. I am sort of enraptured really, and every time I hear the story of the server shutdown, it still sends a chill up my spine. I relive it with them each time it is retold. While each of them lived it once, in some way I have relived it dozens of times because I have relived it through each of their eyes, through multiple subjectivities.

In losing her *Uru* avatar, Raena said she felt like she had experienced a kind of death. In a way it's true. And does Cyan/Ubisoft have that right to kill an avatar? I suppose technically they do, because they own it. Yet who really owns the avatar? The avatar is nothing without the player, but the code that comprises it is owned by the company. It's as if your soul were owned by you, but your body were owned by somebody else. Clearly, losing an avatar is very painful, because it is a part of the person, even if they've only been an avatar for a short period. It is like losing a limb, or perhaps how a child feels when their favorite toy is lost . . . there is an emotional attachment that happens through play . . . That seems like an apt metaphor.

Hmmm . . . that's very interesting. We become emotionally attached to our projected identities. It may be what Holopainen and Myers referred to as "somatic displacement," the ability to project yourself into an object, such as a doll or a toy car (2000). This seems consistent with the ways we project alter-identities into avatars, yet at the same time, there is a sense of being *within* the avatar that I'm not sure somatic displacement accounts for entirely. This type of emotional attachment can be very real and very powerful. When you lose your avatar, you feel as though you have lost a part of yourself. I think this is really interesting. The avatar becomes like a ghost limb—you can feel it even though it is no longer there.

Perhaps this is a variant of "falling in love with our prosthesis" (Stone 1996, 1), but it's also a feeling I have about my own avatar when I'm not logged on. The avatar also serves as a bridge to others, a kind of interpersonal connecting tissue. We know that these connections are real, even if the worlds that facilitate them are virtual. To the people experiencing them, they are very real and intense, and in some ways can be more intense then RL . . . I know this is true. I've experienced it myself. My two hours with Raena were more intense than the dinner I had with my housemate earlier this evening. I learned more in two hours about Raena, who I've never met, than I know about my housemate, who I've lived with for nearly a year. It's mysterious, but amazing.

I'm really excited about this work. There is something important and powerful that I'm uncovering here . . . peeling away like layers: the social . . . the psychological . . . the distributed self, as Turkle calls it (1995), and then the social construction of the self . . . The avatar is a precious entity, because it is an extension of yourself, a social prosthesis, especially when the game embodiment is compensating for a physical embodiment that has broken down (Lynn in her wheelchair, Cola with her arthritis): it's even more important. Because not being able to run and jump isn't just a physically painful experience . . . it's also socially painful. There are aspects of yourself that must be shut down that can be reawakened through an avatar. Lynn can run, jump, ride horses, and be a soccer ball in *There.com*. So in a way Lynn in *Uru* or in *There.com* is more the real Lynn than Lynn in the wheelchair in Cedar County, New Mexico, who has lost part of her identity and her social agency with the loss of her ability to walk. I feel like I know a side of these people that no one in their real lives will ever know. And since I have made it my business to know as much about them as I possibly can, I feel I've taken on a big responsibility. I've become the steward of their collective "self." TGU itself is an avatar in a way. It's the aggregate avatar of all the individual TGU avatars, isn't it? This is a very interesting way to look at it.

"Me and my shadow . . ."

hmmm . . .

Reflections on the Uru Server Shutdown Anniversary (February 9, 2005)

Journal Entry

I gathered with the European contingent at noon, along with a couple of U.S. folks, Lynn among them. She always makes a point to be present with every grouping in every time zone, and I think this is significant to her role in holding the group together.

I was expecting there to be discussion about the shutdown, and there had also been storytelling planned, but we never got around to that. Instead, Lynn suggested hide-and-seek, which took up the next three-plus hours.

It was fascinating. Here we were, this group of adults, mostly over 40, some over 50 even, playing a children's game in a virtual world. How many other occasions do we have to do this? Lynn was even on the phone (we could hear her over Teamspeak) telling her friend we were playing hide-and-seek.

Hide-and-seek had been a favorite activity in *Uru Prologue*, even though it's not really part of the game, but the brand of hide-and-seek they play is very much unique to the *Uru* environment. They particularly like playing in Eder Kemo, the garden Age. I asked them why they never play hide-and-seek in *There.com*. "Because of the nametags," they said.

This subversion of the environment into a playscape is a trademark play style of the group, and they do this in each environment in a different fashion, experimenting with, and sometimes against, the virtual world's given properties, capabilities, and bugs. It is particularly interesting to look at the way that certain game features promote or restrict certain types of subversive play. An interesting research question would be to look at ways of creating features specifically designed with this type of play in mind.

Before we started, there were some rules that had to be sorted out with respect to the new Ki pack everyone received as a Christmas present from the hackers who set up *Until Uru*. The Ki extended features of the game. One of the players, Uno, had invented the "Ki hug." This was done by looking at your Ki (a PDA you wear on your wrist) while chest-to-chest with another player. This created the appearance that the avatars were hugging, but the heads-up display obscured the view such that the hugging players themselves could not really see the hug. The extended Ki figures included a non-Ki hug that allowed hugging players to see themselves, as well as higher jumps the ability to float, among others. For the purpose of hide-and-seek, the group decided it was okay to use the float and higher jump commands to find hiding places, but the person who was "It" could use only higher jumps but not the float command to find people. You were not permitted to spawn to escape detection. All this was negotiated in advance, like game rules in a real-world playground.

Naturally, using my new "participant engagement" method, I played along. This strategy has been somewhat challenging since I am a "noob" by Uruvian standards, and since this was my first time, I fumbled along trying to get the hang of it. On the first round, while looking for a hiding place, I accidentally linked out of the Age. When I returned at the spawn point, Phae'dra was there and immediately said "I found Arte." I explained that I had just spawned in, but it made us all laugh. On the second round, I was slightly less inept at finding a hiding place, although I was one of the first people discovered.

In this version of the game, once you are found, you have to help the "It" person to find the others, which is really much more fun than hiding. One of the things I immediately noticed was the cleverness of some of the hiding places. For example, there was one spot where a couple of people were hiding that was one of those rifts in cyberspace. If you did a particular high jump in the right spot in the tunnel, you could land on the back of the cave ceiling, which wasn't a "real" place in the game. From here you could see the "back of house," as if you'd gone inside the wall of a theme park ride. From this vantage point, you could also see other parts of the Kemo that were not visible from other locales. This was one of a number of ways the new Ki commands introduced some new possible hiding scenarios to the game.

Since the Uruvians all know the space so well, and have spent a lot of time looking for hidden clues, they know all the nooks and crannies. The know the cubbyholes, the backs of things, the weird ledges that require runs and jumps to get to, arcane combinations for getting on top of things that would otherwise seem inaccessible.

The best hiding place of all was by Kellor, who figured out a way hide *inside* the trunk of a Braintree. The trunk collision detection was flawed in some way and it was the exact width of an avatar. As a result, he was able to just stand inside the tree trunk, and though visible from the waist up, he was hard to detect because he was not discernable as a geometric element. Everyone gathered round to express their appreciation for the cleverness of this hiding place. This was a big part of the experience—trying to come up with a really clever hiding place that everyone else would appreciate for its creativity. Since the group places such high value on solving puzzles, finding hidden things, and being clever about it, it was a real pleasure to play the Uru variation of hide-and-seek because it turned out to be a very sophisticated version of the game.

This is another case of the ways in which players subvert or reframe the virtual environment to their own ends. So in a sense the virtual world becomes more like a playground than a game, a terrain that can morph or take on a variety of shapes, that can be adopted at will by simply changing the game terms. This week *Uru* is a hide-and-seek game; maybe another week it is a treasure hunt. This week *There.com* is a card game; next week it is a cross-country race. The playing board is constantly being redefined. This is significantly different from a game like Monopoly where the game board is fairly static, even if the theme changes, whereas on a checkers/chess board, you can play a couple of different games, and of course with playing cards, a seemingly infinite number. It's like a playground in which a vertical wall, a ball, some rope, and a piece of chalk allow you to constantly reconfigure the play parameters of the space.

This causes me to question this notion of the magic circle a bit. How finite is it, really? The magic circle is really nothing more than a mutual agreement to abide by a set of social constraints. These can be independent of the terrain, and they can also be highly malleable and contingent on people and context. In some cases, the social constraints are terrain-dependent; for example, we play Monopoly on a Monopoly board, but there is no reason we could not make up a new set of rules to play on the same board, and no reason we can't play that same set of rules on a different board, depending on its configuration. Monopoly could be played with chalk in a playground, or even on the city streets, as long as you had some markers to represent player progress and some form of currency. This is the principle behind the "Big Game" "Pac-Manhattan," in which the rules of Pac-Man are played out in full scale in the streets of New York City (Delio 2004). In fact, Thereians later invented a series of board games in which avatars served as playing pieces. I think one of the phenomena at play here is that players run out of things to do as prescribed by the game. The TGUers have already solved all the puzzles in *Uru*, so now they explore and invent new modes of play.

The most noteworthy thing about the anniversary gathering was that it was not a grieving of the past. There was some passing reference to the initial loss of *Uru*, but they also reminded each other of what they had gained. The flavor of the event, stated by Lynn up front, was really more a celebration of play and community than anything else.

And under that lies this new theory I am formulating. One of the reasons the emotional bonds of social play can be so intense is because in these liminal zones people "let their hair down," as Lunar pointed out in my interview with him. And people can do things, like Teddy's gender-bending, that in any other space would have profoundly different connotations. Teddy's cross-gender play in a virtual world is very distinct from what we traditionally think of of transgender practices in the real world. Because this is a liminal space, framed by make-believe, experimentation and subversion are accepted as part of the territory—although hurting others is not tolerated, at least not among this group. Even in a virtual world, deception can be an egregious crime, but deception is often reframed in the context of imagination.

In addition to the *Until Uru* event, there was also an event hosted by the *Uru* refugees in *Second Life*. At the behest of some of the *Second Lifers*, I invited a few of my Uruvian-Thereian friends, including Lynn, with whom I had now become good friends, and we all went to the event together. Although I seldom saw anyone but the creators in the *Uru* area of *Second Life*, this event had the largest turnout of any event I had attended in any area of *Second Life*. It was impossible to actually count the number of people present. As usual, the high traffic also revealed the prime vulnerability, the Achilles tendon of virtually all MMOGs: it's not clear exactly how many people gathered in the *Second Life* Hood, perhaps as many as 100, because at a certain point, we were all ejected into a barren desert. Once again, the server had failed. This was unfortunate because this was one of those highly emotional occasions where people really wanted to be together.

More Presentations (February 2005)

Journal Entry

Over the course of doing several presentations as Artemesia, I've evolved the technique significantly. Because of the voice versus text controversy among the TGUers since the first presentation, which was done purely with text, I have shifted to giving presentations with voice. I also now shift back and forth between Celia and Artemesia, rather than keeping Celia silent in the background. While this is awkward and uncomfortable, I think it makes for a more interesting presentation, and it's more aligned with my new methodology.

In one presentation I gave in Holland, an audience member came up to me afterward and said "when you were switched to the avatar, you were more boring." I realize there are some language issues here, but after talking to some other people present, I think what he was trying to say was that when in avatar persona, I project *through* the avatar, so my real-life avatar is not as expressive.

After my presentation in Copenhagen, T. L. Taylor told me that she found the fissures between the real-life and the online avie to be interesting. I think what makes this type of presentation challenging is that I am almost always alone when I'm "being Artemesia" and I often feel embarrassed or awkward if even one other person enters the room. I suppose this is in part because most of the people I deal with in my daily life do not really understand what I'm doing; they think it's strange. In addition, while being in-world is a highly social activity, at the same time it feels very private. So while it is very uncomfortable to do this in public, to perform the act of being Artemesia with both real-life and virtual avie simultaneously, I think that awkwardness is precisely what makes it interesting. It might be comparable to a puppeteer pulling away the curtain. Usually a puppeteer is not that interesting to watch for the same reason—she is usually channeling her persona through the puppet. I suppose when you channel your persona through the avatar, there is a visible shift in energy, or charisma, or whatever you want to call it—you can see the life force move from being inside the body to being extended into the embodiment of the avatar. I can feel this happening myself, but it's interesting that it is also visible to an audience.

Philosophical Conversations (February 2005)

Journal Entry

So much of the ethnographic process has to do with being in the right place at the right time; there is a certain amount of kismet I suppose to this work. Today, in the course of exploring, I accidentally stumbled on exactly the sort of situation that every ethnographer dreams of encountering. Wingman, Nature_Girl, and Bette were having a deep philosophical conversation about the nature of their *Uru/There.com* experience.

On the one hand, says Wingman, Lynn wants there to be a re-creation of D'ni Ae'gura in *There.com*. But there is a difference, he says, between *re-creating Uru* versus *extending* the world into *There.com*. The former approach entails making facsimiles of *Uru* artifacts, the latter is an approach to making *Uru*-like objects that is more like creating new Ages. (This is what Damanji is trying to do).

Nature_Girl, being the group's rabbi, as usual, covers the theological and historical perspective of the story. The D'ni chose Earth to build the cavern, the underground city of D'ni Ae'gura. They came to Earth, to New Mexico, when their world was destroyed.

But, Wingman argues, the world we are standing in right now (*There.com*) is not Earth. Nature_Girl says it's kind of a linking book that leads to another Age. We put our hand on the *There.com* book and came here from Earth.

But, I think, maybe like the D'ni who chose to come to New Mexico when their world was destroyed, the TGUers chose to come to *There.com* when their world was destroyed. At this point, though, I say nothing. I am just listening.

Nature_Girl suddenly turns to me and says: "Arte, what do you think?" Bette says: "Art is just taking it all in. She's typing frantically, wondering where the chat log is." I laugh because she is right; my fingers are flying across the keyboard trying to capture every word they are saying.

Is *There.com* the same "place" as the cleft in *Uru*? Is it another Age of *Uru*? Is it the "real world" in relation to *Uru*? Or is it a place for a new Age to be "written?" Nature_Girl of course will argue that we cannot write Ages; only D'ni can do that. But to Damanji, writing Ages is the next logical step, especially in an environment like *There.com*, which is extensible by players. Why not write Ages? We have all the tools we need here. What's to stop us?

St. Patrick's Day Parade (March 12, 2005)

Journal Entry

One Sunday when we were having our usual noontime *Until Uru* meet-up, one of the members of the Tapestry Shard popped into our hood and wanted to know if TGU wished to participate in a St. Patrick's Day parade they were planning. Petrova, the deputy mayor and coadministrator (with D'evon) of the TGU *Until Uru* shard, agreed to take the lead on making this happen.

Although having a parade doesn't seem like that big a deal, in *Uru*, because server and client interactions are not always well synchronized, coordinated formations of any kind are extremely challenging. Thus this enterprise entailed a great deal of strategic planning and rehearsal time to compensate for the flaws in the server architecture.

First, it was not possible for the entire group to parade concurrently in a single shard because of continual crashing. Instead, each group was to be "warped" (teleported) by an administrator into the Tapestry Event Shard, where they would march one length of the parade route, then be "warped' back into their hood to make way for the next group. There were no spectators allowed, as this would cause crashes. Two players were assigned as cameramen to stream the parade out to the web, not only so spectators could watch, but also so those organizing the parade could monitor what was happening.

The "no spectator" rule really highlighted the importance of this new participant methodology approach I was developing. Here was a case where it would be impossible to just observe the situation; it was simply not allowed. The only possible way to study this event was to actually participate in the parade.

I also quickly discovered that this was a case where actually participating was the only way to really understand this client-server architecture problem in an experiential way. D'evon and Petrova led the numerous rehearsal sessions, which mostly entailed practicing walking in a straight line. But in reality, or perhaps more aptly, in virtual reality, this relatively simple task was actually impossible. While you might appear to be walking in a straight line on your own screen, to others, you may be "rubber banding," sliding forward and backward in the scene. You may see your avatar as following another player's, while at the same time she may see her avatar as walking behind yours. So from a perceptual perspective, there is no way to really walk a parade that looks right to everyone because each person is seeing something different on his or her client screen. Simply walking in a coordinated straight line required numerous rehearsals and coordination from Petrova, D'evon, and others.

The parade itself turned out to be a grueling ordeal. It took much longer than expected, and while it officially began at noon, TGU wasn't warped into place until well after 2:00 p.m. We were the last leg of the parade, and the largest group to participate. As soon as we arrived at our final destination behind the library, everybody crashed and the parade was over. Crashing is now humorously referred to as "linking to the Desktop Age."

While not a game per se, the difficulties of orchestrating something as seemingly simple as a parade on a highly unstable server infrastructure presented players with a feat so challenging that, in the end, it became its own kind of game. Had I not participated both in rehearsals and the parade itself firsthand, I would never have understood the complexity of the task, nor the mastery and tenacity required to execute it.

The St. Patrick's Day Parade also provided another instance of the conflation of meanings between real and imaginary worlds. When I first heard about it, it made me uncomfortable, in part because it felt like real-world cultures intruding on the fantasy of *Uru*. It was another example of porousness in the magic circle, a phenomenon I became progressively more used to, and eventually came to fully accept as part of the transludic lifestyle.

Shifting Worlds (May–June 2005)

Journal Entry

Over the past few months, there has been some dissatisfaction with *There.com*. This seems to happen in cycles, but this time, the result is that Lynn, Leesa, and Nature_Girl have started spending more time in *Second Life*. Nature_Girl, who has mastered a number of content creation skills in *There.com*, seems to like the building features because it gives her a new challenge. Lynn has purchased some coastal land and put out a houseboat, along with Uno, who has also been spending more time in SL. I ended up buying the adjacent land, so now we have a little Uruvian-Thereian waterside enclave.

This has caused a little tension with Raena, who is concerned that others will follow Lynn into *Second Life*. I'm less worried, as my impression is that *Second Life* has taken on the role of an after-hours club or a vacation home for Lynn. She tends to go there after most of the Thereian community has gone to bed. We hang out and play SL's version of Mah Jongg, which is fun because it is a two-player cooperative game modeled after Mah Jongg Solitaire. Her husband Frank and RL friend Henry, who was responsible for setting up the Koalanet forum, also hang out there. I guess I am getting to know a different side of her as her SL neighbor.

Our neighborhood in SL reminds me a bit of Sausalito. I've always wanted to live on a houseboat, so I ended up buying a galleon and setting myself up a pirate ship. *Second Life* is a little more conducive to fantasy role-playing than *There.com*. Clothes and costumes are much cheaper and people run around in all manner of avatar forms. Unlike *There.com*, where your avatar is pretty much fixed, in *Second Life* you can keep as many different avatar versions in one account as you want. So while your identity remains the same (your nametag is persistent), your visual representation is a lot more malleable. Our neighbor, Thomas Tuffnell, is a Victorian steampunk inventor with a giant mansion filled with wacky gadgets and works in progress. There is something kinky going on upstairs, but I haven't ventured forth to investigate yet.

High up in the air, above Lynn's and my boats, is a western saloon complete with playable piano, owned by Sam Smith, who is modeled after an historical character of the same name. Across the bay are a variety of houses, and someone has plopped a very cool submarine just offshore. Various avatars show up presenting as robots, children, and even animals, although it does not seem as populated as *There.com*. It's sort of like being at a twenty-four–hour costume party. We don't know very many people, but we like our neighbors just fine. Lynn likes to come there because of the dancing animations, and she also has some snuggle poses she gets to do with her husband. As much as she complains about *There.com* management, I don't get the feeling she will abandon *There.com* for SL; she still doesn't much care for the kinky culture in SL. She and I like to sit on the deck of her boat and play Mah Jongg when we are online together. I also sometimes sit and play alone on mine. It's funny to go into a virtual world to play what is essentially a single-player game, but it's sort of a nice break from the other worlds I go to where I'm always "working."

Secrets Revealed

One evening I was sitting with Teddy and Raena in Raena's house when Leshan popped in somewhat abruptly. Leshan was a fairly new member, having left another Hood in *Until Uru*. Since joining TGU, she had become close with a number of members, including Raena and myself.

Leshan was one of the few in the group who continued to use text even though voice was the communication mode of choice. She was very agitated when she entered the house and said she had something very important to tell us. The information she had to impart, via text chat, was that she was, in real life, a man. I do not think Leshan was aware of Teddy's past at this juncture, and as I sat there I could not help but observe the irony of the interchange. In some sense, she had unwittingly come to the right place. Needless to say, the three of us were extremely blasé about the confession.

Leshan's reasons were quite a bit different from Teddy's: she had been playing female avatars in games for many years in response to her lifelong experience of gender dysphoria. Following the precedent set by Teddy, and the recommendation of the three of us, Leshan discussed this first with the group's leaders, primarily Leesa and Lynn, as well as a handful of other close friends, and then posted her confession on the group's forum. Since the community had already been through this once, it was not such a big deal the second time around, although frankly, it was not such a big deal the first time either. Similar to the first case, it was a much bigger deal to the person revealing their true gender than to the other members of the group. Unlike Teddy, Leshan chose to continue to play her female avatar, but now spoke with her natural, male voice.

More Presentations

Journal Entry

I finally have got the hang of giving in-world presentations in *There.com*, although presenting in situ requires some funny tricks. For instance, if I want my avatar to face the audience, I have to use mirror view and walk backwards, so this is something I need to practice. This is not possible with *Second Life*: even though you can change your view with camera controls, once you start walking, the camera snaps into standard view.

I've done a couple of presentations to the PhD cohort and at the Banff Centre, much more intimate settings predominately consisting of artists and designers (as opposed to the academics and lawyers at some of my previous presentations.) These have been much easier and more laid-back. They are generally smaller events where I know everybody in the audience, in a context where performance tends to be a natural part of the mix. They are therefore more interested in and more tolerant of performative experimentation. I've also developed a pretty fluid technique of switching back and forth between Artemesia and Celia, which still reveals the ruptures and boundaries, but gives me a little more leeway and mitigates some of the awkwardness of being in-game on stage. Artemesia is much more nervous on stage than Celia, but I think she's getting over that slowly, with practice.

One thing that always makes these presentations more interesting is when the Uruvian-Thereians themselves show up. I always let them know when I'm planning an in-world presentation. Initially I did this so they could have the option to avoid being seen, but it turned out that they actually liked it, and would often show up to be part of the presentation. One on occasion, a flotilla of hoverboats descended upon me moments after rezzing on Yeesha Island. The players jumped out and waved at the audience. It's very sweet and really demonstrates their *level* of involvement in the research, which is always gratifying to me. I think to some extent, they also find it amusing to be famous.

True Confessions (Haselmere, Surrey, July 2005)

Journal Entry

Raena is a man.

I was sitting on the sofa after a long session in the UK with the other PhD candidates, about to close things down for the night, when I got a Skype from her wanting to talk. It took forever for her to get it out. There was a long preamble . . . but eventually she told me: "My real-life avie is a man."

Once she got that part out, we talked a little about the ramifications. I told her I didn't care, which I really don't. To me, this really has very little impact on our friendship. What interested me more about it was the fact that she had been at the center of the two other gender revelations in the group and had managed to keep this to herself the entire time. It also amazed me that she had been able to master the female voice. Re-gendering your voice is really challenging, not just because of pitch, but also cadence and social style. Women and men just talk differently, and so Raena has managed not only to shift the voice pitch, but also get the social style and the cadence down. My God, she even sings in-world!

I suppose as a researcher, this should somehow taint her credibility as an informant, but it really never even crossed my mind. For one thing, all of the things she has told me about the group have been corroborated by other interviews and observation. This speaks well for the crystallization method. But more than that, I know Raena is totally reliable and totally honest. I suppose to anyone else this would seem outrageous. How could you trust someone who "lied" about something so crucial? But I guess it doesn't really seem like a lie to me. And this is one of those issues where knowing about the real-life avie naturally adds another dimension to the person, but in the long run, it does not have any impact on what happens in-world. Just because the real-life avie is a man doesn't make the virtual-world avie any less of a woman. I know that sounds contradictory, but it makes perfect sense to me.

We talked about how she was going to handle it with the group. As seems to be the pattern, a "true gender confession" seems to be a much bigger deal for the person confessing than for everyone else. She had already discussed it with Leesa and Lynn, who were fine about it. Following the precedent set by Teddy and Leshan, they decided the best thing to do would be to post on the forum, in the same way that Teddy and others have done in the past. I guess she wanted to tell me, as well as her other close friends, in person before she did this. The real question now is whether she is going to keep being Raena, as Leshan did, or switch to a male avie, as Teddy did. To test this out, she created a male avie, Raenen, who she is going to take out for a spin.

I did not feel in any way betrayed by her confession, but when she told me about Raenen, I found myself feeling sad. It reminded me of how Raena had reacted when she found out Daisy was not available to say good-bye on the last day of *Uru*. I tried to be really tactful and supportive. My main thrust was, I support whatever you choose do, but I would really miss Raena.

Raena's priority has always been the community, and this is one of the things I respect about her. So even though I think she feels the same way about it as I do, I think she would switch to the male avie even if she didn't really want to, if she felt that was what the group preferred. This really reinforces what I've been saying about the social construction of identity. She has basically put her identity up for group consideration, and as is always the case with TGUers, began by consulting with the leadership.

This revelation of course causes me to see every conversation and story involving Raena in a new light. Her grief at losing her avatar, while no different from anyone else's, had special significance because a part of her was dying that was unique to that place. She is also a pillar of the community, and has had a major behind-the-scenes role in everything significant that has happened to this group. She was instrumental in the move into *There.com*. While she has some male friends, she mainly hangs out with women (who as far as we know are also women in RL), although she's been at the center of the two other gender-switching narratives within the group. The artwork she creates in *There.com* is very feminine in its content and style. Even the way she dresses, her modest attire, is unusual for a man playing a woman. Most men tend to create female avatars that are sexy, and wear flamboyant or frilly clothes. She mostly wears jeans and sweaters in-world, just like a real woman in real life.

Well, this is an interesting turn of events, and I will be curious to see the outcome.

Following the custom set by Teddy and Leshan, Raena, aka Steve, posted a confession on Koalanet. He described his reason for the gender switch as stemming from a house rule he had made to protect his daughter from predators online: that any online activity would be conducted with disguised identities without revealing any real-life information.

After the post, there ensued a period of discussion and negotiation. Most members of the group had had no idea Raena was not a female as presented via the female avatar, although a few said they had suspected as much. By and large everyone was supportive, and while he was encouraged to do whatever felt appropriate, there seemed to emerge a general consensus among the community that Raena was a well-loved and pivotal member and if she were to go, she would be missed. While this discussion was under way, Raena made a go of trying to present as a male avatar.

Raena introduced me to Raenen, her male alter ego, in *There.com*. She is practicing talking like a man. She told me she practiced talking like a woman when she made Raena and now she is used to relating in that way and the male voice is hard. She also said something about how you can have different cubbyholes in your mind to accommodate the multiple identities of avatar life. This awareness came to her through meeting Leshan and his wife. Raena talked about listening to Leshan "talk about us as if we were RL people." His wife knows all of us of course, but only from him. And so in her mind, the avies are all "real." To her, we each have only one cubbyhole, as characters in her husband's stories.

Even though I now know differently, I prefer to still think of Raena as a woman. The *There.com* Real Life Gathering is imminent, which is in part what motivated her confession. Soon I will meet the man behind the avatar . . . and then I will have to make some adjustments internally, I suppose. I continue to call her, and all other cross-gendered avatars, by their avatar pronouns.

Raena is part of the man behind her, a part of his persona that gets to come out and play in this context. In this case, it's not a sexual thing, but it's a very risky and dangerous thing to do nonetheless . . . to explore parts of your personality that are not available to you in RL. You really have no idea where it will take you.

I am very uncomfortable with my reaction to Raenen. I find myself resenting him because I feel like he is replacing my friend Raena. It's irrational, but I feel like he represents a negation of Raena. Since that first introduction, Raenen has been hanging out intermittently in both *Until Uru* and *There.com*. I am having a really hard time with it. I want to be nice to him; I guess in some ways he's a newbie, but in reality, I just want Raena back. On a couple of occasions, he's managed to get both avatars into *There.com* at the same time. This has been very strange, because the struggle to create a male identity becomes so clear . . . his attempts to talk like a man are both poignant and amusing. At the same time, it's somehow easier for me to be comfortable with Raenen when Raena is around.

We've seen pictures now. Raena has a beard. And yet when in avie, he's just a woman. That's all. The odd part is, I know they are the same person, but to me Raenen is not Raena. He's an entirely different person. But they are both Steve. Yet somehow I don't see Raenen as a male version of Raena.

As a result of the discussion on Koalanet, a kind of consensus has emerged. By and large, TGU members expressed that they would prefer to see Raena remain part of the community, even though they continued to leave the final decision up to Steve to do what he felt was right. This, combined with his personal struggles with switching to a male avatar, prompted Steve to maintain his identity as a female avatar and continue to use the female voice. Most community members and friends know Raena is male, but they treat her as if she is a woman, and she has memberships in a number of female-dominated groups.

There.com Real Life Gathering (September 2005)

Journal Entry

In the end, we did what we always did: laughed, explored, talked for hours, and played spades until 2:00 in the morning.

The first thing that struck me was that the voice became the bridge from the real-life avie to the in-world avie. And the voice carries them between worlds now. I know the voices so well, I sort of wallowed in them. From the first moment I heard Lynn's smoky voice and Blossom's English accent from the bathroom stalls, I connected immediately with the real-life avatars. Leshan had the same voice, but this time coming out of a male body. Wingman was dressed as his avie, so that was easy, but his voice kept wafting between the rooms the whole time. Nature_Girl, possibly the most distinctive voice of the lot . . . Raena was the only one who sounded nothing like herself, although I could hear just a glimmer of Raena coming through the voice of Steve, the man standing there before me. The real-world hug . . . that's the one I remember the most. Really she's my best friend in-game. There is no way around that. "My best girlfriend is a guy," I thought. "Sounds like an episode of Oprah."

Later, when we sat at dinner, the conversation was like those we have in-game. I kept picturing the avatar gestures that Raena uses, the cadence of the speech, the pauses to think, the "I'm thinking" gesture which is done by typing in "hmmm." I could also see in Steve, the man, the male RL avie, the ghost of the woman inside. These things are hard to explain if you have not experienced them. It's not a gender confusion thing . . . Raena explained it best when she talked about the cubbyholes. I have two cubbyholes in my mind for this person—Raena, the game persona, and Steve, the real-life avatar. They are one, and yet they are two. Each is a facet of the other.

There were a few real-life social conventions to sort out. One was what to call each other, but we quickly fell quite comfortably into calling each other by our avatar names. This was reinforced by the fact that those were the names on our nametags. And it was fun to see how each had a glimmer of his or her avatar. Nathan8 wore a tie-dye shirt. Shaylah's body was different from her avatar, but her eyes were the same. Nature_Girl wore braids, just like in *There*. Maesi wore the same glasses in RL as in-game and her gestures seemed oddly similar to the procedural movements of her avatar. People were actually doing a variety of avatar gestures and dances all weekend, which was hilarious. A few wore floating There-style nametags on their heads.

Ultimately, I think humor may be the key to the soul. After voice, humor was the next distinctive personality trait that persisted outside of the game. Everyone's humor was precisely the same as in-game. This is something you can't really hide. Just as Raena said (ironically, now) that she had always suspected Daisy of really being a man because of his sense of humor, humor is unique: it's spontaneous; it's like a fingerprint of the personality.

It was particularly special to meet Leesa. We had a moment of mutual appreciation. I really admire how she has developed as the reluctant leader of this group. And she expressed her appreciation for the work I have been doing with her community, which meant a lot to me after the controversy back in November. I think the outcome has been positive for everyone. In the end, the project really did feel like the collaboration I had always intended it to be.

I was both surprised and unsurprised to find that nearly half the gathering consisted of TGU members. This is a measure not so much of their numerical representation in *There.com*, but of their influence and their commitment to both *There.com* and each other. *There.com* was their refuge, it was their safe harbor . . . not entirely safe . . . but yet they stuck to it with admirable tenacity. They never let up, even after all the moves, even after *There.com* seemed on the verge of closure. As Raena said to me at dinner, "People were afraid we would take over. It looks like maybe we have."

But it also attests to the power of play. In sessions, people kept saying "It's not just a game." I kept wanting to say "Why 'just'?"

I think we need to stop belittling play like it's something unimportant. Play is important, it's deep, it's human. The shared values of Leesa's rules are about play. They are guidelines for the playground. They are a philosophy of play. And they were powerful enough to keep this group of people together for this protracted period of time, through trials and tribulations, well beyond the initial context in which their bond was formed. Each step of the way, they prevailed. They remained together. Why? Because they were guided by shared values and a philosophy of play that was robust and continues to sustain them.

Most of the RLG program was planned by the *There.com* staff. There were panels and sessions on "The Care and Feeding of the Servers" and "Theronomics." There were discussions about community management, perhaps reminiscent of Member Advisory Board meetings. There were screenings of films made in-world and performances by members.

All of these things were interesting, but they were different from what we would do together ordinarily; that felt somewhat odd and a little bit overly restrained.

The most interesting part of the gathering was the last day, which was for the unofficial events. There was a dinner planned at San Francisco's Fisherman's Wharf. It was here, in these open-ended, unstructured activities, that you could see the natural patterns of behavior emerge. The first challenge was finding a place to park, especially Lynn's van, which had a handicapped sticker but was too large to fit in a conventional parking spot. We were on mobile phones to each other trying to coordinate this, scouting for parking, and arranging to meet up. This was very similar to the way we use the IM box in *There.com*, or Teamspeak in the background of *Until Uru*.

Once we convened, we broke up into various exploratory groups, including a chocolate quest led by Lynn. Here was a case where the play style was consistent . . . Lynn the explorer was alive and well in realspace. The challenge was navigating her wheelchair through the hilly streets of San Francisco, which were decidedly lacking in adequate accessibility affordances. But the group quickly turned this into a puzzle, and everyone contributed to the search for ramps and lifts. We were determined to get Lynn to the Ghirardelli Chocolate shop, regardless of the obstacles. A number of inventive solutions were found, many of which required group effort, and some of which involved contraptions, such as a wheelchair lift. The relationship to space could be seen clearly: the questing, the puzzle-solving, the collaboration, and the relentless search for a solution. And above all, one could see the dedication of the group to Lynn and to each other. Others with disabilities or special needs were treated the same way. We all took care of and looked after each other.

After dinner we headed back to the hotel. In the car, I told conavigator Wingman that something had been missing for me throughout the proceedings, and I had finally realized what it was: play. We had done everything imaginable together but play. When we got back to the Marriott, we took over the hotel lobby and quickly transformed it into a play space. We appropriated furniture, making our own spades tables, and just like every other space TGU has been in, they turned it into a *There .com* "Fun Zone."

Spades said it all. It was the same but different. We all played in the same styles as we always play. We said the same things we always say. But the avatar fidelity was different. You could see the eyes, the smiles, the sidelong looks, the hand gestures. Throughout the two days, whenever I was with someone, I would have brief "avatar flashbacks" (cognitive haunting, again) where I would picture the person's avatar talking. But it was not until we were playing spades that I realized that from here on out, whenever I play spades in-game with them, I will experience cognitive haunting of their real-life avies as well.

It's all quite an adventure. They are a quirky lot, each to varying degrees more or less like his or her avie. But as Leesa and everyone always say, the soul shines through, both good and bad. I don't think anyone expected to see a bunch of Disneyesque cartoon Barbie dolls there. We all knew it would be a motley group, but part of what you find is you know something about a person's inner life that transcends his or her appearance, and this awareness translates into the physical. And there we were, a bunch of people who would probably have no other occasion to have known each other calling each other family.

What is that? How can we say, "It's just a game?" Play is important. It's spiritual. It can create a type of bond that happens nowhere else, a bond between strangers. It can create friendships that emerge quickly but can also be sustained over the long term. Regardless of what goes on in our real lives, what our established roles are, here we are just playmates.

There is something magical in that, the freedom to play, and to play wherever and whenever we want, to be silly, to horse around, to explore, to experiment. This proves perhaps the final contention of my dissertation: that play styles are mobile, that they can move across virtual worlds and even into the real world; that it is in play that the style of interaction is fully rendered, fully realized, and its personality both transcends and transforms the context, whether it be inside a virtual world or in the lobby of a hotel.

There is so much more to all of this than meets the eye.

Community Awards

In October, about a month after the Real Life Gathering of *There.com*, Leshan invited us all to attend the first annual Community Achievers of *There* Award. We had been informed about these awards about a month earlier, but the announcement was made official at the RLG. The basic idea was to award selected Thereians for community achievement by having Imagina design a gown named for each award recipient. I had been awarded one of these gowns during the year. Now, all the recipients were to be gathered together for the first formal award ceremony, where trophies would be distributed. I was very touched that Leshan had given me an award, but until this ceremony was called, the award had felt more personal (perhaps based on friendship) than socially significant. Having the honor announced made real my sense of contribution to the community.

On the night of the ceremony, Leshan and Imagina alternated giving short statements about why each of us had been given the award. When my turn came up, I was very touched and surprised by what was said. Leshan began by saying "I don't know if you are all aware of the work Arte does . . ." She then went on to say that I was doing great things for *There.com* by giving presentations to the outside world and trying to impart a deeper understanding of the online lifestyle Thereians, beyond the screen. Over the past eighteen months, I had traveled around the world and written papers describing their experience to people in a variety of settings. It had never occurred to me that this was being perceived as a contribution to the community itself. However, Leshan's speech revealed that I (both Celia and Artemesia) had taken on the role as a kind of ambassador to the outside world, giving testimony to what had happened to the *Uru* community, and hopefully providing a more nuanced and less stereotyped view of what it meant to be part of an online community in a virtual world. Being acknowledged and honored for this contribution also imparted in me a renewed and extended sense of responsibility, which I carry forward into my current and future work.

| V |

BEYOND *URU*: COMMUNITIES OF PLAY ON THEIR OWN TERMS

CODA: *URU* RESURRECTION—APPLIED
CYBERETHNOGRAPHY AS ACTION RESEARCH

In the spring of 2006, as I was completing the PhD thesis for which this research was initially conducted, I received a phone call from a woman at Turner Broadcasting who wanted to talk with me about the possibility of my consulting for the company. She could not say what the project was, but she requested a meeting with me on a subsequent trip to Atlanta that I was planning in order to participate in a symposium at Georgia Tech. I was also in progress on a job negotiation there, which I eventually accepted and where my current real-life avatar is an assistant professor at this writing.

During the symposium, I was bustled into a conference room for a private meeting and asked to sign a nondisclosure agreement. I was then introduced to a gentleman who told me that they wanted to hire me to assist them in researching the possibility of reopening *Uru*.

Those present still recall with amusement the expression on my face. Early in my encounters with the Uru Diaspora, I had often imagined ways to assist them. At one point, I even had access to a large university research server that could have easily hosted a version of the game. I was not clear on whether or not an intervention on my side would be a breach in ethics, and it would certainly reflect a radical shift into action research, a mode of ethnography that involves engagement with the community in active problem solving. It soon become evident, however, that the Uruvians were resourceful enough on their own to have instigated the Atmosphere Hood, *Until Uru*, and many other player-led hacking and creation initiatives, so I had laid those thoughts aside. Now I was placed in the unusual and privileged position of being asked to actually contribute to helping the community I had been studying for the past two-plus years in a very tangible way. I was assigned the role of official *Uru* anthropologist.

Over the course of the months that followed, and while completing my dissertation, I was given three main tasks. The first was to help galvanize the current Uru

Diaspora and bring them together to make a business case for the reopening of *Uru*. The second was to continue my ethnographic work and monitor how that process was progressing. The third was to generate a survey to capture some demographic, play pattern, and marketing-related data the team needed for design, planning, and business development.

As this effort was under way, I had a providential encounter at the E3 Game Expo in Los Angeles. A man who was videotaping the speakers at a panel asked me to watch his camera, and when he returned to his seat, I noticed that his badge indicated he was the "Uru Community Manager, Ubisoft." This was remarkable in and of itself considering the game had been closed for over two years at this point. I immediately roped Ron Meiners into assisting in the conspiracy, and we later started a blog together titled "Virtual Cultures."

The plan was to make a business case to GameTap and its parent, AOL, for the reopening of *Uru* by reconvening a very much alive and active fan base in a single *Until Uru* shard (server). Along with other members of the community who had been drafted into service by Cyan, I was tasked with getting the word out among *Uru* refugees that they should make an effort to gather in the D'mala shard. Two years earlier, after *Uru's* initial closure, players had also instigated an online petition. A new one was started by players in support of a relaunch. Additional *Until Uru* software keys, which had been discontinued for some time, were now made available to new players to enable as many players as possible, both new and old, to participate in the D'mala shard.

The entire scenario was framed within the context of the *Uru* storyline, with the Cyanists appearing as members of the D'ni Restoration Council to announce the possibility of obtaining new funding to resume its restoration efforts on the City of D'ni Ae'gura. Throughout this process the identity of the owners of D'mala was kept secret, as was that of the mysterious stranger who now appeared in-cavern as their potential benefactor.

It did not take long for the band of resourceful and tech-savvy world-class puzzle-solvers to reveal the identity of the mysterious stranger or the company he worked for. They looked up the IP address of D'mala and found it was registered to Turner Broadcasting, then did some research and figured out that Turner was behind the initiative. Virtually overnight, fans updated the *Uru* page in Wikipedia. As resident ethnographer, I was amused to inform the mysterious stranger, Blake Lewin, that he had been "outed." In grand Uru Diaspora tradition, players began to take the D'mala challenge as a game.

This process represented an unusual intersection between top-down corporate organization and bottom-up emergent processes. Those of us who were deeply engaged with the community helped to instigate a viral communication campaign based on what we already knew about the Uru Diaspora, where they were, and how to reach them. With a relatively small amount of effort on our parts, we were able to seed the D'mala initiative, and players took over from there. Uruvian-Thereians began actively recruiting not only Uru immigrants, but players who had played the single-player *Uru Prime* but never experienced the multiplayer version, as well as entirely new players who had never tried either. In *Second Life*, we generated virtual note-cards and passed them around within the *Uru* community. Over the course of about a month, via fan forums and *Uru* communities in other games, we were able to register 3,000 players on D'mala.

At the 2006 E3 Expo, GameTap officially announced that it would be launching *Myst Online: Uru Live* (MOUL) as part of its subscription-based game portal service. In February 2007, three years to the month after the plug was pulled on the original *Uru Prologue* servers, *Myst Online: Uru Live* was opened under "GameTap Originals."

What happened after was an interesting and arguably unprecedented collaboration between a very large corporate entity and a vibrant, though small, fan community, the marriage of enterprise and emergence. We have already seen how *There.com* players had learned that they could "talk with their feet" by staying in a virtual world rather than leaving it. They also understood that the vitality and sustainability of the new *Uru* would depend on its gaining a strong following. Completely on their own and with no provocation from GameTap or its agents (including their cyberethnographer-for-hire), Uruvian-Thereians began launching a viral marketing campaign. They placed signs by *Uru*-inspired artifacts and areas, set up an *Uru* travel center with information about how to join GameTap and play the game, and conducted regular tours of the new *Uru* for uninitiated Thereians.

I have no doubt that the same would have happened in *Second Life*, if not for the fact that the D'ni Island had been forced to close down during the D'mala experiment. *Second Life* islands are notoriously expensive to maintain and the small handful of artisans could no longer sustain their creation. They had, however, had the forethought to engage Linden Lab's assistance in archiving the project. When I began to see the emergent marketing campaign take off in *There.com*, I connected the *Uru* builders from *Second Life* with GameTap, who decided to sponsor the reopening of D'ni Island as part of their *Myst Online* promotion effort. With some minor modifications, including interactive billboards directing *Second Life* players to *Myst Online*, D'ni Island was reopened as *Myst Online* Island, with a major launch party in conjunction with the opening of MOUL (figure 15.1).

| **Figure 15.1** |
Aerial view of *Myst Online* Island in *Second Life*. (Image: Pearce)

Now that *Uru* was back, one would have assumed, as many at GameTap and Cyan did, that *Uru* refugees would abandon their new homes and return to their homeland. But as I had already observed with *Until Uru*, such was not the case. *Uru* refugees continued to flourish within their adopted homes, and new patterns and transludic synergies emerged. In addition to the emergent marketing of *MOUL* in other games, new *MOUL* players also started visiting the settlements of *Uru* refugees and forming new *Uru* communities in *There.com* and *Second Life*, following the now well-established custom of creating transludic identities.

This second wave of Uru immigrants, which had begun on a smaller scale during the *Until Uru* period, now began to join their compatriots in these new worlds, even while continuing to frequent *MOUL*. Longtime *Uru* refugees for whom *Uru* was their first online game also started to branch out into the more traditional MMOGs such as *World of Warcraft*, *Guild Wars*, and *Lord of the Rings Online*. For some, *Uru* had set the stage for becoming full-fledged MMOG gamers, even though they had previously shunned these more traditional, combat-based games.

These multiworld transludic practices fly in the face of conventional wisdom about consumption patterns among MMOG players. Among the traditional demographic described in book I, primarily male college students and recent grads, intergame cannibalization is a well-known fact. Players in this oversaturated market migrate en masse into new games, often taking entire guilds with them. So-called hardcore players typically maintain only one subscription at time, canceling prior subscriptions in the process.

The Uru Diaspora, on the other hand, because of its older, predominately baby boomer demographic, follows an entirely different pattern. As a follow-up study I conducted with baby boomer gamers revealed, this demographic has both more disposable income and more free time than the primary audience to which most MMOGs are targeted (Pearce 2008b). As a result, they can afford to maintain multiple game and virtual world accounts. Furthermore, community-minded players are often willing to outlay significant expenditures in *addition* to subscription fees, sometimes in the hundreds or even thousands of dollars per month, to engage in productive play and community-building, buy real estate, and shop for virtual items, such as fashions and furnishings. So, far from a mass exodus to *Uru*, the Uru Diaspora continued to expand and grow in other games.

As with all MMOGs, the relationship between creators and players is an important and often overlooked dynamic. Ever since the days of *Ultima*'s "Lord British" (Richard Garriott's pseudonym in the games he created), MMOG players have viewed their game's designers as deities of sorts. When Rand Miller appeared in-world, as he did for events such as the *Second Life* MOUL Island opening, or the St. Patrick's Day parade in *Uru*, it was as if players were getting a glimpse of the king. Other Cyanists were also treated with reverence, although they were perceived as being more accessible. The status of the game designers in a fixed synthetic world like *Uru*, where the designers' imagination is foregrounded, is particularly high because players have become so attached to the designer's vision. In-world sightings of lead designers in co-created worlds, such as *There.com*'s Michael Wilson, or *Second Life*'s Corey Ondrejka, are equally momentous, but players seem to view the gods of such worlds as more approachable. Michael Wilson and Linden CEO Philip Rosedale frequently make in-world appearances to give "state of the virtual world" addresses and speak to their denizens after the fashion of elected leaders.

One year after the opening of *MOUL*, in February 2008, GameTap announced that *Uru* would be, once again, closing. While players noted the coincidence of this announcement taking place exactly four years after the original *Uru* closure, they also appreciated that GameTap had chosen to make the announcement in a much more timely and respectful fashion than its predecessors. Players were given two months to say their good-byes and make other preparations, and were even given an extension in order to have an extra weekend to enjoy their beloved world together.

Unlike the original closure, where players had virtually no warning and no place to go, the "third wave" of *Uru* immigrants had options. Those who had already settled in other games and virtual worlds continued to maintain their enclaves. In the *Uru* tradition of helping newbies, many of these first- and second-generation *Uru* refugees began mentoring and even recruiting newer players, taking them on tours to find new homes within established *Uru* communities in other virtual worlds. The *MOUL* forums, much like the Koalanet forum for TGU, became the primary extravirtual communication hub for the new Uru Diaspora, including a full-blown debate about the merits and deficiencies of the various virtual worlds to which players were emigrating.

During the last days of *MOUL*, players from around the world gathered in-cavern to say goodbye. Many stayed online to the final moments, staging what some players referred to as a "wake." European players who could not be online for the shutdown at midnight Eastern time parked their avatars in their hoods, watched over by their friends.

TGU had already made a plan: similar to their immediate transition to the Koalanet chat room following the first closure, they would all go to *There.com* after the shutdown. Players stayed in the hood; their previous experience with server instability and being unable to log on after crashing, or being unable to link between Ages, made them cautious. They all wanted to be together when the plug was pulled.

A few Cyanists visited throughout the day to spend time with players, a gesture that was deeply appreciated. Even Rand Miller himself came in briefly. These visitations gave players a clear signal than unlike in the previous circumstance, the gods of their world actually cared about them. The server administrators sent off warnings at the fifteen– and five–minute points, and even inserted humorous quips to soften the blow. Finally, at 12:01 Eastern time on April 10, 2008, once again—or in some cases, for the first time—players saw the message on their screen that had devastated them over four years earlier.

| Figure 15.2 |

The final screen of *Myst Online Uru Life*, as experienced firsthand by the author. (Image: Pearce)

For me, it was an eerie moment: to experience firsthand, as a member of the community, the story I had heard numerous times over the previous four years, seemed strangely surreal and ironic (figure 15.2).

But unlike the first end of *Uru*, within minutes, players had logged on to other virtual worlds, many convening in *Uru*-themed areas in *There.com* and *Second Life*. When *Uru* initially closed in 2004, it was literally the end of the world for many players who had never been in an online game before and were surprised by the strength of the bonds that had formed there. Now, after four years of creating their own emergent cultures, the Uru Diaspora had developed a sense of self-determination, autonomy, and empowerment. Rather than seeing this as the end of *Uru*, many viewed it as an opportunity to reclaim *Uru* and continue to cast it in their own likeness.

The *Uru* narrative is enfolded in many layers of poetic irony, in which a fictional premise interweaves with its real-life experience in virtually every imaginable way. The Cyanists, like the powerful D'ni Age writers they invented, had the power to create and destroy entire worlds and peoples (in this case avatars) at a whim. Yet through their puzzles, its designers had also trained their players to outsmart them using their own emergent play patterns. The theme of *Uru* is the restoration of a lost culture, the precise metagame in which the Uru Diaspora has been engaged ever since the initial closure. Even the reopening of *Uru* was a game of sorts: players were challenged by Cyan and GameTap to reconvene and bring their numbers up, a goal at which they succeeded. Since the closure of MOUL, after a protracted negotiation with GameTap, Cyan announced it would launch yet a third iteration of Uru titled *Myst Online: Restoration Experiment*, or *MORE*. The main aim of this experiment would be to provide tools to enable players to begin "restoring" (in other words, building) their own Ages. Cyan had already set up guilds in *MOUL*, such as the Guild of Writers (to create such Ages) and the Guild of Maintainers (for testing them), as a precursor to this direction. However, the effort has been indefinitely postponed due to financial problems at Cyan. At this writing, the status of *Uru* remains in flux, but there is no doubt that the interplay between the imagination of its designers and the emergent cultures of its players will continue for years to come.

CRAFTING CULTURES: EMERGENCE AS DESIGN MATERIAL

As game designers, what are we to make of emergent cultures? They appear to be a fact of life of any entertainment environment genre in which players are given the power to participate in a consequential way. We see them in social networking sites, Web 2.0 applications, and all manner of fan cultures. The defining characteristics of virtual worlds identified in chapter 2—contiguous spatiality and explorability; persistence, particularly persistent, embodied identity; inhabitability and consequential participation; populousness; and worldness—all predispose these environments to serve as ecosystems for certain types of emergent behavior. As we've seen, how this emergence plays out will vary based on the affordances of the design of these ecosystems, depending on whether they are ludic, goal-based games, or paidiaic, open-ended, creative worlds, regardless of where they fall on the fixed synthetic/co-created world spectrum. Even before the world is inhabited, the seed is planted by the very players who are attracted to it. Once let loose on our designs, communities of play can be powerful engines for collaboration—they can build or enhance our worlds, or send them on trajectories we don't care for or which are not particularly good for business. As second-order designers, the agony and the ecstasy of our craft is the very fact that we cannot fully anticipate the outcomes of our creations. Play has a life of its own. It can be guided, but never controlled.

How then do we guide emergent cultures? How do we actively participate in bottom-up processes? The most recent chapter in the tale of the Uru Diaspora illustrates a growing need for ongoing, culturally engaged research throughout the design, testing, and implementation of virtual worlds. As we've learned, once these delicate play ecosystems are open to the public, they become subjected to emergent cultures and processes that designers may not have anticipated, and which can be challenging if not impossible to avert or redirect once under way.

Designers of these worlds are quickly discovering that MMOGs and MMOWs are not products in the traditional sense. The classic model of CD-based game production entails spending multiple years to design, produce, test, and finally release a product, which, much like a book or film, is fixed once it enters into the marketplace. Not so virtual worlds. These environments are more like real estate developments, particularly theme parks, mixed-use entertainment retail centers, or even residential neighborhoods, than they are like traditional games. Because they are persistent and inhabited, they evolve over time. They are more of a service industry than a product, but in truth, they are both.

Even fixed synthetic worlds require ongoing maintenance and the regular updating and refreshment of content. They sometimes require special events, live performers, and other elements to reflect seasonal visitation patterns, or to maintain the interest of return visitors. Some, like *Myst Online: Uru Live* have adopted the episodic structure of television, releasing content at regular intervals. This allows for a more rapid release of an initial build, and also provides a framework for a dynamic interplay between designers and players. In this manner, feedback loops that fuel emergence can also be leveraged to help improve design. Blizzard, for instance, added ten new levels to its maximum of sixty in order to enhance the *World of Warcraft* experience for its higher-level players. In *MOUL*, new Ages were solved quickly and posted on fan gaming guide sites. Players could also make their own marker quests. Co-created worlds typically rely on players to keep content fresh, and include regular software updates to fix bugs and add features. *Second Life* treats this process as collaborative, allowing players to submit and vote on proposed software features, which the "Lindens" (as its owners are called) review for implementation.

On the other hand, when designers try to step in to fix games that are already in the midst of emergent processes, the results are often catastrophic, especially if they are not deeply engaged on a day-to-day basis with players. *Star Wars: Galaxies'* midstream redesign failed to expand its audience while at the same time alienating its existing fanbase. The transition of the foundering *The Sims Online* to *EA-Land* was a disaster, contributing to the game's ultimate, and possibly inevitable, demise. TSO is a prime example of a complete disconnect between designers and emergent cultures. The original *Sims* series has the most vibrant emergent fan culture of any single-player game in history. From the beginning, the game integrated user-created content, allowing players to skin game characters, furniture, and other items. *The Sims* fan culture is well studied (Pearce 2002a, Pearce 2002b, Poremba 2003, Prügl and Schreier 2006) and could have easily been leveraged in crafting the culture of its multiplayer spin-off. Instead, its designers opted against creating an affordance for players to bring their own skins into the game, a fatal mistake that any knowledgeable researcher could (and in fact did) recommend.

Community managers have an important role to play, but are typically brought in after the fact, working largely under the customer service paradigm. At their best, they serve as evangelizers, event organizers, den mothers and fathers, and sounding boards, providing designers with insights once the game has launched, which may be too late. Even with the best intentions, fatal mistakes can be made by simply not understanding the community's emergent cultural dynamics. For instance, community managers often work conventional office hours of 9 to 5, precisely the time period when the fewest number of players are typically online. As a result, faux pas often result from community managers being woefully unaware of cultural practices among their constituents. Player representation can help. *There.com* has appointed its Member Advisory Board from pools of player-nominated candidates. Forums are also a source for gathering user feedback, although they tend to follow the "squeaky wheel" pattern, where players who are the most comfortable voicing their (often negative) opinions are most visible, even though they do not necessarily represent the community as a whole. Good community managers are relied upon by players to galvanize the community; however, they also run the risk of being viewed as representing management, which can either place them in the position of authority figures, or worse yet, make them subject to grievances and even abuse from players for decisions that are seldom of their making. At present, there is virtually no formal training for a career in community management, a field that is certain to grow as Web 2.0 applications and online games become more prevalent.

This is where cyberethnographers can come in. Working in tandem with designers and community managers, they make it their business to understand the game community on its own terms. Unlike community managers, an anthropologist or sociologist has the ability to step back from a personal investment in the success or failure of a world and provide a broader view, one less tied to business interests. Players will often orient themselves differently toward someone perceived as an anthropologist because they do not associate them with management, even, as was the case with my GameTap work, if they are known to be in management's employ. The credibility I had built up in advance of *Uru*'s reopening aided me in gathering information that would not have been available to people who were perceived as representing management.

Most importantly, both community managers and cyberethnographers have a vital role to play in the *design* process. Ethnography has long been an integrated component in a number of design practices. Fields such as industrial design, human-computer interaction, and computer-supported cooperative work have a tradition of integrating ethnographers into the design process, as exemplified by research groups in successful IT companies such as IBM, Microsoft, Apple, Intel, Xerox, PARC, and others. Methods such as participatory and community design and action research, which engage users throughout the design process, can also be an effective way to guide emergent cultures. The game industry has no such research tradition, but it would do well to adopt some of these practices.

Experienced cyberethnographers can also bring to the table their extensive experience in studying a variety of games from an objective viewpoint. Transludic research is particularly valuable in this regard. For instance, my own work with players trying to make decisions about whether to migrate to *Second Life* or *There.com* has made me privy to player perceptions of both worlds that neither community managers nor designers of either would be exposed to. One finding was that many *There.com* players, particularly those in the baby boomer demographic (a highly lucrative audience), are turned off by *Second Life* because they see it as a virtual red-light district. This is not information that people directly affiliated with either company would have access to.

As a game designer myself, I am particularly interested in the notion of emergence as a design material. How can we actually use emergence—consider it, learn from it—to shape the next generation of MMOGs and virtual worlds? All too often, virtual world and game designers reinvent the wheel, failing to build on prior work. This is particularly true in the metaverse space, which tends to operate on a basis of historical amnesia, whereas MMOG designers tend to build games that are more derivative of their forebears. In either case, they sometimes miss valuable lessons from precedents, and as a result may be missing the opportunity to advance the field. Metaphorically, they reinvent the wheel rather than inventing the car. Designers are fortunate as MMOG research is the fastest growing sector of game studies. Now available with a simple Google search are numerous highly accessible and informative studies that can help designers better understand emergent cultures in online virtual worlds and games and make better decisions as a result. More and more students are emerging from universities equipped to assist in the design process through the use of ethnography and related research skills. This research can also help them to rethink the design process as they begin to reframe the essence of their craft as a collaborative process of creating cultures. When framed in this way, emergence can become a powerful engine to make games that are wildly more innovative, interesting, and successful than many of the copycat games and virtual worlds we see today.

This is particularly important when we consider current and anticipate future trends. If the top two in each genre—*MapleStory* and *Habbo Hotel*, with their combined 160 million subscriptions—are any indication, we can anticipate that the challenges of crafting emergent cultures in virtual worlds will only increase exponentially as more and more tweens come of age as regular denizens of virtual worlds and multiplayer games. How can we approach these issues creatively? How can game designers, whose fundamental craft is to envision something they can never really entirely control, learn to adapt and respond to emergent cultures at the very start of the design process, and throughout the life of an online virtual world or online game?

One way to do this is to study emergence in other virtual worlds, as I have done here. There are many principles that can be taken away from the *Uru* case study that can be applied across other play ecosystems. User-created content is of course the most obvious, but thinking more deeply about tools for both creating and distributing user-created content will help us to amplify their emergent effects to enhance both the player experience and our own goals as designers. At the same time, we must be wary of forms of emergence that are undesirable, as these are almost impossible to reverse once they are under way.

Other examples include simple features that have been discussed here: persistent nametags, for instance, prevent players from certain types of gameplay, such as hide-and-seek. Loose objects that can be moved around can be transformed into play props, such as the *Uru* traffic cones being adapted as bowling pins. (In one of the later *MOUL* Ages, Cyan actually included a soccer ball and some strategically placed posts to enable soccer playing.) These are just two examples of seemingly minor design features that had a significant impact on emergent behavior. Understanding players' underlying interests, motivations, and play styles can also help us in this process. Notions introduced here such as spatial literacy, intersubjective flow, and productive play give us conceptual tools with which to enhance the emergent potentialities of our virtual worlds.

These issues will become increasingly important as play becomes a more pervasive part of culture, not only in virtual worlds, but in every aspect of life.

GLOBAL PLAYGROUNDS AND THE "PLAY TURN" IN CULTURE

If the story of the Uru Diaspora tells us anything, it is that the more things change, the more they stay the same (Karr 1849). The essential qualities of human culture, of people's desire for affinity, for identity, for expression, and for the liminal space of ritual and alternative personas, is a persistent theme throughout many cultures and historical periods. How these needs are expressed may vary, and as the world becomes concurrently larger and smaller, the "global village" (McLuhan 1964) is being reconfigured in some sectors as a global playground.

Indeed, a global village powered by the Internet and wireless technologies is very different from the global village of McLuhan's day when all the world's populace could passively watch the same events at more or less the same time, whether it be the Vietnam War, the assassinations of presidents and civil rights leaders, or man's first step on the moon. Today's global village is discursive, collaborative, emergent, and highly social. New research has shown that far from being isolated and alienated by technology, today's wired and wireless youth are more social and more connected than ever before. Instant messaging, mobile phone texting, and virtual worlds enable kids to remain in constant contact with their friends and families. According to a recent study by the Pew Trust, about two-thirds of teenagers have their own web sites, blogs, or MySpace pages (Lenhart et al. 2007). Virtual worlds are becoming a growing part of this media mix.

One of the key factors in this growing global village is the issue of identity. As early as the late 1960s, McLuhan and Fiore anticipated that rapid global mediation would make identity the single most important issue of the next century, leading to worldwide wars and conflict (1968). Indeed, today we see violent conflicts that expose these rifts as people increasingly try to define national or religious identities and boundaries in a world that seems increasingly boundaryless. These trends are also emergent, and often take us by surprise because they don't fit the top-down paradigms to which most of Western culture is accustomed.

For online gamers, this instinct finds its expression in play rather than war, and sometimes through play war. In the alternative universes of virtual worlds, games, and fan cultures, players may adopt fictive ethnicities that provide them with a sense of belonging and community. These alternate identities are not mutually exclusive with real-world identities, and, as we've seen, online gamers are not, by definition, people "without lives." Rather, they adopt multiple lives, multiple identities, and multiple bodies through their avatar instantiations (Taylor 1999).

Is this new, is this somehow posthuman? Not in the least. Among children, we regard role-play and imaginary identities as a natural part of growing up. But in Western culture, adult play other than sports, and particularly imaginary play, has traditionally been viewed as transgressive. However, if this research is any indication, this is in the process of changing. With populations of both multiplayer games and metaverses on the rise, it is clear that for the next generation, online lives and alternative personas will soon be as commonplace as watching television has been to their parents.

If we telescope out to the larger picture, we find that networked play is not simply confined to the game worlds that have been the focus of this book. In fact, network play has insinuated itself into many other aspects of life. It could be argued that You-Tube is a networked playground of sorts, even more so when we take note of the numerous machinima films created in games by players. Another emergent form of culture, these films take a range of forms, from the infamous "All Your Base Are Belong to Us" meme phenomenon, riffing on a poor translation in the Sega game *Zero Wing*, to "Dance, Voldo, Dance," a player-created music video that uses fighting moves from the Dreamcast game *Soul Calibur* as dance steps (Brandt 2002), to "Male Restroom Etiquette," a mockumentary created in *The Sims 2* (Overman 2006), and its female retort.

But these trends move far beyond traditional gamer fan culture. They point to a growing "play turn" in which, far from being a marginalized fringe activity, play is beginning to pervade every aspect of our lives. We see games and play increasingly embedded in social networks, in mobile phones, on web sites, and in domains as diverse as education, military and corporate training, activism, even politics.

Nowhere is this "play turn" more evident than in the emerging genre of alternate reality games (ARGs), or "big games." These games reconfigure both the physical world and the network as a game board in which anything can be co-opted as a game piece, blurring the boundary between play and real life. Pioneering games like *Majestic*, *Big Urban Game*, *The Beast*, *Pac-Manhattan*, and *I Love Bees* turn the world into a giant playground where public payphones and billboards deliver clues, and players engage in large-scale puzzle-solving by collecting information from the real world.

In *Big Urban Game*, players voted online to select the routes of giant, inflatable game pieces that moved through the Minneapolis/St. Paul area. In *Pac-Manhattan*, students of New York University's Interactive Telecommunications Program enacted a giant tag-like version of the classic eighties game *Pac-Man* in the streets of New York.

These types of games, like the MMOGs and MMOWs described in this book, are increasingly merging with the content creation of Web 2.0 to inspire diverse forms of productive play. In addition to the creative efforts illustrated among players in *There .com* and *Second Life*, players are also engaging with elaborate knowledge-building enterprises that might provide some clues on how to improve these types of applications in "serious," real-life applications, such as education. For instance, using a special plug-in and forum-style entries, thousands of *World of Warcraft* players contribute to Thottbot, a Wikipedia-style database of game guides and maps. For the ARG *Chain Factor*, integrated into an episode of the television show *Numb3rs*, players built a communal wiki deciphering the game's elaborate math puzzles. To commemorate the closure of MOUL, *Uru* players created a *Myst*-style walk-through from still images of the game, as well as a number of videos.

Thus man the player is also man the creator, who plays with, subverts, and reconfigures media, inscribing it with new goals and cultural meanings. In this sense, one could argue that the new global village is a distributed playground, less passive and more collaborative than what McLuhan initially envisioned. Everyone who inhabits the global village-as-playground is at once performer and audience, merging the sense of play-as-performance with gameplay. At the same time, as content creators, they are empowered to redesign the game to their own liking.

Looking at these cultures of play through an anthropological lens suggests that this new global playground brings us closer to the more traditional notion of a village: a small community whose collective unity is held as a high priority, and in which individual and group identity are inextricably intertwined. It might also cause us to question if the Cartesian, paradigmatically modern, model of the individual as paramount is misdirected and even failing humanity in some essential way.

The story of the Uru Diaspora illustrates the unique bonds and connections that can form within a play community. These bonds suggest that one's role in the real world, though *real*, might not be entirely *true*; it might fail to provide for the full expression of the true self. This is the power of the play community, where the true self is manifested through the selves of others. Thus we find new insights into ourselves through play and in particular play with others in the shared space of imagination.

Play is not just for kids anymore, as Leesa's call at the end of book II suggests. But as more and more children and adults engage with networked play communities, we are also faced with a nagging dilemma. All of the play ecosystems described in this book are global villages that are run by corporations. Some of these global villages have expanded to the status of mini-nations. *World of Warcraft* has a population the size of Belgium, and *Habbo Hotel* has more "citizens" than Germany.

Being implicated in this process myself through aiding in the *Uru* relaunch, I am also well aware of the complexities of this dynamic. While people may feel empowered by their new communities in the global playground, the bottom line is that their communities, their property, indeed their very bodies, are owned by corporations. And yet these corporations are providing a service and resources that players want: the creative talents of Rand Miller and the Cyanists cannot be underrated, for it is their vision that galvanized the *Myst/Uru* community in the first place. Yet the narrative of the Uru Diaspora also illustrates this challenging and sometimes heartbreaking side of the equation: global playgrounds and the communities they house are ultimately at the mercy of "shareholder value." Nonetheless, this tension, this rupture, is in constant play. In the case of the Uru Diaspora, we see the unique case of a community whose profound connection to each other and the content that gave them their new home and identities has transcended its creators and their institutional framework.

This is the power of emergence. Bottom-up processes have a mind of their own: they cannot be controlled. Emergence, once under way, is very hard to undo. And just as it has proven nearly impossible to regulate the Internet, companies who engage in the creation of emergent play cultures are likely to find that they have lost control over the very communities they create. We have seen this in game economies where one bad design decision, one bug, or one hacker vulnerability can lead to an irrevocable downward spiral of one kind or another.

As the writing of this book was coming to a close, the status of *Uru* was still in flux. Cyan and GameTap had resolved their legal negotiations, reflecting traditional notions of media ownership between developer and publisher, and Cyan was poised and yet fiscally unable to begin the next phase of the *Uru* legacy: the move to player-created content. Yet in some sense this negotiation and its outcome are moot. What both corporate entities have failed to entirely comprehend is that *Uru* no longer belongs to either of them. There seems little question concerning who the true owners of *Uru* really are. The fate of *Uru* is in the hands of the emergent cultures of its players. These will live well beyond the game itself in any official, corporate-sanctioned form, and the Uru Diaspora will continue to find new and ingenious ways to become the masters of their play community's own destiny.

But at the end of the day, how much power *do* the corporations that own these networked play spaces within the ludisphere, the global playground, really have? In some sense, they have it all; in another sense, they have none. In Cyan's case, having trained players to solve complex problems and intricate puzzles with the goal of restoring a lost culture, their own role has perhaps become subordinate to that of their players. Ultimately, *Uru is* its players. The game's very name, *URU (you are you): Ages Beyond Myst*, seems apocryphal now. And we can only hear the echo of Yeesha's final words as we contemplate the future of *Uru* and what it portends for the future of game communities within the new global playground of the ludisphere and its distributed playgrounds:

"Perhaps the ending has not yet been written."

Games and Virtual Worlds Cited

Active Worlds (originally *Alphaworld)*, 1995, Worlds, Inc. (Ron Britvich, designer).

Age of Empires, 1997, Ensemble Studios/Microsoft.

Anarchy Online, 2001, Funcom/Funcom.

Asheron's Call, 2001, Turbine Entertainment Software/Microsoft Game Studios

The Beast, 2001, 42 Entertainment (Jordan Weisman, Elan Lee, and Sean Stewart, designers)/Microsoft

Big Urban Game (B.U.G.), 2003, University of Minnesota Design Institute (Nick Fortuno, Frank Lanz, and Katie Salen, designers).

Blaxxun (originally *Black Sun)*, 1996, Blaxxun Interactive (originally Black Sun Interactive).

Chain Factor, 2007, Area+Code (Frank Lanz, designer)/CBS.

Civilization (aka *Sid Meier's Civilization)*, 1991, MPS Labs (Sid Meier, Bruce Campbell Shelley, designers)/MicroProse Software, Inc.

Cybertown, 1996, Cybertown (Pascal Baudar).

Dark Age of Camelot, 2001, Mythic Entertainment; Wanadoo (Mark Jacobs, designer)/Vivideni Universal.

Diablo, 1997, Blizzard Entertainment/Ubisoft, Electronic Arts.

Dungeons & Dragons Online, 1974, TSR (Gary Gygax and Dave Arneson, designers)/TSR and Wizards of the Coast.

EVE Online, 2003, CCP Games/CCP Games.

EverQuest, 1998, 989 Studios/Verant (Brad McQuaid, Steve Clover, Bill Trost, designers)/ Sony Online Entertainment.

Gaia Online, 2003, Gaia Interactive, Inc.

Grand Theft Auto III, 2002, Rockstar Games (Chris Rothwell, Craig Filshie, William Mills, James Worrall, designers).

Guild Wars, 2005, ArenaNet (Mike O'Brien, Patrick Wyatt, Jeff Strain, designers)/NCSoft

Habbo Hotel, 2000, Sulake (Sampo Karjalainen Aapo Kyrölä, designers).

Habitat (also LucasFilm Habitat, Fujitsu Habitat and WorldsAway), 1986, Lucasfilm Games, Quantum Link, Fujitsu (Chip Morningstar and Randy Farmer, designers)/Quantum Link, Fujitsu

HiPiHi, 2007 (beta), HiPiHi Co. Ltd.

I Love Bees, 2004, 42 Entertainment and Bungie Studios/Microsoft.

Kaneva, 2006, Kaneva, Inc.

Lineage, 1998, NCsoft (Jake Song, designer)/NCsoft.

LlambdaMOO, 1990, Xerox PARC (Pavel Curtis, designer).

Lord of the Rings Online, 2007, Turbine Entertainment Software/Midway.

Majestic, 2001, Anim-X (Neil Young, designer)/Electronic Arts.

MapleStory, 2003, Wizet/Nexxon.

Meridian 59, 1996, Archetype Interactive/3DO Studios; and 2004, Near Death Studios.

MUD, 1979, Roy Trubshaw and Richard Bartle, designers.

Myst Online: Uru Live, 2007, Cyan Worlds (Rand Miller, designer)/GameTap Originals.

Myst, 1993, Cyan Worlds (Robyn and Rand Miller)/Brøderbund.

OnLive! Traveler (Currently *Digitalspace Traveler*), 1996, OnLive! (Steve DiPaola, Ali Eb-tekar, Stasia McGehee, designers).

Pac-Man, 1980, Namco (Toru Iwatani, designer)/Namco and Midway.

Pac-Manhattan, 2004, New York University Interactive Telecommunications Program (Frank Lanz, instructor).

The Palace, 1995, Time Warner (Jim Bumgardner, designer).

Planetside, 2002, Sony Online Entertainment/Sony Online Entertainment.

Pong, 1972, Atari Inc. (Allan Alcorn, designer).

Puzzle Pirates, 2003, Three Rings Design (Daniel James, designer)/Three Rings Design, Ubisoft.

Ragnarok Online, 2002, Gravity Interactive, Inc.

Riven: The Sequel to Myst, 1997, Cyan/Brøderbund, Acclaim, Ubisoft.

Ryzom, 2003, Nevrax/Nevrax.

PlayStation Home, 2008, Sony Computer Entertainment London Studio/Sony Computer Entertainment.

Second Life, 2003, Linden Lab (Cory Ondrejka, designer).

The Sims Online (Later *EA-Land*), 2002, Maxis (Will Wright, Chris Trottier, designers)/ Electronic Arts.

The Sims, 2001, Maxis (Will Wright, designer)/Electronic Arts.

The Sims 2, 2004, Maxis/Electronic Arts.

Spacewar!, 1962, MIT (Steve "Slug" Russell, Martin "Shag" Graetz, Wayne Wiitanen, designers, with Alan Kotok).

Spore, 2008, Maxis (Will Wright, Alex Hutchinson, designers)/Electronic Arts.

Star Wars: Galaxies, 2003, Sony Online Entertainment (Raph Koster, Richard Vogel, and John Donham, designers)/LucasArts.

Tennis for Two, 1958, Brookhaven National Laboratory (William Higinbotham, designer).

There.com, 2003, There, Inc. (Will Harvey and Jeffrey Ventrella, designers); 2005, Makena Technologies.

Toontown Online, 2003, Disney Interactive, Inc.

Ultima I: The First Age of Darkness, 1980, Origin Systems (Richard Garriott, designer)/California Pacific Computer Company.

Ultima Online, 1997, Origin Systems (Raph Koster, designer)/Electronic Arts.

Uru: Ages Beyond Myst, 2003, Cyan Worlds (Rand Miller, designer)/Ubisoft.

Virtual Magic Kingdom, 2005, Walt Disney Parks and Resorts, Sulake/ Walt Disney Parks and Resorts.

Whyville, 1999, Newmedeon (Jen Sun, designer).

World of Warcraft, 2003, Blizzard Entertainment (Rob Pardo, Jeff Kaplan, Tom Chilton, designers)/Vivendi Universal.

Zero Wing, 1992, Toaplan Co., Ltd.

References

Aarseth, Espen. 2000. "Allegories of Space: The Question of Spatiality in Computer Games." In *Cybertext Yearbook 2000*, eds. M. Eskelinen and R. Koskimaa, 152–171. Watertown, MA: Eastgate Systems.

American Heritage® Dictionary of the English Language, 4th ed. 2000. "Diaspora." Boston, MA: Houghton Mifflin.

Anderson, Benedict. 1991. *Imagined Communities: Reflections on the Origin and Spread of Nationalism*. Rev. Ed. London: Verso.

Appelcline, Shannon. 2004. "If You Build It, They Might Come: Critical Mass and Other User Buzzwords." Trials, Triumphs & Trivialities. Skotos Gaming & Storytelling Community. Available at http://www.skotos.net/articles/TTnT_/TTnT_143.phtml.

Appelcline, Shannon. 2000–2006. Trials, Triumphs & Trivialities. Skotos Gaming & Storytelling Community. Available at http://www.skotos.net/articles/TTnT.shtml.

Ashe, Suzanne. 2003. "Exporing Myst's Brave New World." *Wired* 11.06, June.

Au, Wagner James. 2002. "Playing Games with Free Speech." *Salon.com*, May. Available at http://dir.salon.com/story/tech/feature/2002/05/06/games_as_speech/.

Au, Wagner James. 2008. "Lindens Limit Libertarianism: Billboard Advertising Restricted, Continuing Rollback of Laissez Faire Politics." *New World Notes*, February 14. Available at http://nwn.blogs.com/nwn/2008/02/lindens-limit-l.html

Barab, Sasha, Michael K. Thomas, Tyler Dodge, Kurt D. Squire, and Markeda Newell. 2004. "Reflections from the Field: Critical Design Ethnography: Designing for Change." *Anthropology and Education Quarterly* 35, no. 2: 254–268.

Bartle, Richard. 1996. Hearts, Clubs, Diamonds, Spades: Players Who Suit MUDs. Available at http://www.mud.co.uk/richard/hcds.htm

Bartle, Richard. 2003. *Designing Virtual Worlds*. Indianapolis: New Riders.

Bartle, Richard. (Forthcoming). "Alice and Dorothy Play Together." In *Third Person*, eds. Noah Wardrip-Fruin and Pat Harrigan. Cambridge, MA: MIT Press.

Bar-Yam, Yaneer. 1997. *Dynamics of Complex Systems (Studies in Nonlinearity)*. Boulder, CO: Westview Press.

Bar-Yam, Yaneer. 1999. "Virtual Worlds and Complex Systems." In *Virtual Worlds: Synthetic Universes, Digital Life, and Complexity*, ed. J.-C. Heudin. Reading, MA: Perseus Books.

Bar-Yam, Yaneer. 2000. "Concepts in Complex Systems." New England Complex Systems Institutute. Available at http://necsi.edu/guide/concepts/.

Bar-Yam, Yaneer. 2003. "Unifying Principles in Complex Systems." In *Converging Technology for Improving Human Performance*, eds. M. C. Roco and W. S. Bainbridge, 380–409. Amsterdam: Kluwer.

Bateson, Gregory. 1972. "A Theory of Play and Fantasy." In *Toward an Ecology of Mind*. New York: Ballantine.

Bateson, Gregory. 1988. "Play and Paradigm." *Play & Culture* 1, no. 1:20–27.

Baudrillard, Jean. 1994. *Simulacra and Simulation*. Ann Arbor: University of Michigan Press.

Behar, Ruth. 1993. *Tranlsated Woman: Crossing the Border with Esperanza's Story*. Boston, MA: Beacon Press.

Behar, Ruth. 1996. *The Vulnerable Observer: Anthropology that Breaks Your Heart*. Boston, MA: Beacon Press.

Bell, David, and Barbara M. Kennedy, eds. 2000. *The Cybercultures Reader*. London, UK: Routledge.

Berger, Peter L., and Thomas Luckmann. 1966. *The Soical Construction of Reality: A Treatise on the Sociolog of Knowledge*. Garden City, NY: Doubleday.

Blumer, Herbert. 1937. "Social Psychology." In *Man and Society: A Substantive Introduction to the Social Science*, ed. E. P. Schmidt. New York: Prentice Hall.

Blumer, Herbert. 1969. *Symbolic Interactionism: Perspective and Method*. Englewood Cliffs, NJ: Prentice-Hall.

Boal, Augusto. 1985. *Theatre of the Oppressed*. New York: TCG.

Boal, Augusto. 1992. *Games for Actrs and Non-Actors*. London, UK: Routledge.

Boellstorff, Tom. 2006. "A Ludicrous Discipline? Ethnography and Game Studies." *Games & Culture* 1, no. 1: 29–35.

Boellstorff, Tom. 2008. *Coming of Age in Second Life: An Anthropologist Explores the Virtually Human*. Princeton, N.J.: Princeton University Press.

Bolter, Jay David, and Richard Grusin. 2000. *Remediation: Understanding New Media*. Cambridge, MA: MIT Press.

Born, Georgina. 1995. *Rationalizing Culture: IRCAM, Boulez, and the Institutionalization of the Musical Avant-Garde*. Berkeley: University of California Press.

Bourdreau, Kelly. 2007. *Pixes, Parts & Pieces: Constructing a Digital Identity*. Saarbrüken, Germany: VDM Verlag Dr. Müller.

Brand, Stewart. 1972. "Spacewar." *Rollilng Stone*, December 7.

Brand, Stewart. 1994. *How Buildings Learn: What Happens After They're Built*. New York: Penguin Books.

Brandt, Chris. 2002. "Dance, Voldo, Dance." Machinima film made inside *Soul Calibur* (Namco, 1998). Available at http://www.milkandcookies.com/link/17611/detail/.

Bruckman, Amy. 1992. "Identity Workshop: Emergent Social and Psychological Phenomena in Text-Based Virtual Reality." Cambridge, MA: MIT Media Lab.

Bruckman, Amy. 1997. "MOOSE Crossing: Construction, Community and Learning in a Networked Virtual World for Kids." PhD diss., Media Lab, Massachusetts Institute of Technology (MIT).

Caillois, Roger. 1961. *Man, Play and Games.* Trans. M. Barash. New York: The Free Press. Original edition, 1958.

Campbell, Douglas. 2008. "Virtual Economics: Economists Explore the Research Value of Virtual Worlds." *Region Focus*, The Federal Reserve Bank of Atlanta, Winter: p. 18. Available at http://www.richmondfed.org/publications/research/region_focus/2008/winter/pdf/feature1.pdf.

Carroll, Jon. 1994. "Guerrillas in the Myst." *Wired* 2.08, August. Available at http://www.wired.com/wired/archive/2.08/myst_pr.html.

Castronova, Edward. 2001. "Virtual Worlds: A First-Hand Account of Market and Society on the Cyberian Frontier." Working Paper No. 618, CESifo, Munich. Available at http://papers.ssrn.com/sol3/papers.cfm?abstract_id=294828.

Castronova, Edward. 2004. "The Right to Play." *New York Law School Law Review* 49, no. 1: 185–210.

Castronova, Edward. 2005. *Synthetic Worlds: The Business and Culture of Online Games.* Chicago: University of Chicago Press.

Caughey, Shanna. 2005. *Revisiting Narnia: Fantasy, Myth, and Religion in C. S. Lewis' Chronicles.* Dallas, TX: Benbella Books.

Chen, Jenova. 2007. "Flow in Games (and Everything Else)." *Communications ot the ACM* 50, no. 4: 31–34.

Chicago Public Radio. 1998. This American Life, "*Notes on Camp,* (episode 109)."

Chuang, Tamara. 2004. "Cyber Sociology: A UCI Researcher Looks Into Lives Lived Online, and One Culture Revived." *The Orange County Register,* October 29.

Clifford, James. 1983. "On Ethnographic Authority." *Representations* 2: 118–146.

Clifford, James. 1994. "Diasporas." *Cultural Anthropology* 9, no. 3: 302–338.

Clifford, James, and George E. Marcus, eds. 1986. *Writing Culture: The Poetics and Politics of Ethnography.* Berkeley: University of California Press.

Crawford, Chris. 1984. *The Art of Computer Game Design.* New York: McGraw-Hill Osborne Media.

Csíkszentmihályi, Mihály. 1990. *Flow: The Psychology of Optimal Experience.* New York: Harper & Row.

Curtis, Pavel. 1992. "Mudding: Social Phenomena in Text-Based Virtual Realities." In *Proceedings of the 1992 Conference on Directions and Implications of Advanced Computing,* 26–34.

Cushman, Dick, and George E. Marcus. 1982. "Ethnographies as Texts." *Annual Review of Anthropology* 11: 25–69.

Damer, Bruce. 1997. *Avatars! Exploring and Building Virtual Worlds on the Internet*. Berkeley, CA: Peachpit Press.

Damer, Bruce, Stuart Gold, Karen Marcelo, and Frank Revi. 1999. "Inhabited Virtual Worlds in Cyberspace." In *Virtual Worlds: Synthetic Universes, Digital Life, and Complexity*, ed. J.-C. Heudin, 127–152. Reading, MA: Perseus Books.

Danet, Brenda. 2001. *Cyberpl@y: Communicating Online*. Oxford, NY: Berg.

de Certeau, Michel. 1984. *The Practice of Everyday Life*. Berkeley: University of California Press.

De Landa, Manuel. 1997. *A Thousand Years of Nonlinear History*. Cambridge, MA: MIT Press.

DeKoven, Bernard. 1978. *The Well-Played Game: A Player's Philosophy*. New York: Anchor Press.

DeKoven, Bernard. 1992a. "CoLiberation." Available at http://www.deepfun.com/colib.htm.

DeKoven, Bernard. 1992b. "Of Fun and Flow." Available at http://www.deepfun.com/funflow.htm.

Delio, Michelle. 2004. "Manhattan Gets Pac-man Fever." *Wired*, May 10. Available at http://www.wired.com/gaming/gamingreviews/news/2004/05/63400.

Denzin, Norman K. 2003. *Performance Ethnography: Critical Pedagogy and the Politics of Culture*. Thousand Oaks, CA: Sage Publications.

Diamond, Jared. 1997. *Guns, Germs and Steel: The Fates of Human Societies*. New York: W.W. Norton.

Dibbell, Julian. 1993. "A Rape in Cyberspace: How an Evil Clown, a Haitian Trickster Spirit, Two Wizards, and a Cast of Dozens Turned a Database Into a Society." *Village Voice*, December 23. Available at http://www.juliandibbell.com/texts/bungle_vv.html.

Dibbell, Julian. 1995. "MUD Money: A Talk on Virtual Value and, Incidentally, the Value of the Virtual." Presented at Stages of the Virtual Conference, Center for the Critical Analysis of Contemporary Culture, Rutgers University, April. Available at http://www.juliandibbell.com/texts/mudmoney.html

Dibbell, Julian. 1998. *My Tiny Life: Crime and Passion in a Virtual World*. New York: Henry Holt & Company, Inc.

Dibbell, Julian. 2006. *Play Money: Or, How I Quit My Day Job and Made Millions Trading Virtual Loot*. New York: Basic Books.

Dibbell, Julian. 2007. "The Life of the Chinese Gold Farmer." *The New York Times Magazine*, June 17. Available at http://www.nytimes.com/2007/06/17/magazine/17lootfarmers-t.html.

DiPaola, Steve. 1997–2005. "Steve DiPaola: A Body of Work." Available at http://www
.dipaola.org/steve/.

DiPaola, Steve. 2008. "Authoring the Global Self: Identity, Expression and Role-Playing
in Virtual Communities." Paper read at Proceedings of the Canadian Game Studies
Association, Vancouver.

DiPaola, Steve, and David Collins. 2002. "A 3-D Virtual Environment for Social Telepres-
ence." Paper read at SIGGRAPH conference, Orlando, FL, July.

DiPaola, Steve, and David Collins. 2003. "Social Metaphor-based 3-D Virtual Environment." Paper read at SIGGRAPH conference, San Diego, CA, July.

Dourish, Paul. 1998. "Introduction: The State of Play." *Computer Supported Cooperative
Work* 7, no. 1–2: 109–155.

Dourish, Paul. 2001. *Where the Action Is: The Foundations of Embodied Interaction*. Cambridge, MA: MIT Press.

Dragon*Con. 2008. "A Brief History of Dragon*Con." Available at http://www.dragoncon
.org/history.php.

Entertainment Software Association. 2008. "Industry Facts." Available at http://www.theesa
.com/facts/index.asp.

Farmer, Randy, and Chip Morningstar. 1991. "Lessons of Lucasfilm's Habitat." In *Cyberspace: First Steps*, edited by M. Benedikt, 273–302. Cambridge, MA: MIT Press.

Ferris, Duke. 2004. "Myst IV: Revelation—PC Review". In *Game Revolution*. Available at
http://www.gamerevolution.com/review/pc/myst_iv_revelation

Fine, Gary Alan. 1983. *Shared Fantasy: Role-playing Games as Social Worlds*. Chicago: University of Chicago Press.

Fisher, Michael M. J. 1990. *Debating Muslims: Cultural Dialogues in Postmodernity and Tradition, New Directions In Anthropological Writing*. Madison: University of Wisconsin
Press.

Fluegelman, Andrew, ed. 1976. *The New Games Book*. Tiburon, CA: Headlands Press.

Freeman, Derek. 1983. *Margaret Mead and Samoa: The Making and Unmaking of an Anthropological Myth*. Canberra, Australia: Australian National University Press.

Friedman, Batya, and Helen Nissenbaum. 1996. "Bias in Computer Systems." *ACM Transactions on Information Systems* 14, no. 3: 330–347.

Fron, Janine, Tracy Fullerton, Jacquelyn Ford Morie, and Celia Pearce. 2007a. "Playing
Dress-Up: Costumes, Roleplay and Imagination." Paper read at Philosphy of Computer Games, University of Modena and Reggio Emilia, Italy, January 25–27.

Fron, Janine, Tracy Fullerton, Jacquelyn Ford Morie, and Celia Pearce. 2007b. "The
Hegemony of Play." Paper read at Situated Play: Proceedings of the Digital Games
Research Assocation Conference, Tokyo, Japan, September 24–28.

Fullerton, Tracy, Christopher Swain, and Steven Hoffman. 2004. *Game Design Workshop:
Designing, Prototyping and Playtesting Games*. Berkeley, CA: CMP Books.

Garfinkel, Harold. 1967. *Studies in Ethnomethodology*. Englewood Cliffs, NJ: Prentice-Hall.

Gee, James. 2003. *What Video Games Have to Teach Us about Learning and Literacy*. New York: Palgrave Macmillan.

Geertz, Clifford. 1973. *The Interpretation of Cultures*. New York: Basic Books.

Gell, Alfred. 1998. *Art and Agency: An Anthropological Theory*. Oxford, UK: Clarendon Press.

Gibson, William. 1984. *Neuromancer*. New York: Ace Press/Berkeley Publishing Group.

Gilmore, Lee, and Mark Van Proyen, eds. 2005. *AfterBurn: Reflections on Burning Man*. Santa Fe: University of New Mexico Press.

Goffman, Erving. 1959. *Presentation of Self in Everyday Life*. Garden City, NY: Doubleday & Company, Inc.

Goffman, Erving. 1963. *Behavior in Public Places: Notes on the Social Organization of Gatherings*. New York: Macmillan/The Free Press.

Goffman, Erving. 1974. *Frame Analysis: An Essay on the Organization of Experience*. London: Harper and Row.

Halberstam, David. 1996. *The Amateurs: The Story of Four Young Men and Their Quest for an Olympic Gold Medal*. New York: Ballantine Books.

Haro, Sulka. 2007. Keynote Address. Austin Game Developers Conference, Austin, Texas, September 6.

Heim, Michael. 1993. *The Metaphysics of Virtual Reality*. Boulder, CO: NetLibrary, Incorporated.

Helmreich, Stefan. 1998. *Silicon Second Nature: Culturing Artificial Life in a Digital World*. Berkeley: University of California Press.

Herz, J. C. 1997. *Joystick Nation: How Videogames Ate Our Quarters, Won Our Hearts, and Rewired Our Minds*. New York: Little, Brown and Company.

Hine, Christine. 1998. "Virtual Ethnography." Paper from Internet Research and Information for Social Scientists Conference. University of Bristol, UK, March 25–27.

Hof, Robert D. 2006. "My Virtual Life (Virtual World, Real Money)." *BusinessWeek*, May 1, p. 70.

Hofer, Margaret K. 2003. *The Games We Played: The Golden Age of Board and Table Games*. Princeton, N.J.: Princeton Architectural Press.

Holopainen, Jussi, and Stephan Meyers. 2000. "Neuropsychology and Game Design." Paper read at Consciousness Reframed III, Centre for Advanced Inquiry in the Interactive Arts (CAiiA), University of Wales College, Newport, August 24–26.

Horn, Stacy. 1998. *Cyberville: Clicks, Culture, and the Creation of an Online Town*. New York: Warner Books.

Horwitz, Tony. 1998. *Confederates in the Attic: Dispatches from the Unfinished Civil War* New York: Vintage.

Howard, Robert E., L. Sprague de Camp, and Lin Carter. 1989. *The Conan Chronicles*. London: Sphere Books. Works by Howard originally published 1932–1969.

Huberman, A. Michael, and Matthew B. Miles. 1994. *Qualitative Data Analysis.* Thousand Oaks, CA: Sage.

Huizinga, Johan. [1938] 1950. *Homo Ludens: A Study of the Play-Element in Culture.* Translation of the original. New York: Roy Publishers.

Hurston, Zora Neale. 1937. *Their Eyes Were Watching God.* New York: J.B. Lippincott.

Hurston, Zora Neale. 1935. *Mules and Men.* Philadelphia: J.B. Lippincott Company.

Hyatt-Milton, Katherine. 2005. "The Alpha Learner and Cognitive Haunting." PhD diss., College of Education, Arizona State University.

Iacovoni, Alberto. 2004. *Game Zone: Playgrounds between Virtual Scenarios and Reality.* Basel, Switzerland: Birkhäuser.

Jackson, Michael. 1998. *Minima Ethnographica: Intersubjectivity and the Anthropological Project.* Chicago: University of Chicago Press.

Jacobs, Jane. 1961. *The Death and Life of Great American Cities.* New York: Random House.

Janesick, Valerie J. 1999. "A Journal About Journal Writing and a Qualitative Research Technique." *Qualitative Inquiry* 5, no. 4: 505–524.

Janesick, Valerie J. 2000. "The Choreography of Qualitative Research Design: Minuets, Improvisations, and Crystallization." In *Handbook of Qualitative Research,* eds. N. K. Denzin and Y. S. Lincoln, 379–399. Thousand Oaks, CA: Sage Publications.

Jenkins, Henry. 1992. *Textual Poachers: Television Fans and Participatory Culture.* New York: Rutledge.

Jenkins, Henry. 1998. "'Complete Freedom of Movement': Video Games as Gendered Play Spaces." In *From Barbie to Mortal Kombat: Gender and Computer Games,* eds. J. Cassell and H. Jenkins, 262–297. Cambridge, MA: MIT Press.

Joas, Hans. 1993. *Pragmatism and Social Theory.* Chicago: University of Chicago Press.

Johnson, Steven. 2001. *Emergence: The Connected Lives of Ants, Brains, Cities and Software.* New York: Scribner.

Juul, Jesper. 2002. "The Open and the Closed: Games of Emergence and Games of Progression." Paper read at Computer Games and Digital Cultures, Tampere, Finland, June.

Juul, Jesper. 2004. "Introduction to Game Time." In *First Person: New Media as Story, Performance and Game,* eds. N. Wardrip-Fruin and P. Harrigan, 131–142. Cambridge, MA: MIT Press. Available at http://www.jesperjuul.net/text/timetoplay/.

Juul, Jesper. 2005. *Half-Real: Video Games Between Real Rules and Fictional Worlds.* Cambridge, MA: MIT Press.

Karr, Jean-Baptiste Alphonse. 1849. *Les Guêpes.*

Kay, Alan. 1998. "The Computer Revolution Hasn't Happened Yet." Paper presented at the Third Asian Pacific Conference on Computer and Human Interaction, Kanagawa, Japan, July 15–17.

Kay, Alan. 2003. "Interview with Alan Kay." *Computers in Entertainment* 1, no. 1: 8.

Kendall, Lori. 2002. *Hanging out in the Virtual Pub: Masculinities and Relationships Online.* Berkeley: University of California Press.

Kim, Amy Jo. 1997. "Ritual Reality: Social Design for Online Gaming Environments." Paper read at Computer Game Developers Conference, April.

Klastrup, Lisbeth. 2003a. "Towards a Poetics of Virtual Worlds—Multi-User Textuality and the Emergence of Story, Digital Aesthetics and Communication." PhD diss., IT University, Copenhagen.

Klastrup, Lizbeth. 2003b. "A Poetics of Virtual Worlds." Paper read at Digital Arts and Culture, Melbourne, Australia, May 19–23.

Klein, Norman. 1997. *The History of Forgetting: Los Angeles and the Erasure of Memory.* London: Verso.

Konzack, Lars. 2006. "Sub-creation of Secondary Game Worlds." Paper read at iDiG—International Digital Games Conference Proceedings, Portalegre, Portugal, September 27–29. Available at http://www.vrmedialab.dk/~konzack/subcreation2005.pdf

Koster, Raph. 1998–2006. "Raph Koster's Web Site." Available at http://www.raphkoster.com/.

Koster, Raph. 2001. "Narrative Environments: Worlds That Tell Stories." Paper read at Entertainment in the Interactive Age, University of Southern California, Los Angeles, January 29–30.

Laurel, Brenda. 1991. *Computers as Theater.* New York: Addison-Wesley.

Lave, Jean, and Etienne Wenger. 1991. *Situated Learning: Legitimate Peripheral Participation.* Cambridge, UK: Cambridge University Press.

Lazzaro, Nicole. 2004. "Why We Play Games: Four Keys to More Emotion Without Story." XEODesign White Paper. Available at http://www.xeodesign.com/xeodesign_whyweplaygames.pdf.

Lenhart, Amanda, Mary Madden, Alexandra Rankin Macgill, and Aaron Smith. 2007. "Teens and Social Media: The Use of Social Media Gains a Greater Foothold in Teen Life as They Embrace the Conversational Nature of Interactive Online Media." Pew Report: Family, Friends & Community. Washington, D.C.: Pew Research Center. Available at http://www.pewinternet.org/PPF/r/230/report_display.asp

Levy, Steven. 1993. *Artificial Life: A Report from the Frontier Where Computers Meet Biology.* New York: Vintage.

Liatowitsch, Daniel, director. 2002. *Avatars Offline* (documentary). Dallica Pictures, Inc.

Losh, Elizabeth. 2006. "Making Things Public: Democracy and Government-funded Videogames and Virtual Reality Simulations." Paper read at ACM Siggraph Video Game Symposium, Boston, MA, July 29–30.

Losh, Elizabeth. 2009 [forthcoming]. *Virtualpolitik: An Electronic History of Government Media-Making in a Time of War, Scandal, Disaster, Miscommunication, and Mistakes.* Cambridge, MA: MIT Press.

Luckmann, Thomas. 1983. *Life-World and Social Realities*. Oxford, UK: Heinemann Educational Books.

Ludlow, Peter. 2004. "Coming Soon to an MMORPG Near You! The Gambino Family." *The Second Life Herald*, June 21. Available at http://www.secondlifeherald.com/slh/2004/06/coming_soon_to_.html.

MacKinnon, R. C. 1995. "Searching for the Leviathan in Usenet." In *Cybersociety: Computer-mediated Communication and Community*, ed. Steven G. Jones, 112–137. Thousand Oaks, CA: Sage.

Malaby, Thomas. Forthcoming. *Making Virtual Worlds: Linden Lab and Second Life*. Ithaca, NY: Cornell University Press.

Malinowski, Bronislaw. 1967. *A Diary in the Strict Sense of The Term*. New York: Harcourt, Brace & World.

Manning, Frank E. 1988. "Anthropology and Performance: The Play of Popular Culture." *Play & Culture* 1, no. 3: 180–190.

Marcus, George E. 1995. "Ethnography in/of the World System: The Emergence of Multi-Sited Ethnography." *Annual Review of Anthropology* 24: 95–117.

Markham, Annette N. 1998. *Life Online: Researching Real Experience in Virtual Space*. Walnut Creek, CA: AltaMira Press.

Mason, Bruce Lionel. 1996. "Moving Toward Virtual Ethnography." *American Folklore Society News* 25, no. 2: 4–5.

McLuhan, Marshall. 1964. *Understanding Media: The Extensions of Man*. New York: Mentor.

McLuhan, Marshall, and Quentin Fiore. 1968. *War and Peace in the Global Village*. New York: McGraw-Hill.

Mead, Margaret. 1949. *Coming of Age in Samoa*. New York: Penguin Group.

Miller, Kimberly A. 1998. "Gender Comparisons within Reenactment Costume: Theoretical Interpretations." *Family and Consumer Sciences Research Journal* 27, no. 1: 35–61.

Mills, C. Wright. 1959. *The Sociological Imagination*. New York: Oxford University Press.

Mnookin, Jennifer L. 1996. "Virtual(ly) Law: The Emergence of Law in LambdaMOO." *Journal of Computer-Mediated Communications* 2, no. 1. Available at http://jcmc.indiana.edu/vol2/issue1/lambda.html.

Montessori, Maria. [1900] 1964. *The Montessori Method*. New York: Schocken Books.

Montessori, Maria. [1917] 1964. *The Montessori Elementary Material*. Cambridge, MA: R. Bentley.

Morabito, Margaret. 1986. "Enter the On-Line World of Lucasfilm." *Run Magazine*, August, 24–28.

Mortensen, Torill, and Hilde Corneliussen. 2005. "The Non-sense of Gender in Neverwinter Nights." Paper read at Women in Games Conference, University of Abertay Dundee, August 8–10.

Mortensen, Torill Elvira. 2003. "Pleasures of the Player: Flow and Control in Online Games." PhD diss., Department of Humanistic Informatics, Volda University College, Norway.

Mulligan, Jessica, and Bridgette Patrovsky. 2003. *Developing Online Games: Insiders Guide.* New York: Prentice Hall.

Mumford, Lewis. 1961. *The City in History: Its Origins, Its Transformations and Its Prospects.* New York: Harcourt, Brace & World, Inc.

Murray, Janet H. 1997. *Hamlet on the Holodeck: The Future of Narrative in Cyberspace.* Cambridge, MA: MIT Press.

Nardi, Bonnie. 2005. "Beyond Bandwidth: Dimensions of Connection in Interpersonal Communication." *Computer-Supported Cooperative Work* 14, no. 2: 91–130.

Nardi, Bonnie, and Justin Harris. 2006. "Strangers and Friends: Collaborative Play in *World of Warcraft*." Paper read at Computer Supported Cooperative Work, Banff, Alberta, Canada, November 4–8.

Nardi, Bonnie, and Vicki O'Day. 1999. *Information Ecologies: Using Technology with Heart.* Cambridge, MA: MIT Press.

Nardi, Bonnie, Steve Whittaker, and Erin Bradner. 2000. "Interaction and Outeraction: Instant Messaging in Action." Paper read at Computer Supported Cooperative Work, Philadelphia, PA, December 2–6.

NDP Group. 2007. "Expanding the Games Market." NDP Special Reports. Port Washington, NY: The NDP Group.

Nielsen. 2007. "The State of the Console: Video Game Console Usage, Fourth Quarter 2006." New York: The Nielson Company.

Nocera, Jose L. Abdelnour. 2002. "Ethnography and Hermeneutics in Cybercultural Research Accessing IRC Virtual Communities." *Journal of Computer Mediated Communication* 7, no. 2.

Ondrejka, Cory R. 2004. "Escaping the Gilded Cage: User Created Content and Building in the Metaverse." *New York School Law Review* 49, no. 1: 81–101.

Opie, Iona, and Peter Opie. 1969. *Children's Games in Street and Playground.* London: Oxford University Press.

Orbanes, Philip. 2003. *The Game Makers.* Cambridge, MA: Harvard Business School Press.

Ortiz, Fernando. 1947. *Cuban Counterpoint.* New York: Knopf.

Overman. 2006. "Male Restroom Etiquette." Machinima film made inside *The Sims 2* (Maxis/Electronic Arts, 2004). Available at http://www.youtube.com/watch?v=IzO1m CAVyMw

Paccagnella, Luciano. 1997. "Getting the Seats of Your Pants Dirty: Strategies for Ethnographic Research in Virtual Communities." *Journal of Computer-Mediated Communication* 3, no. 1. Available at http://jcmc.indiana.edu/vol3/issue1/paccagnella.html.

Papert, Seymour. 1993. *Mindstorms: Children, Computers and Powerful Ideas*. New York: Basic Books.

Papert, Seymour, and Idit Harel. 1991. *Constructionism*. Stamford, CT: Ablex.

Patience, Allan, and Joseph Wayne Smith. 1986. "Derek Freeman and Samoa: The Making and Unmaking of a Biobehavioral Myth." *American Anthropologist* 88, no. 1: 157–162.

Pearce, Celia. 1997. *The Interactive Book: A Guide to the Interactive Revolution*. Indianapolis, IN: Macmillan Technical Publishing.

Pearce, Celia. 2002a. "Emergent Authorship: The Next Interactive Revolution." *Computers & Graphics* 26, no. 1: 26–29.

Pearce, Celia. 2002b. "Sims, BattleBots, Cellular Automata, God and Go: A Conversation with Will Wright." *Game Studies Journal* 2, no. 1. Available at http://www.gamestudies.org/0102/pearce/.

Pearce, Celia. 2002c. "Story as Play Space: Narrative in Games." In *Game On: The History and Culture of Video Games*, ed. L. King, 112–119. London: Lawrence King.

Pearce, Celia. 2005. "A Conversation with Raph Koster." *Game Studies Journal* 5, no. 1. Available at http://www.gamestudies.org/0501/pearce/.

Pearce, Celia. 2006a. "Games as Art: The Aesthetics of Play." In *Visible Language: After Fluxus* 40, no. 1 (special issue, eds. K. Friedman and O. F. Smith.).

Pearce, Celia. 2006b. Productive Play: Game Culture from the Bottom Up. *Games & Culture* 1 (1):17–24.

Pearce, Celia. 2006c. "Seeing and Being Seen: Presence and Play in Online Virtual Worlds." Paper read at Online, Offline & The Concept of Presence When Games and VR Collide, University of Southern California Centers for Creative Technologies, October 25–27.

Pearce, Celia. 2007. "Narrative Environments from Disneyland to World of Warcraft." In *Space, Time, Play: Computer Games, Architecture and Urbanism: The Next Level*, eds. Friedrich von Borries, Steffan P. Walz, and Matteas Bottger, 200–205. Basel: Birkhauser.

Pearce, Celia. 2008a. "Spatial Literacy: Reading (and Writing) Game Space." Paper presented at Future and Reality of Gaming (F.R.O.G) conference, University of Vienna, October 17–19.

Pearce, Celia. 2008b. "The Truth About Baby Boomer Gamers." *Games & Culture* 3, no. 2: 142–174.

Pearce, Celia. 2008c. "Identity-as-Place: Trans-Ludic Identities in Mediated Play Communities—The Case of the Uru Diaspora." Presented at Internet Research 9.0: Rethinking Communities, Rethinking Place, Association of Internet Researchers, Copenhagen IT University, October 15-18.

Pearce, Celia, and Artemesia. 2007. "Communities of Play: The Social Construction of Identity in Persistent Online Game Worlds." In *Second Person: Role-Playing and Story in Games and Playable Media*, eds. N. Wardrip-Fruin and P. Harrigan, 311–318. Cambridge, MA: MIT Press.

Piaget, Jean. 1962. *Play, Dreams and Imitation in Childhood*. New York: Norton.

Plant, Sadie. 1992. *The Most Radical Gesture: The Situationist International in a Postmodern Age*. London/New York: Routledge.

Poremba, Cindy. 2003. "Player as Author: Digital Games and Agency." Master's thesis, Department of Computing Arts and Design Sciences, Simon Frasier University, Vancouver, Canada.

Powdermaker, Hortense. 1966. *Stranger and Friend: The Way of the Anthropologist*. New York: W. W. Norton.

Prügl, Reinhard, and Martin Schreier. 2006. "Learning from Leading-edge Customers at *The Sims*: Opening Up the Innovation Process using Toolkits." *R&D Management* 36, no. 3: 237–250.

Raybourn, Elaine M. 1997. "Computer Game Design: New Directions for Intercultural Simulation." *Developments in Business Simulation and Experiential Exercises* 24: 144–145. Available at http://sbaweb.wayne.edu/~absel/bkl/vol24/24bk.pdf.

Red Rock LLC. 2007. "Burning Man: What is Burning Man?: Timeline."Available at http://www.burningman.com/whatisburningman/about_burningman/bm_timeline.html.

Reed, Adam. 2005. "'My Blog Is Me': Texts and Persons in UK: Online Journal Culture (and Anthropology)." *Ethnos* 70, no. 2: 220–242.

Reynolds, Ren. 2007. "Ethics and Practice in Virtual Worlds." Paper read at The Philosophy of Computer Games, University of Modena and Reggio Emilia, Italy, January 25–27.

Rheingold, Howard. 1993. *The Virtual Community: Homesteading on the Electronic Frontier*. New York: Addison-Welsey.

Rheingold, Howard. 2002. *Smart Mobs: The Next Social Revolution*. New York: Basic Books.

Richardson, Laurel. 1994. "Writing: A Method of Inquiry." In *Handbook of Qualitative Research*, eds. N. Denzin and Y. S. Lincoln, 923–948. Thousand Oaks, CA: Sage.

Rouse, Roger. 1991. "Mexican Migration and the Social Space of Postmodernism." *Diaspora* 1, no. 1: 8–23.

Rudofsky, Bernard. 1965. *Architecture without Architects: A Short Introduction to Non-Pedigreed Architecture*. New York: Museum of Modern Art.

Ryan, Marie-Laure. 2001. *Narrative as Virtual Reality: Immersion and Interactivity in Literature and Electronic Media*. Baltimore, MD: Johns Hopkins University Press.

Safran, William. 1991. "Diasporas in Modern Societies: Myths of Homeland and Return." *Diaspora* 1, no. 1: 83–99.

Salen, Katie, and Eric Zimmerman. 2004. *Rules of Play: Game Design Fundamentals*. Cambridge, MA: MIT Press.

References

Salvador, Tony, Genevieve Bell, and Ken Anderson. 1999. "Design Ethnography." *Design Management* 10, no. 4: 35–41.

Salvador, Tony, and Michael Mateas. 1997. "Design Ethnography: Using Custom Ethnographic Techniques to Develop New Product Concepts." Paper read at CHI 97: Conference on Human Factors in Computing Systems, at Atlanta, GA, March 22–27.

Sanders, T. Irene, and Judith A. McCabe. 2003. "The Use of Complexity Science: A Survey of Federal Departments and Agencies, Private Foundations, Universities, and Independent Education and Research Centers." Washington, D.C.: Washington Center for Complexity & Public Policy.

Santa Fe Institute. 2008. "Santa Fe Institute." Available at http://www.santafe.edu/.

Santino, Jack. 1983. "Halloween in America: Contemporary Customs and Performances." *Western Folklore* 42, no. 1: 1–20.

Schechner, Richard. 1988. "Playing." *Play & Culture* 1, no. 1.

Schechner, Richard, and Mady Schuman. 1976. *Ritual, Play and Performance: Readings in the Social Sciences/Theater*. New York: Seabury Press.

Schelling, Thomas C. 1971. "Dynamic Models of Segregation." *Journal of Mathematical Sociology* 1, no. 2: 143–186.

Schiano, Diane J. 1999. "Lessons from LambdaMOO: A Social, Text-Based Virtual Environment." *Presence: Teleoperators & Virtual Environments* 8, no. 2: 127–139.

Schindler, Henri. 1997. *Mardi Gras: New Orleans*. Paris: Flammarion.

Seale, Clive, ed. 2004. *Researching Society and Culture*. Second ed. London: Sage Publications.

Seay, A. Fleming, Bill Jerome, Kevin Lee and Robert E. Kraut. 2001–2008. *Project Massive*. Available at http://www.projectmassive.com/.

Seay, A. Fleming, Bill Jerome, Kevin Lee and Robert E. Kraut. 2004. "Project Massive: A Study of Online Gaming Communities." In *CHI '04: Extended Abstracts on Human Factors in Computing Systems*, 1421–1424. New York: ACM Press.

Shils, Edward. 1957. "Primordial, Personal, Sacred and Civil Ties." *British Journal of Sociology* 8, no. 2: 130–145.

Shostak, Marjorie. 1981. *Nisa, the Life and Words of a !Kung Woman*. Cambridge, MA: Harvard University Press.

Sidel, Robin. 2008. "Cheer Up, Ben: Your Economy Isn't As Bad as This One: In the Make-Believe World of 'Second Life,' Banks Are Really Collapsing." *Wall Street Journal Online*, January 23.

Smith Bowen, Elenore (aka Laura Bohannan). 1964. *Return to Laughter*. 2nd ed. Garden City, NY: Doubleday & Company, Inc.

Spence, Edward H. 2007. "Meta Ethics for the Metaverse: The Ethics of Virtual Worlds." Paper read at The Philosophy of Computer Games, University of Modena and Reggio Emilia, Italy, January 25–27.

Star, Susan Leigh, and James R. Griesemer. 1989. "Institutional Ecology, 'Translations' and Boundary Objects: Amateurs and Professionals in Berkeley's Musem of Vertebrate Zoology, 1907–1939." *Social Studies of Science* 19, no. 3: 387–420.

Steinkuehler, Constance A. 2005. "Cognition and Learning in Massively Multiplayer Online Games: A Critical Approach." PhD diss., University of Wisconsin-Madison. Available at http://website.education.wisc.edu/steinkuehler/thesis.html.

Steinkuehler, Constance A., and Kurt D. Squire. 2006. "Generating Cyberculture/s: The Case of *Star Wars Galaxies*." In *Cyberlines: Languages and Cultures of the Internet*, eds. D. Gibbs and K.-L. Krause, 177–198. Albert Park, Australia: James Nicholas Publishers.

Stephenson, Neal. 1992. *Snow Crash*. New York: Bantam Books.

Stone, Allucquere Rosanne. 1991. "Will the Real Body Please Stand Up?: Boundary Stories About Virtual Cultures." In *Cyberspace: First Steps*, ed. M. Benedikt, 81–118. Cambridge, MA: MIT Press.

Stone, Allucquére Rosanne. 1996. *The War of Desire and Technology at the Close of the Mechanical Age*. Cambridge, MA: MIT Press.

Strathern, Marilyn. 2004. *Commons and Borderlands: Working Papers on Interdisciplinarity, Accountability, and the Flow of Knowledge*. Oxford: Sean Kingston.

Suellentrop, Chris. 2007. "Will Wright: I Am Not a Game Maker." *Wired Epicenter (Blog Network)*, March 9.

Suits, Bernard. 1967. "What Is a Game?" *Philosophy of Science* 34, no. 2: 148–156.

Suits, Bernard. 1978. *The Grasshopper: Games, Life and Utopia*. Toronto, Ontario: University of Toronto Press.

Surowiecki, James. 2004. *The Wisdom of Crowds: Why the Many Are Smarter Than the Few and How Collective Wisdom Shapes Business, Economies, Societies, and Nations*. New York: Doubleday.

Sutton-Smith, Brian. 1981. *A History of Children's Play: New Zealand, 1840–1950*. Philadelphia: University of Pennsylvania Press.

Sutton-Smith, Brian. 1997. *The Ambiguity of Play*. Cambridge, MA: Harvard University Press.

Sutton-Smith, Brian, and Elliott M. Avedon. 1971. *The Study of Games*. New York: J. Wiley.

Sutton-Smith, Brian, and Anthony D. Pellegrini. 1995. *The Future of Play Theory: A Multidisciplinary Inquiry into the Contributions of Brian Sutton-Smith*. Albany: State University of New York Press.

Sweetser, Penny. 2007. *Emergence in Games*. Boston, MA: Charles River Media.

Taylor, T. L. 1999. "Life in Virtual Worlds: Plural Existence, Multimodalities, and Other Online Research Challenges." *American Behavioral Scientist* 43, no. 3: 436–449.

Taylor, T. L. 2002a. Living Digitally: Embodiment in Virtual Worlds. In *The Social Life of Avatars: Presence and Interaction in Shared Virtual Environments*, ed. R. Schroeder, 40–62. London: Springer.

Taylor, T. L. 2002b. "'Whose Game Is This Anyway?': Negotiating Corporate Ownership in a Virtual World." Paper read at Computer Games and Digital Cultures, Tempere, Finland, June 6–8.

Taylor, T. L. 2003. "Intentional Bodies: Virtual Environments and the Designers Who Shape Them." *International Journal of Engineering Education* 19, no. 1: 25–34.

Taylor, T. L. 2005. Keynote Address. Paper read at Digital Games Research Association 2005 Conference: Changing Views - Worlds in Play, Vancouver, Canada, June 16–20.

Taylor, T. L. 2006. *Play Between Worlds: Exploring Online Game Culture*. Cambridge, MA: MIT Press.

Taylor, T. L., and Mikael Jakobsson. 2003. "*The Sopranos* Meets *EverQuest*: Social Networking in Massively Multiplayer Online Games." Paper read at International Digital Arts and Culture Conference, Melbourne, Australia, May 19–23.

Teilhard de Chardin, Pierre. 1961. *The Phenomenon of Man*. New York: Harper & Row.

Tiscali. 2003. "10 Years and Counting." In *Tiscali Games*. Available at http://www.tiscali.co.uk/games/myst/history.html.

Tolkien, J. R. R. 1954. *The Fellowship of the Rings*. London: Allen & Unwin.

Tolkien, J. R. R. 1954. *The Two Towers*. London: Allen & Unwin.

Tolkien, J. R. R. 1955. *The Return of the King*. London: Allen & Unwin.

Tolkien, J. R. R. 1983. *The Monsters and the Critics and Other Essays*. Reprinted with additional material, New York: HarperCollins, 1997.

Tönnies, Ferdinand. [1887] 1988. *Community and Society*. Translation from the original, *Gemeinschaft and Gesellschaft*. New Brunswick, N.J.: Transaction Publishers.

Tuan, Yi-Fu. 1977. *Space and Place: The Perspective of Experience*. Minneapolis: University of Minnesota Press.

Turkle, Sherry. 1984. *The Second Self*. New York: Simon and Schuster.

Turkle, Sherry. 1995. *Life on the Screen: Identity in the Age of the Internet*. New York: Simon & Schuster.

Turner, Jeremy, Donato Mancini, and Patrick "Flick" Harrison. 2003. *Avatara* (DVD). USA: (Self-Distributed).

Turner, Victor Witter. 1982. *From Ritual to Theater: The Human Seriousness of Play*. New York: Performing Arts Journal Publications.

University of California, Los Angeles (UCLA). 2008. "UCLA Human Complex Systems Degree Program." Available at http://www.hcs.ucla.edu.

van Gennep, Arnold. 1909. *The Rites of Passage*. London: Routledge & Kegan Paul. English edition translated by Monika Vizedom and Gabrielle L. Caffee, 1960. Chicago: University of Chicago Press.

Visweswaran, Kamala. 1994. *Fictions of Feminist Ethnography*. Minneapolis: University of Minnesota Press.

Wells, H.G. 1913. *Little Wars: A Game for Boys from Twelve Years of Age to One Hundred and Fifty and for That More Intelligent Sort of Girl Who Likes Boys' Games and Books*. London: F. Palmer.

Wiener, Norbert. 1948. *Cybernetics or Control and Communication in the Animal and the Machine*. Cambridge, MA: MIT Press.

Willis, Paul. 1978. *Profane Culture*. London: Routledge.

Willis, Paul. 1981. *Learing to Labour: How Working Class Kids Get Working Class Jobs*. New York: Columbia University Press.

Willis, Paul. 2000. *The Ethnographic Imagination*. Cambridge, UK: Polity Press.

Winge, Theresa. 2007. "Costuming the Imagination: Origins of Anime and Manga Cosplay." In *Mechademia 1: Emerging Worlds of Anime and Manga*, ed. F. Lunning. Minneapolis: University of Minnesota Press.

Winnicott, D. W. 1971. *Playing and Reality*. London: Tavistock.

Wittgenstein, Ludwig. 1953. *The Philisophical Investigations*. 3rd edition published by New York: Prentice-Hall, 1999.

Wolcott, Harry F. 1990. *Writing Up Qualitative Research*. Newbury Park, CA: Sage Publications.

Wolf, Margery. 1992. *A Thrice Told Tale: Feminism, Postmodernism, and Ethnographic Responsibility*. Stanford, CA: Stanford University Press.

Yalom, Marilyn. 2004. *Birth of the Chess Queen: A History*. New York: HarperCollins Publishers.

Yee, Nicholas. 2001. "The Norrathian Scrolls: A Study of *EverQuest*," version 2.5. Available at http://www.nickyee.com/eqt/report.html.

Yee, Nicholas. 2003. "The Demographics of Gender-Bending." Available at http://www.nickyee.com/daedalus/archives/000551.php.

References

Index